Subject Knowledge and Teacher Education

THE DEVELOPMENT OF BEGINNING TEACHERS' THINKING

Viv Ellis

continuum

For A. G. and V. P.

Continuum International Publishing Group

The Tower Building
11 York Road
SE1 7NX

80 Maiden Lane, Suite 704
New York, NY 10038

www.continuumbooks.com

© Viv Ellis 2009
First published in 2007

British Library Cataloguing-in-Publication Data
A catalogue record for this book is available from the British Library.

ISBN: 0826419887 (paperback)

Library of Congress Cataloging-in-Publication Data
A catalogue record for this book is available from the Library of Congress.

Typeset by Free Range Book Design & Production Ltd
Printed and bound in Great Britain by MPG Books Ltd, Bodmin, Cornwall

Subject Knowledg

ONE WEEK LOAN

Contents

List of Tables and Figures

Tables

Figures

Acknowledgements

My thanks are due first and foremost to the various settings in which I have worked as a teacher and teacher educator, especially the English departments of Woodway Park and Castle High Schools, the Schools of Education at the Universities of Brighton and Southampton, and the Department of Educational Studies at Oxford. I owe specific debts of gratitude to many creative individuals who have challenged and inspired me as teacher and researcher in each of these settings and elsewhere. I am especially grateful to Tony Burgess at the London University Institute of Education, who guided me through the research with a rare combination of wisdom, patience and good humour, and also to Anne Edwards (University of Oxford), Carol Fox (University of Brighton), Rosalyn George (Goldsmiths College, University of London), Peter Smagorinsky (University of Georgia), Ilana Snyder (Monash University) and Bridget Somekh (Manchester Metropolitan University) for their critical and insightful feedback at different stages in the development of the manuscript. Above all, this book would not have been possible without the commitment of Ann, Grace and Liz and the support of their university tutors, teacher mentors and other colleagues in schools.

Foreword

Teacher educators, like those throughout the educational system, have often looked for 'the answer' to vexing problems with teaching and learning. In the US, reductive initiatives such as the No Child Left Behind legislation for students and the National Council of Accreditation of Teacher Education (NCATE) reviews for teacher education programmes take one-size-fits-all approaches to assessing the widely divergent teaching and learning conducted in schools with disparate populations, resources, missions and other facets of institutional make-up. These efforts are praised by those who seek to homogenize teaching and learning across the spectrum of communities and people served. Yet they operate from premises that are rejected by those for whom these evaluations represent grossly ill-informed and poorly executed efforts to standardize instruction according to limited visions of education, and stifle creative thinking among the teachers who produce the field's most intriguing innovations.

In this book, Viv Ellis takes a situated perspective on teacher education, looking closely and carefully at a small set of teachers as they experience the settings in which they learn to teach. These settings include the relatively rarified environment of the university department of education and the teeming, gritty world of the schools. Making the transition from universities to schools has often made for a bumpy ride for teachers. Universities tend to emphasize the theoretical and ideal while schools must deal with the immediate, moiling, conflict-ridden days of children and adolescents and their infinite problems and contradictions. Ellis takes us into the crucible of this conflict, providing detailed accounts of early-career teachers' experiences as they try to negotiate the multiple value systems that compete for their allegiance.

Doing so requires a theoretical approach that allows one to provide a comprehensive account of the situated nature of human development. Ellis's clear, thoughtful appropriation of sociocultural theory grounded in the work of Vygotsky enables him to make sense of the ways in which the settings of learning to teach mediate teachers' conceptions of how to teach. Many studies of teacher education look for single, universal explanations for shared experiences. And so one study will argue that teachers are so well apprenticed to business-as-usual that they reject the progressive values of teacher education programmes; another will posit that teachers learn a progressive pedagogy in college but that schools crush them with their emphasis on control; and so on. Taking a sociocultural approach enables Ellis to find that no single reason can account for the tendency for teachers to gravitate to the norms of their schools. Rather, one must look to the specific cultural practices of particular universities and schools to account for why any teacher might embrace one value system or another. In his research, Ellis highlights the personal yet socially channelled trajectories of beginning teachers' experiences in the conceptual morass of multiple settings and traces the complex, 'twisting path' of teachers' concept development (Smagorinsky, Cook and Johnson 2003, Vygotsky 1987).

This meticulous set of case studies will make a great contribution to the field's understanding of early-career teachers' knowledge and thinking in relation to the settings in which they learn to teach. Viv Ellis has provided both an essential study of teachers' early-career concept development and a model for how future such studies might be conducted. This valuable research should strongly influence the ways in which teacher educators think about their work in terms of the situated nature of learning to teach.

Peter Smagorinsky
University of Georgia

1

Introduction

When I became a university-based teacher educator in England in the late 1990s, one of my first tasks was to implement a subject knowledge auditing procedure for a Postgraduate Certificate of Education (PGCE) course in English.[1] This procedure was then a new requirement made by Department for Education and Skills (DfEE) Circular 4/98 and the Initial Teacher Training National Curricula (ITTNCs) (DfEE 1998a). The rationale provided in the Circular was that there was such variation in the subject knowledge 'covered' in university courses, that the bachelor's degree could be no guarantee that graduates would be prepared – in terms of 'content' – to teach the subjects they were being trained to teach. The Circular's assumptions were that certain bits of subject knowledge were prerequisite to teachers being able to teach effectively in schools, that these bits of knowledge could be specified and atomized in advance by the government's Teacher Training Agency (TTA), and that the more of these bits teachers accumulated in their heads, the better they would eventually be able to teach.

For my first go at making a subject knowledge audit, I used Microsoft Word to produce little boxes for my students to tick. In my grand design, two ticks suggested expertise in one of the content areas specified by 4/98; one tick indicated confidence; and no ticks … well, no ticks highlighted a 'gap' into which I would leap with handouts on word classes and syntax. My second effort clustered many of the 'auditable' areas together and invited my students to think about what they *did* know. And then, of course, to tell me what they didn't. This led to targets, monitoring and, finally, assessment. My course was inspected by the Office for Standards in Education (Ofsted) and deemed 'compliant'. I kept my job.

The reforms of initial teacher education (ITE) in England towards the end of the twentieth century – along with government interventions in teaching through, for example, the National Literacy Strategy (DfEE 1998b) and, later, the Key Stage 3 English Framework (DFES 2001) – were founded upon an objectivist view of knowledge as a static and universal commodity that could be fragmented, accumulated and transferred. In these times of heightened vertical accountability, as the New Labour government sought to reconstruct the teaching profession (Furlong *et al.* 2000, Hextall and Mahony 2000), knowledge became a *thing* the volume of which had to be measured in order to demonstrate compliance. Only compliance ensured continued government funding. Non-compliance led to the closure of courses and programmes and, in some cases, university departments of education.

As I had never believed subject knowledge existed as an object, as some sort of packing material or viscous fluid that could be 'boosted', 'topped up' or measured, my audit procedures were a good example of what Edwards *et al.* (2002) refer to as the 'duplicitous discourse' in which teacher educators at the time of the 4/98 Standards were implicated. In satisfying Ofsted with little boxes to tick, I was simplifying 'what is eminently complex' and encouraging my students to accommodate unhelpfully to 'apparent certainties' (Edwards *et al.* 2002: 4). My students knew better, however, and that is how the idea for the research presented in this book grew. I became interested in how student teachers tackled the systems teacher educators contrived for them and how their thinking about the concept of subject knowledge figured as an aspect of their work on becoming a teacher. I became interested in how beginning teachers thought about subject knowledge outside of practice – the very kind of thinking required by the statutory instruments of auditing.

This book presents a study of three beginning teachers' thinking about the subject knowledge of English at the time of the 4/98 Standards. The subject English was chosen for pragmatic reasons: it was the subject in which I was working as a teacher educator and which I had taught as a schoolteacher. However, as expected, it also proved to be an especially good site for exposing and exploring conflicting epistemologies against the background of contemporary reforms of teaching and teacher education. The research took place over a two-year period and the teachers with whom I worked – Ann, Grace and Liz – were not my own students. Two questions guided my research: first, what did these beginning teachers think about the subject knowledge of English and did this thinking change or develop over the period? And second, in more abstract and theoretical terms, how might this thinking and the way it developed be conceptualized?

Framing the research I: epistemological issues

How can one claim to describe what people think?
In claiming to describe what people think, my fundamental premise is the Vygotskian understanding that there is a reciprocal relationship between thinking and language, 'a continual movement back and forth from thought to word and from word to thought ... Thought is not merely expressed in words; it comes into existence through them' (Vygotsky 1986: 218). Speech is not simply an externalization of thought but a tool in its development, hence the 'movement back and forth'. Language (or, more specifically, speech) is seen as a means (a tool, if you

wish) for cognitive work. My study traces the development of three beginning teachers' thinking in the context of their interviews with me as researcher. The analysis is therefore primarily of what they said to me (their spoken language) – but also of 'maps' they drew and narratives they wrote (see Chapter 4) – about the subject knowledge of English rather than everything that they ever thought everywhere.

What is the difference between teacher thinking and teacher knowledge?
Often in the teacher education literature, thinking and knowledge are used interchangeably; sometimes cognition is used in preference. In this research, although I don't regard the terms as entirely distinct, I use the terms separately to indicate different kinds of knowing, as suggested in Davis and Sumara's (2000) distinction between individual knowing and collective knowledge. Thinking (a gerund) is used to indicate how the individual makes sense of and works on concepts using language as a mediational tool.[2] Knowledge is used to indicate that which exists at the level of the culture in terms of materials and resources that are appropriated as tools in practice. What counts as knowledge has been evaluated as justified and true in communities of practice working on the same object[3] and seeking the same cultural identity.

Framing the research II: traditions of research

From the 1970s onwards, especially in US and to an extent in UK, there has been a growth in interest in teachers' thinking (Clark 1989, Calderhead 1987). This is partly associated with a recognition that it is inadequate to try to understand teachers' behaviours without also trying to understand their reasoning and beliefs (McIntyre and Morrison 1977). In their seminal review of the research on teachers' thinking, however, Clark and Peterson (1986) delineated three broad categories of research within this tradition: 1 teachers' planning (or their 'pre-active' and 'post-active' decision-making); 2 teachers' interactive thoughts and decisions in the moment of practice; 3 teachers' theories and beliefs when not engaged in practice. My research is situated partly within the third category, with the important caveat that much of the research within this category is characterized by a focus on thinking as a purely 'inside-the-head' process whereas mine attempts to understand knowledge and thinking more ecologically.

There is also a tradition of research in psychology that seeks to trace the epistemological development of subjects. This tradition is influenced by Piaget's concept of 'genetic epistemology' (Piaget 1971, 1950) and his theories of intellectual development. The aim of this research tradition – at the intersection of philosophy and psychology – is to schematize how individuals come to know and how their beliefs about knowledge relate to how they think and reason. Perry's (1970) longitudinal studies of the epistemological development of groups of almost exclusively male, white, middle-class students at Harvard University allowed him to propose a developmental scheme that moved from the subject's initial 'dualism' through 'multiplicity' to 'relativism' and, finally, to 'relativism with commitment'. The exclusive nature of Perry's sample provoked Belenky *et al.* (1986) to design a study to focus on 'women's ways of knowing'. They extended the phenomenographic perspective of Perry's clinical research design by including structured interviews and elaborated a developmental scheme that proposed that women's epistemological development moved from 'silence' to 'received knowledge' to 'subjective knowledge' to 'procedural knowledge' to 'constructed knowledge'.

Although they operated rather different definitions of knowledge and knowing, the purpose of Perry's and Belenky *et al.*'s research – and the research of others (e.g. Baxter Magolda 1987) that followed – was to develop Piagetian-like stage schemes that could describe the epistemological development of relatively large samples. With specific reference to teacher education, Fuller and Bown (1975) put forward just such a stage scheme of teacher development (see also Kagan 1992). The purpose of my research was rather different. I wanted to describe the distinctive richness and complexity of a few individual beginning teachers' thinking and then interpret the development of this thinking in theoretical terms so as to be able to claim 'prototypical' generalizability (Langemeyer and Nissen 2005) for my conceptualization.

Situating my research within the existing traditions

The line I have taken in the research reported here is sociocultural in that it regards the individual as a person-in-context (see Cole 1996) and the development of knowledge as being 'stretched over' (Lave 1988) individuals, communities and environments over time. My research sought to understand what three beginning teachers of English thought about the subject knowledge of English over a two-year period (the PGCE to the Induction year) and their crossings of borders between university departments of education and nine school English departments. It started from the assumption that what teachers think is intellectually interesting and not entirely independent of their participation in settings as members of communities of practice (even though, in this research, their practice was not the focus). It attempts to bring a more sociocultural approach to bear on teachers' thinking and knowledge than traditions that have either conceptualized cognition as an individualistic, 'in the head' process or conceptualized development as a series of distinct, genetic stages against which an individual's progress (or even their adequacy) might be measured.

In the chapters that follow, through studying these beginning teachers' accounts and perceptions of their participation in multiple educational settings, I identify key dynamics (in terms of intellectual tensions) in the development of the individual teachers' thinking about subject knowledge and common dimensions to development. I also explore the processes underlying the development of the beginning teachers' thinking at a theoretical level and suggest how this development might be conceptualized and understood prototypically.

The book in outline

In Chapter 2, I outline a perspective on knowledge and cognition that informed my inquiry. The chapter proposes a view of knowledge as emerging from the 'shared procedures' of a community working towards the same object and identity (Toulmin 1999). By addressing some foundational, epistemological questions at the outset, this chapter sets a direction for the book as a whole.

Chapter 3 places the research in its cultural-historical context through a discussion of the reforms of teacher education in England in the late 1990s, with specific reference to the concept of subject knowledge. In this discussion, questions of historical variation, values, purpose and 'epistemological stance' (Hillocks 1999) are explicitly addressed.

In Chapter 4, I elaborate a theoretical framework of knowledge creation within a dynamic system that is built out of my argument in the preceding chapters. I show how this framework for understanding informed my research design and the generation of data.

Chapters 5, 6 and 7 are in-depth case studies of the three beginning teachers' thinking about the subject knowledge of English and how this thinking developed over the two-year period. They reveal the distinctiveness and complexity of their thinking and expose a strongly affective dimension. As narratives structured by theoretical concepts, the chapters seek to foreground contradictions and tensions. These extended case studies offer a substantive answer to the question *what* these beginning teachers thought about the subject knowledge of English and how this thinking developed over the period of the research. They also begin to answer the second question as to *how* this development might be conceptualized.

Chapter 8 takes these ideas forward and offers an analysis of the underlying processes of development across the three cases that represents a conceptual answer to the second, more theoretical question. There is no attempt here to 'isolate variables' but rather to identify key dynamics and common dimensions and to interpret the developmental process as a personal trajectory of participation in the practices of multiple settings, oriented and informed by what I refer to (after Dreier (1999) and Damasio (2000)) as stances or dispositions.

In Chapter 9, I consider how this research might contribute to our understanding of teachers' subject knowledge and teachers' thinking and to the concept of development. I also suggest some of the pedagogical implications of the research in terms of how teacher education programmes might better reflect an understanding of subject knowledge as being *amongst* participants in a field as much as it is *within* them. The professional (and, indeed, political) implications of this understanding are profound for if we believe that knowledge can only be created and achieve value within a dynamic system that is capable of *being worked on* as well as *working on* its participants, then teaching must be seen as a collective enterprise and a relational practice embedded in specific social, cultural and historical conditions. To say that this is not how the government in England conceived of teachers and teaching at the time of research would be something of an understatement.

2

Working on and being worked on: developing knowledge in practice

The research problems addressed in this book are concerned with teachers' knowledge and teachers' thinking. How knowledge and thinking are conceptualised will, therefore, be of central importance. This chapter begins by addressing these foundational questions and does so, by way of a brief introduction, through a critical engagement with the work of Edwards *et al.* in *Rethinking Teacher Education: Collaborative responses to uncertainty* (2002). Edwards *et al.* considered a number of the dilemmas and opportunities for 'duplicitous discourse' presented to teacher educators in England at the time of Circular 4/98 (DfEE 1998a). In doing so, they considered three possible answers (expressed as *objectivist, subjectivist* and *reflective* categories) to the question 'What is the knowledge-base that beginning teachers acquire from their teacher education?' that they rejected before proposing a fourth ('the *contextualist* answer') which they considered best reflects the complexities of teaching and learning and the contestable and shifting nature of knowledge.

These answers to the question about the beginning teacher's knowledge-base represent different orientations to knowledge. These different orientations make different claims to justification and truth and the terms used to describe them come, in the main, from the branch of philosophy concerned with the study of knowledge as a subject in its own right – epistemology. As such, they are not unique or original to Edwards *et al.* nor do they address the more psychological (and indeed social) question of how we acquire, develop or come to knowledge. As will become clear, these categories are a useful starting point only; the tensions produced by attempting to draw together some of the philosophical and psychological research on knowledge and cognition will show that there are points at which the boundaries between categories merge. An important factor in the production of this tension is, of course, that philosophy and psychology attempt to answer two very different sets of questions about knowledge and knowing: philosophy (epistemology) is concerned with evaluating claims to knowledge in terms of justification and truth; psychology is concerned with describing how we (expressed as learners) come to know or develop knowledge. My contention is that both sets of questions are relevant to any consideration of teachers' knowledge and thinking and, especially, of how we learn to teach. I also suggest that the epistemological and psychological questions achieve common ground in answers that foreground the sociocultural – object- or goal-oriented, systemic activity in settings – in accounts of how we come to knowledge.

Foundational: perspectives on knowledge and teaching

Objectivism and rationalist perspectives on 'principled and context-free knowledge'

Philosophically, objectivism has its origins partly in rationalism and the philosophy of Plato and Descartes. Rationalism assumes the possibility of *a priori* knowledge – that is, knowledge not based on or arising out of the world around us – and the existence of general and necessary truths. Scheffler, discussing the rationalistic tradition in education, refers to Plato's dialogue *Meno* and the supposition therein that the 'source of genuine knowledge' is within the individual mind:

> ... and the knowledge itself to be capable of elicitation by questioning and suggestion which merely draw the mind's attention to that which it already possesses. The ideal education, for Plato, is a mathematical education, in which the mind comes to an apprehension of necessary truths and ideal forms. (1965: 3)

Davis and Sumara associate the idealism of Plato's logic with the classical forms of Euclidean geometry and note their profound influence in shaping the predominant contemporary understandings of the structures of schooling and curriculum (2000: 823–5). With reference to teacher education, Edwards *et al.* suggest that:

> The very question 'What is teacher knowledge?' presupposes an answer that will provide some sort of objective list of knowledge? ... Such a knowledge-base would be objective in that it was unchanging, a source of certainty, providing a firm foundation for clear-cut unconditional statements about teacher knowledge and the justification for a single and unchanging national curriculum for teacher education. (2002: 33–4)

In their review of research into 'Cognition and Learning', Greeno *et al.* also identify a rationalist perspective on knowing and learning.[1] They associate rationalism with cognitive perspectives on knowledge:

> The cognitive/rationalist perspective on knowledge emphasizes understandings of concepts and theories in different subject matter domains and general cognitive abilities, such as reasoning, planning, solving problems, and comprehending language. (1996: 16)

They identify constructivism as one of the important intellectual traditions within this perspective, where the focus – after Piaget (1971, 1950) – is on characterizing the stages of development in conceptual understanding. *Gestalt* psychology and symbolic information-processing are identified as other important traditions within the cognitive/rationalist perspective – 'all three traditions emphasize the importance of organised patterns in cognitive activity' (Greeno *et al.* 1996: 16).

In a discussion of the mathematical explanations of primary school teachers, Leinhardt refers to 'principled and context-free knowledge [that] is detached and generally true' (Leinhardt 1988: 148) and distinguishes it from other, 'situated' forms of knowledge. The 'principled and context-free' knowledge is associated with algorithms (explained as the 'generative and always correct procedure') and situated knowledge with heuristics (a set of problem-solving procedures) (*ibid.*: 147–8), both with reference to teacher thinking. The assumption is that the 'principled and context-free' knowledge is in some sense *a priori* and has been elicited and is articulated in the process of education.

Objectivism, in this sense partly informed by rationalist and cognitive perspectives, regards knowing as a process of recognition and construction of concepts, and knowledge as 'some *third thing* – to be grasped, held, stored, manipulated, and wielded' (Davis and Sumara 1997: 110). An important limitation of the objectivist position in any analysis of teacher education and development is that knowledge (especially knowledge of the subject to be taught) becomes a stable, detached and universal entity that is presented to teachers and students *as given*. Objectivism can be contrasted with the position Edwards *et al.* (2002) describe as subjectivism.

Subjectivism – contrasted with the behaviourist/empiricist tradition of objectivism and postmodern perspectives

Edwards *et al.* contrast 'the absolute objectivity of knowledge' proposed by an objectivist position with 'the absolute autonomy of the individual' and 'the primacy of direct experience as the foundation of all knowledge claims' asserted by subjectivism (2002: 35). Philosophically, subjectivism contends that knowledge may reasonably be based upon individual views of the world. In other words, a subjectivist epistemology asserts that claims to justification and truth can be properly evaluated solely on the ground of an individual's direct experience. With reference to teacher education, Edwards *et al.* contend that critics of the universities' role prioritize 'on-the-job' learning and 'experience in the classroom' and denigrate attempts to make learning to teach an intellectual, knowledge-based activity. Although they would not identify themselves as subjectivists, Edwards *et al.* suggest that such critics are just that, 'arguing for the primacy of direct experience as the foundation of all knowledge claims' (*ibid.*: 35–6).

In its assertion of individual experience as the ground for evaluating claims to knowledge, subjectivism may falsely appear to be related to the philosophy of empiricism. Scheffler, using Locke's phrase, explains the empiricist view of the mind as *tabula rasa* (a blank slate) to which phenomena are revealed by experience:

The ideal education suggested by an empiricist view is one which supplies abundant and optimally ordered phenomenal experiences ... The ideal education, further, trains the student not only in proper logical habits but in traits requisite for learning from experience – accurate observation, reasonable generalisation, willingness to revise or relinquish purported laws which fail to anticipate the actual course of events. (1965: 3)

Greeno *et al.* link the empiricist view with the psychological tradition of behaviourism. In the behaviourist/empiricist view, 'knowing is an organised accumulation of associations and components of skills' (1996: 16). The traditions of associationism (the association of ideas building new associations = knowledge), behaviourism (knowledge as the observable and reinforced connections between stimuli and responses) and connectionism (knowledge as the pattern of connections between elements) are seen as contributing to this view (*ibid.*).

However, it is clear that empiricism/behaviourism accepts some of the assumptions of an *objectivist* epistemology – knowledge is objectified in that it is seen as the 'accumulation of discrete pieces of evidence' (Hood 2002), what Kelly (1955, 1963) termed 'accumulative fragmentalism'. Moreover, empiricism/behaviourism (like the cognitive/rationalist perspective) works within the positivist tradition; that is, it accepts that there is the possibility of 'a complete and scientific explanation of physical and social reality' (Pring 2000: 223). In this way, we might discern two traditions of objectivism – cognitive/rationalist and behaviourist/empiricist – but distinguish subjectivism (as proposed by Edwards *et al.*) by its proximity to solipsism. Indeed, in Edwards *et al.*'s account, subjectivism in relation to teacher knowledge and teacher education is more usefully a stick with which to bash critics of the university's role in initial teacher education, than a philosophical position on teacher knowledge.

Lyotard's theory of the postmodern condition of knowledge might initially be seen to be situated within the subjectivist view. Lyotard proposed that the production and dissemination of knowledge, once legitimized through the deployment of metanarratives or 'grand narratives', has, since the 'cultural transformations' at the end of the nineteenth century, 'dispersed' into fractured and individualistic personal narratives (1984: xxiii–iv). The individualistic and relativistic aspects (and, for some critics, the 'anything goes' implications) of postmodernist accounts of knowledge could lead them to be classified as subjectivist. However, the postmodern position – at least, the 'optimistic' version (Usher and Edwards 1994) – is informed by the concept of a test of *shared credibility*, not against an external and observable reality but in the context of shared activities and procedures. In radical constructivism, this test is referred to as the notion of 'fitness' for purpose; in postmodernist accounts of knowledge it is the concept of 'language games' (Wittgenstein 1972, Usher and Edwards 1994). And it is the notion of shared credibility that links these theories of knowledge to Edwards *et al.*'s fourth orientation: contextualism. The importance of the subjectivist position in Edwards *et al.*'s argument is that it presents them with an opportunity for a critique of the proposition that teacher education is merely a 'practical' activity or even a sub-intellectual one. Subjectivism also offers a good point of contrast with the reflective position.

The Reflective perspective: pragmatism and the concepts of 'professional' or 'practical' knowledge
The reflective perspective on knowledge is strongly associated with the work of Donald Schön (Edwards *et al.* 2002: 36–7). Schön rejected 'technical rationality' as a way of understanding cognition and learning in the professions; through a series of case studies, he proposed the concept of 'ordinary practical knowledge' (Schön 1983: 54). Edwards *et al.* suggest that he is:

> … in effect rejecting objective knowledge. At the same time he is not accepting the chaos of subjectivism (what he calls 'no knowledge at all' – Schön and Rein 1994: 42), for he wants to argue that professionals work with a tacit form of knowledge which he terms 'knowing-in-action' and which surfaces through a process he terms 'reflection-in-action'. (2002: 37)

Reflective practice is subject to critique in Edwards *et al.*'s analysis (see also Gilroy 1993). In Schön's work they see the attempt to 'reconstruct the knowledge-base of teacher education' (after the decline of the 'grand narratives of the disciplines') through the presentation of 'niche narratives … personal histories presented as reflective practice' (*ibid.*: 46) as a false dichotomy.

Philosophically, the reflective position can be seen to have grown out of pragmatism, associated with Peirce, James and Dewey. Scheffler notes that, for Dewey, the educational process is 'one of trying and undergoing – trying an idea in practice, and learning from the consequences' (1965: 4). The pragmatic view suggests that:

> To learn something significant about the world, we must do more than operate logically upon basic truths that appear to us self-evident, and we must go beyond reasonable generalisations of observed phenomenal patterns in our past experience. Experimentation involves active transformation of the environment, in a manner dictated by leading ideas put forward in response to problems and directed toward the resolution of these problems. (*ibid.*: 3–4)

The pragmatic origins of Schön's theories of professional learning and professional knowledge can be seen in the concepts of reflection-in-action and reflection-on-action as heuristics for practical problem-solving. The key test for knowledge from within the reflective position is whether it works in practical situations.

Greeno *et al.* group the pragmatic perspective on knowledge with the 'socio-historic' to form the compound 'situative/pragmatist-sociohistoric' (1996: 17). Taking Dewey as typical of the pragmatist perspective and Vygotsky as typical of the sociohistoric, they bring the two together as influential in the new 'situative perspective' on knowing and learning in that they both '... emphasise that knowledge is constructed in practical activities of groups of people as they interact with each other and their material environments' (*ibid.*: 16).

Greeno *et al.*'s compound formulation suggests that this is a point at which the boundaries of Edwards *et al.*'s four categories bleed into each other. Within the reflective position, this can be said to take place at two points: first, the individual agent's interaction with their setting; and second, the classification of 'working knowledge' or 'practical knowledge' as unique categories that are separate from – and in some senses inferior to – 'academic' or disciplinary knowledge. It is worth briefly considering the work of Eraut here.

Eraut could be said to bridge the reflective and contextualist positions. Through the concept of 'professional performance in context', he argues that 'the nature of the context affects what knowledge gets used and how' (1994: 20) and that 'transferring from one context to another requires further learning and the idea itself will be transformed in the process' (*ibid.*). He also distinguishes 'professional knowledge' from 'the knowledge from traditional disciplines' and makes a distinction between 'technical' or 'practical' knowledge (sometimes referred to as 'craft knowledge' (McNamara and Desforges 1978, Tom 1984)) and 'discipline-based' forms of knowledge. Eraut claims that the former ('practical' knowledge) depends for its validity on its use value in context (its relevance) whereas the latter ('discipline-based' knowledge) doesn't depend on use value and relevance and may therefore be described objectively.

It is through this false dichotomy (and through the one-way conceptualization of the context-individual relationship) that Eraut's work makes itself distinct from the contextualist perspective. Although there is an appeal to interaction and context, the distinction between 'practical' and 'discipline-based' knowledge allows Eraut to maintain an essentially objectivist epistemology. There is no sense that contexts themselves may be reconfigured through the participation of individuals. As I will show, such a division would not be a feature of a contextualist, sociocultural perspective and, as such, I believe locates Eraut within the reflective position.

In summary, the reflective perspective, closely associated with Schön's 'epistemology of practice' (Schön 1983: 113) and Dewey's pragmatism, views knowing not as acquiring fixed neural connections but as an ongoing process of developing understanding in practical situations. Knowledge, in this perspective, can arise out of 'doing' and, to some extent, interactions. To varying degrees, it may therefore be thought of as both an individualistic and collective orientation to knowledge, although it is clear that its identification of 'practical knowledge' –

knowing-in-action – as a distinct category allows it alone to develop in relation to context and for other, more objectivist – and transcendental – forms of knowledge to exist individualistically, inside the head of the knower without reference to contexts of any sort. The reflective perspective allows for an individual's practical knowledge to be developed as a consequence of working in a particular setting but not for the setting itself (specifically, the forms of knowledge held within that context) also to be changed. Edwards *et al.*'s final position, contextualism, offers a perspective on knowledge *per se* that is premised on just such a reflexive and transactional relationship between individual and setting.

Contextualism: language games and systemic activity

In answering the question 'What is the knowledge-base that beginning teachers acquire from their teacher education course?', Edwards *et al.* reject the three previous perspectives before mounting a defence of a fourth – the contextualist perspective. Their approach contrasts with that of Greeno *et al.*, a source I have referred to throughout this brief discussion, who, whilst outlining three general perspectives on knowing and learning from the psychological research (behaviourist/empiricist, cognitive/rationalist and situative/pragmatic-sociohistoric), acknowledge the 'considerable strengths of all three' and propose the 'value and importance of using their resources pluralistically in considering educational problems' (Greeno *et al.* 1996: 16). Rather, Edwards *et al.* see their version of contextualism as bridging the dichotomy of objectivism and subjectivism whilst simultaneously providing a more cogent, sociocultural theorization of the reflective position's focus on practice.

The philosophical origins of the contextualist position can be traced to the later work of Wittgenstein (Edwards *et al.* 2002: 38–46, Wittgenstein 1972). Wittgenstein, Edwards *et al.* argue, abandoned the search for objective truth and certainty '… arguing that it is the social system we operate in that provides the criteria against which we judge whether something is perceived as being knowledge or falsehood' (2002: 38).

They use Wittgenstein's notion of *language game* – a system, bounded by a shared purpose, 'consisting of language and the actions into which it is woven' (Wittgenstein 1972: 5§) – to describe the social process by which knowledge is legitimized and disseminated. This is 'rule-governed behaviour' that varies from context to context (Edwards *et al.* 2002: 39) so, from the contextualist perspective, it would be a mistake to generalize from these language games in order to compile a universal codification of teacher knowledge. With reference to teacher education, Edwards *et al.* suggest that:

> The rule-governed nature of the 'game' of teaching requires first practice and second the understanding of the criteria that guide this practice, which would include

experiencing and grasping the shifting and varied nature of the criteria guiding their practice. It is the first of these requirements that student teachers naturally concentrate on as they work at surviving in the classroom, but it is the second that would allow them to begin to see the ways in which their practice is rule-governed, connected to a social context and thus subject to change. (*ibid*.: 40)

Earlier, in my discussion of subjectivism, I pointed out the importance of the idea of a test for shared credibility. Contextualism is not subjective relativism nor does it imply that 'anything goes'. Edwards *et al.* argue for the distinctive contribution of a contextualist answer to the question of a knowledge-base for teaching:

> What has to be avoided is both a context-free (transcendental) argument for objectivity and a context-bound (socially subjective) argument for the relativity of knowledge. By arguing that knowledge claims are to be located within language games which have their life within various social contexts, one avoids any attempt at some sort of supra-objectivity, only a straightforward description of how knowledge is to be found in practice. By arguing that language games are governed by rules provided by criteria, one avoids any attempt at accepting that 'anything goes' for knowledge. (*ibid*.: 44)

It is important to note, however, that 'certain limited and temporary objectivities' within the language game are necessary in order to provide an agreement on the basis on which the game can be played (*ibid*.: 46). This is one way – through the incorporation of a temporary and contingent objectivism – in which Edwards *et al.*'s contextualist perspective can be seen to encompass elements of the three other perspectives they have dismissed and which they assert that contextualism supersedes. Similarly, the induction of new teachers into a form of 'knowing-in action' (Schön 1983) can be seen as immersion into the activity of a language game 'followed by critical illumination of that activity's context' (reflection-on-action) (Edwards *et al.* 2002: 47). In this way, Edwards *et al.* would reinterpret reflective practice as '*contextualist* practices' (*ibid*.).

Greeno *et al.* developed the compound formulation of 'situative/pragmatist-sociohistoric' (1996: 17) to emphasize the situated (i.e. contextual) character of knowledge arising out the interactions of people and their environments over time. Drawing on the research traditions of ethnography, ecological psychology and situation theory, they proposed a view of knowledge and knowing that is focused on activity and on 'the processes of interaction with other people and with physical and technological systems' (*ibid*.). The sociohistoric dimension to this theory is represented by the understanding – from Vygotsky (1974) via Bruner (1986) – that 'mind is transmitted across history by means of successive mental sharings' (Roth 1999: 10).

In his account of the development of epistemology over the last 350 years, Toulmin proposed that the contributions of Wittgenstein and Vygostky are mutually supportive. For Toulmin, it was in a concern with 'shared procedures' and practice that their work converges:

> For both men, language has a definite meaning only when it is related to a given constellation of practical activities. Each lexical term is meaningful within a *sprachspiel* (or 'language game'); but a language game is meaningful only if construed in the context of a given *Lebensform* (or 'form of life'). (1999: 59)

So it is in the intersubjectivity of collective situations that meanings are realized and through language that we 'internalise the meanings and patterns of thought that are current in our culture or profession' and, over time, 'acquire inner experiences modelled on the public activities of our culture and society' (*ibid.*: 58). Theoretically, within this perspective on knowledge, the pragmatic and individualist orientation towards practical problem-solving situations is linked to the sociohistoric theory of mind.

Once again, the notion of a test of shared credibility is important. From Toulmin's perspective, 'meaning is determined by its place in a given typified action sequence' (*ibid.*: 60), that is, by its place within a practical context. Knowledge is meaningful, knowledge is said to be developed from within intentional activity and knowledge comes to be seen as systemic, 'shared procedures' for evaluating meaning:

> So understood, shared procedures are neither the exclusive property of collective professions nor the exclusive property of individual agents. Rather, the rational history of a human discipline involves a continuing interchange between the innovations of creative individuals and their acceptance or rejection by the professional community. (*ibid.*)

This notion of the importance of the professional community's evaluation and the relationships between creative individuals and the community is worth developing further at this point as it informs my theorisation of the development of beginning teachers' thinking about subject knowledge. In this way, Toulmin's concept of 'shared procedures' leads us to a consideration of Lave and Wenger's (1991) concept of 'communities of practice'.

Learning, participating and developing a sense of identity

Communities of practice and the existence of knowledge

In *Situated Learning: Legitimate Peripheral Participation* (1991), Lave and Wenger present five studies of learners becoming midwives, tailors, quartermasters, butchers or non-drinking alcoholics through a process of apprenticeship. One of the important contributions of Lave and Wenger's research has been to recover the dynamic complexity of apprenticeship learning from various reductive interpretations and to link the movement to full participation in practice (defined as shared, *conceptual* work) to the formation of the apprentice learner's identity. Within this perspective, apprentices do not just 'acquire the "specifics" of practice through "observation and imitation"'; by being absorbed – peripherally at first – in the 'culture of practice', apprentices develop 'knowledge-in-practice' (1991: 21–4). Knowledge achieves meaning within the 'community of practice'; defining such a community as 'a set of relations among persons, activity, and the world, over time and in relation with other tangential and overlapping communities of practice' (*ibid.*: 23–4), they suggest that:

> A community of practice is an intrinsic condition for the existence of knowledge, not least because it provides the interpretive support necessary for making sense of its heritage. Thus, participation in the cultural practice in which any knowledge exists is an epistemological principle of learning. (*ibid.*: 24)

For Lave and Wenger, all claims to knowledge are evaluated within a community of practice ('the place of knowledge is within a community of practice' (*ibid.*: 25)). This does not mean that all members of that community have to be co-present; it does mean 'participation in an activity system about which participants share understandings' (*ibid.*: 23). They contrast this form of learning with a more didactic form where increasing participation is not the principal motivation for learning but where educational exchange value (i.e. engaging in an activity in order to be awarded a qualification on completion) replaces the use value of increasing participation (*ibid.*: 31). Such a system engenders the 'commoditisation of learning' where 'parasitic practices' such as test-taking are designed to increase the exchange value of learning alone (*ibid.*). Knowledge claims in the commoditized system are evaluated by 'didactic caretakers' (*ibid.*) whereas knowledge claims in the more (in Lave and Wenger's terms) 'authentic' system are evaluated within a community of practice.

However, this position could imply a static notion of knowledge – some stable entity or set of practices – that is merely reproduced by the system. Innovation could be seen as impossible within such a closed system of reproduction, which has certainly been how some critics of school-based teacher education have understood apprenticeship learning (e.g. McIntyre 1997). Lave and Wenger address this issue of the cycle of reproduction of a community and its specialized knowledge by considering the ways in which 'newcomers' and 'old-timers' interact and how their different identities (as newcomers and old-timers) generate productive tensions and contradictions:

> Newcomers are caught in a dilemma. On the one hand, they need to engage in the existing practice, which has developed over time: to understand it, to participate in it, and to become full members of the community in which it exists. On the other hand,

they have a stake in its development as they begin to establish their own identity in its future. (*ibid.*: 33)

They describe this as 'the continuity-displacement contradiction' that involves conflict and tension (between either expert/novices or, more loosely, generations) centred on learning, participating and a developing sense of identity. Knowledge, as a set of shared procedures for evaluating meaning, has a key role to play in this relationship and it is through the 'continuity-displacement contradiction', arising out of the granting of legitimate peripheral participation to 'newcomers with their own viewpoints', that the conditions are established for the generation of new knowledge:

> ... legitimate peripheral participation is far more than just a process of learning on the part of the newcomers. It is a *reciprocal relation* between persons and practice. This means that the move of learners toward full participation in a community of practice does not take place in a static context. The practice itself is in motion. (*ibid.*: 34; my emphasis)

Lave and Wenger's concepts of communities of practice, legitimate peripheral participation and the continuity-displacement contradiction are useful when considering how claims to knowledge can be evaluated and validated and also when considering the relationships between individuals, communities and new knowledge or innovations. Lave and Wenger's work develops our understandings of a contextualist perspective on knowledge in that the learner can be conceptualized as 'both a user and producer of knowledge within a set of social practices' (Edwards *et al.* 2002: 109).

With specific reference to teacher education, Putnam and Borko (2000) developed the theories of knowledge, knowing and learning proposed by Lave and Wenger (1991), Lave (1988), Brown *et al.* (1989) and others to identify possibilities for the design of 'authentic activities' in teacher education programmes. Three conceptual themes are central to their argument: '... cognition is a) situated in particular physical and social contexts; b) social in nature; and c) distributed across the individual, other persons, and tools' (Putnam and Borko 2000: 4).

An important implication of their argument for teacher educators is to identify the '... key characteristics of field-based experiences [school placements/teaching practicums] that can foster new ways of teaching, and determining whether and how these experiences can be created within existing school cultures' (*ibid.*: 10).

In other words, teacher educators need to consider whether existing school cultures and communities of practice are 'open' enough to permit for newcomer teachers the legitimate peripheral participation conceptualized by Lave and Wenger and to allow for the productive tensions generated by the continuity-displacement contradiction. What are the consequences for professional learning, for example, when the community becomes a closed, reproductive system and one where knowledge is understood as static and given?

In order to understand more fully the process by which knowledge is generated within systemic activity and 'stretched over' (Lave 1988) the individual, the community and various aspects of the physical environment, ecological psychology can contribute to our understanding of a contextualist perspective on knowledge. Aspects of ecological psychology were used by Edwards *et al.* (2002) and Greeno *et al.* (1996) in their respective elaborations of contextualism and the situative/pragmatist-sociohistoric view of knowledge as distributed in the world. Given the multiple, multilayered and overlapping dynamic systems in which beginning teachers learn to teach their subjects, ecological psychology can make a useful contribution to the analysis of teachers' development.

The contribution of ecological psychology to perspectives on knowledge and teaching

Informed by the work of Gibson (1966, 1979) and others (for example, Greeno 1994; Greeno *et al.* 1996), ecological psychology proposes that 'knowledge is distributed in the world among individuals, the tools, artefacts, and books they use, and the communities and practices in which they participate' (Greeno *et al.* 1996: 20). Such an account of knowing and learning implies that it is the general characteristics of the context or activity system that determine the generation and evaluation of knowledge. Gibson's notion of *affordances* is important in this respect, where affordance refers to 'whatever it is about the environment that contributes to the kind of interaction [between an 'agent' and a 'system'] that occurs' (Greeno 1994: 338). This idea has emerged from interactionist accounts of cognition. Arising out of situation theory, another concept is useful within the ecological perspective and this is *attunements to constraints* (Greeno 1994, Greeno *et al.* 1996). The concept of *constraint* refers to a regularity involving a situation that may involve a dependent or causal relationship. Knowing that when one perceives smoke there may be a fire involved would be described as an 'attunement to the constraint that *smoke means fire*' (Greeno 1994: 339). Gibson's (1966) theory of perception as the active 'picking up' of information in the environment 'as an aspect of the agent's activity' (Greeno *et al.* 1996: 21) is the foundation of this view of learning and knowledge, where learning could be described as the progressive attunement to the constraints of an activity by the agent (the learner) and knowledge as being afforded by the interaction of an agent with the system (where system is defined as activity system, its tools and communities).[2] The ecological perspective suggests that knowing is both individual and collective in the context of activity and that knowledge emerges in the interaction between agent and system.

With reference to the research on teacher cognition and 'working knowledge in teaching', Yinger and Hendricks-Lee identify a shift in focus from 'individual cognitive processing and technical action' to an interaction between individuals and their environment (1993: 102). They characterize this shift as one towards a view of 'ecological intelligence', within which 'how to characterize and capture knowledge becomes a pertinent issue' (*ibid.*: 104). They offer the following propositions about knowledge:

- Knowledge is inherent and widely dispersed across complex systems of information and action: cultural, physical, social, historical and personal.
- Knowledge within these systems becomes available as working knowledge in particular activities and events.
- Working knowledge is constructed jointly through responsive interaction (conversation) among all the participants (systems) in an activity. (*ibid.*: 112)

At first sight, there may appear to be some similarities with Schön's concept of 'ordinary practical knowledge' (Schön 1983) – for example, the conceptions of 'working' and 'ordinary practical' knowledge and the apparent similarity of 'reflection-on-action' and 'responsive interaction'. An important difference, however, is that Schön's account is essentially individualistic in that the process of reflection and the emergence of 'knowing-in-action' takes place inside the head of the knower, whereas in an ecological account, such as Yinger and Hendricks-Lee's, the conditions for knowledge are set by the attunements of the agent to the constraints and affordances of the activity system.

To explore this relationship between the agent and the system further within a contextualist perspective on knowledge a little more closely, the recent work of Davis and Sumara (2000) and the earlier work of Urie Bronfenbrenner (1979) offer usefully integrative models. Again, this discussion will support my developing argument about the complex ecologies in which beginning teachers think and learn.

A complex view of the 'nestedness' of knowledge in the ecology of human development

In their *Harvard Educational Review* article of 1997, Davis and Sumara proposed a complex and interactive perspective on knowledge for teacher education. They noted what they saw as 'a deeply embedded cultural inability to rid ourselves of the notion that knowledge … has some sort of corporeal existence' (Davis and Sumara 1997: 109). Instead, they argued that knowledge arose out of action and existence in a 'biologically and phenomenologically constituted world' (*ibid.*) and that 'cognition exist[ed] in the interstices of a complex ecology of organismic relationality' (*ibid.*: 110). Distinguishing between 'collective knowledge' and 'individual understanding', they nevertheless described these as 'dynamically co-emergent phenomena' (*ibid.*). The problem for Davis and Sumara is that school systems treat 'such matters as the status of knowledge and the cultural context of education ... as unproblematic givens': 'They arrive, completed, on the teacher's desk in the form of curriculum manuals and standardized textbooks, and their believed-to-be static natures are continuously announced in an unceasing barrage of examinations' (*ibid.*: 121).

Davis and Sumara developed this ecological and cultural perspective on knowledge in their 2000 article, 'Curriculum forms: on the assumed shapes of knowing and knowledge' (Davis and Sumara 2000). Like the 1997 piece, this article makes reference to an eclectic range of literature from biological and genetic science, HIV research and immunology to the philosophy of mathematics, literary anthropology and holistic philosophies. For my present purpose, I will focus on their analysis of the embodied and embodying nature of knowledge and the relationships between different layers or 'nests' of knowing.

They begin by drawing an analogy between the structures of schooling and curriculum (and associated practices such as the pre-planning of learning objectives) and the 'classical' structures required by Plato's logic and Euclid's geometry ('i.e. lines, grids, spirals, and so on' (*ibid.*: 830)). They argue that these 'images and 'metaphors' have been subject to critique 'for the last few centuries' but that this critique has had little impact on the way we think about knowledge in the context of schooling (*ibid.*: 823). Instead they propose fractal geometry (as 'a mathematical analogue to such discourse fields as post-modernism, post-structuralism and ecological theory' (*ibid.*: 821)) as a better way for understanding living systems 'both structurally (in terms of the characters of their sub-systems) and operationally (in terms of the sorts of rules that guide the interactions of these systems)' (*ibid.*: 828). Fractal images are held to be 'far closer to the flexibility of life' (Stewart 1998; cited in Davis and Sumara 2000: 825), and the concepts of scale independence (meaning the same regularity of detail is presented under any magnification) and self-similarity (meaning that one part of the figure resembles the whole) are important.

Davis and Sumara draw on this fractal geometry to provide a visual metaphor for the 'integration of recent but varied discourses on knowing and knowledge' (*ibid.*: 826). Their rationale is that these varied discourses 'rely on very similar dynamics while focusing on very different levels of organism or social organisation' (*ibid.*) The 'varied discourses' under discussion by Davis and Sumara are 'subject-centred constructivism', 'social constructionisms' and 'cultural and critical discourses' (*ibid.*: 831–3). In tracing the commonalities between these discourses, they suggest that the 'metaphoric commitment to the body across interpretive frameworks' is an important integrating factor (*ibid.*). Knowledge is seen to be embodied and embodying (whether in relation to 'a person, a social group or a culture') in that it both arises out of bodily action and gives coherence and 'maintains [the] viability' of a body (*ibid.*: 835). To continue with the fractal metaphors: 'Individual knowing, collective knowledge and cultural identity become three intertwining, self-similar levels of one phenomenon –

ones which, as with the fractal image, can only be understood in relation to one another' (*ibid.*: 834).

In proposing the 'nestedness' of bodies of knowledge and discourses, Davis and Sumara identify the self-similar and scale-independent dynamics that operate at the different 'nests' or layers of knowing, from the 'sub-subjective' (bodily sub-systems) to the 'supra-cultural' (planetary). The embodied and embodying attributes of knowledge and the 'permeability' of the boundaries between the nested layers (that may falsely be seen to separate agents and systems) are important aspects of these self-similar and scale independent dynamics.

The concept of the 'nestedness' of bodies and discourses foregrounds the inter-relationships and interdependence within and between complex systems (at individual, social and cultural/historical levels) at work in the activity of learning to teach. Their account of knowledge – and of learning – in relation to teaching offers a radical challenge to the view that learning to teach consists simply of the individual acquisition of skills and techniques and the filling of 'gaps' in subject knowledge. Their visual metaphor (developed specifically in relation to teaching and learning in schools and pre-service teacher education) also extends Bronfenbrenner's theory of human development and its ecology of 'nested' environments or systems.

Writing in 1979, Bronfenbrenner proposed 'a new theoretical perspective for research in human development' focused on the evolving interaction between the developing person and the environment (1979: 3). Bronfenbrenner conceptualized the 'ecological environment … as a set of nested structures, each inside the next, like a set of Russian dolls' (*ibid.*). He identified and described four systems that constitute the ecological environment:

Microsystem	what is experienced by the developing person in a given setting;
Mesosystem	the interrelations among two or more settings in which the developing person actively participates;
Exosystem	one or more settings in which the developing person is not an active participant but in which events occur that affect or are affected by what happens in the setting containing the developing person;
Macrosystem	consistencies in the form and content of lower-order systems that exist or could exist at the level of the subculture or the culture as a whole. (*ibid.*: 21–6)

Bronfenbrenner's model differs from that of Davis and Sumara in that it is focused on the interaction between the developing person and the ecological environment expressed in terms of these five systems. While they all propose a cultural dimension to knowledge and development, Davis and Sumara's ambitious project attempts to show how dimensions of knowledge that range from bodily subsystems to the planetary are interrelated and reflexive. In their work, however, an important emphasis is also given to the developing person's subjectivity and biography and how these become resources that are drawn upon in the making of knowledge. In Bronfenbrenner's work, an important emphasis is given to the concept of *setting* and how the interrelations among settings are *experienced* (directly or indirectly) by the developing person. Bronfenbrenner also begins to suggest a more direct and reflexive relationship between the individual, the collective and the cultural levels by defining the macrosystem (the cultural or subcultural level) as 'consistencies' in the 'form and content of lower-order systems … along with any belief systems or ideology underlying such consistencies' (*ibid.*: 26). Bronfenbrenner's attention to settings, relationships between settings and how they are experienced is important and it is the concept of setting and the distinction between setting and aspects of the cultural dimension (Bronfenbrenner's macrosystem or what Lave (1988) referred to as *arena*) that will be considered in the next section of the chapter.

Settings, arenas and the development of knowledge

Lave builds on the work of Bronfenbrenner and others in developing our understanding of the concept of setting. In *Cognition in Practice: Mind, Mathematics and Culture in Everyday Life*, Lave sought to understand cognition as 'a nexus of relations between the mind at work and the world in which it works' (1988: 1). To achieve this, she introduces the concept of *arena* – defined as a 'physically, economically, and socially organised space-in-time' (*ibid.*: 150). In her own research into the 'everyday' numeracy practices of shoppers, she describes the concept of the supermarket as an arena: it is 'the product of social formation and political economy' that is 'not negotiable directly by the individual' (*ibid.*: 151). To explain how the individual does come to experience, is affected by *and* affects the arena, Lave uses the concept of setting:

> … for individual shoppers, the supermarket is a repeatedly experienced, personally ordered and edited version of the arena. In this aspect it may be termed a setting for activity. Some aisles in the supermarket do not exist for a given shopper as part of her [sic] setting, while other aisles are rich in detailed possibilities. (*ibid.*)

Lave emphasizes the importance of the dialectical relationship between activity and setting: 'A setting is generated out of a person's grocery-shopping activity and at the same time generates that activity. In short, activity is dialectically constituted in relation with the setting …' (*ibid.*).

Arena, in this analysis, is at the cultural or subcultural level and is a product of 'a particular constitutive order', defined by Lave as a system that 'motivate[s] experience' and is a resource that is 'drawn upon in the fashioning of intentional activity in the lived-in world' (*ibid.*: 178). This suggests the important question: how might the concepts of arena and setting operate in analysis of initial teacher education?

Leach and Moon, in their analysis of 'professional knowledge', have used Lave's concepts of arena and setting to suggest the dynamic and interactive nature of teachers' knowledge (Banks *et al.* 1999; Leach and Moon 2000). They do so in an effort to provide a 'strong focus on learning' in their account of knowledge and to support an analysis of teachers' learning and development that is multi-dimensional (Leach and Moon 2000: 395). In relation to teacher knowledge, they suggest that:

> A pedagogic arena and a pedagogic setting can be explored at a variety of sites and levels. Policy-makers, teachers, software designers, educational website creators and parents, for example, all create pedagogic arenas, their specified 'curriculum' being manifest through these pedagogic dimensions, whether explicitly or implicitly. Arenas are brought to life in particular pedagogic settings – the practices that teachers, together with a particular group of learners, create, enact and experience. Thus the notion of a pedagogic setting can, and should, encompass individuals and the group as a whole as the unit of analysis. Settings just as much reflect teachers' own perceptions of their core task of teaching (and learners' experiences of and interactions with this endeavour) as they are the outcomes of the mediating influences of institutional goals, activities, structures and policies at local and national level. (*ibid.*)

Leach and Moon's development of pedagogic arena and pedagogic setting extends Lave's focus on the interrelationship between the two and the ways in which the setting is constituted dialectically in relation to activity. Settings, for Leach and Moon, can be of different orders and, together with the macrosystemic dimension of arena, make up the ecological environment in the development of teacher knowledge.

Implications for studies of teachers' knowledge and thinking

What Edwards *et al.* refer to as the contextualist perspective on knowledge and learning – informed by 'situative/pragmatist-sociohistoric' (Greeno *et al.* 1996: 17) approaches to cognition – can be generative in analyses of how beginning teachers think about subject knowledge. Contextualist and sociocultural perspectives represents a shift in focus from 'individual cognitive processing and technical action' to interaction between individuals and their environment over time (Yinger and Hendricks-Lee 1993: 102). This perspective emphasises the importance of object-oriented, systemic activity in the development of teacher knowledge and proposes that knowledge itself (rather than just separate – and perhaps lower-status categories such as 'practical' or 'professional' knowledge) is 'stretched over' (Lave 1988) the individual, the community and the environment. A sociocultural perspective proposes that 'individual' knowledge always stands in relation to a community of practice that evaluates its claims to justification and truth; contextualism proposes that 'individual' knowledge stands in relation to the 'shared procedures' (Toulmin 1999) of a community and the 'bodies of knowledge' of a society that have become a cultural resource.

In their integrative model of various discourses on knowledge and knowing, Davis and Sumara offer a visual metaphor that can also inform studies of beginning teachers' development. If we put the biochemical and astronomical layers to one side, their 'nested' model suggests a focus of analysis on 'individual knowing, collective knowledge and cultural identity' (Davis and Sumara 2000: 834) whilst also acknowledging the interplay between these three layers and the permeability of the boundaries between the layers. In other words, their model represents how the individual is situated within the setting and *becomes part of it*. These three layers also conflict and it is against the sometimes contradictory dynamics of individual history or autobiography playing against the activities of a community playing against the layer of cultural resources and political economy that the development of the beginning teachers' thinking about subject knowledge can be examined. Bronfenbrenner's (1979) emphasis on understanding the ways in which the developing person *experiences* their settings and Lave's (1988) distinction between arena and setting can also inform such an analysis of development that isn't founded upon an objectivist epistemology or an individualistic model of mind.

3

Know, understand and be able to do: professionalizing knowledge

In this chapter, I put my research into its cultural-historical context – both in terms of contemporaneous education policy in England and traditions of inquiry within the educational research community. The chapter argues that the objectification and codification of a specialized body of knowledge – specifically, in my research, the category of subject knowledge – is one aspect of the movement to professionalize teaching and that the crisis of professionality that was occurring at the time of the research was also a crisis of knowledge.

Reforming teaching: the codification of professional knowledge

> … initial teacher education has increasingly become a major site for political debate and struggle in recent years. It was not always so. (Furlong *et al.* 2000: 1)

In *Teacher Education in Transition: Re-forming professionalism?*, their analysis of initial teacher education in England since the early 1980s, Furlong *et al.* trace the development of policy in this field towards the apparently diversified but increasingly centralized system that operated in the late 1990s. They see the establishment of the Council for the Accreditation of Teacher Education (CATE), the subsequent revision of conventional training courses and the introduction of new routes into teaching in the 1980s, along with the more directive interventions of the 1990s (such as the establishment of the Teacher Training Agency and the specification of, first, competences (DfE 1993) and then national Standards for the award of Qualified Teacher Status and the Initial Teacher Training National Curricula (DfEE 1998a)), as indicative of unprecedented struggle and debate. Moreover, they state that:

> … most of the changes introduced in the 1990s have been concerned to influence the nature of professional knowledge, skills and values that student teachers are expected to have … The assumption behind policy within this area has been that changes in the form and content of initial teacher education will, in the long run, serve to construct a new generation of teachers with different forms of knowledge, different skills and different professional values. (Furlong *et al.* 2000: 6)

Whilst it is certainly the case that government policy in this area in the late 1990s sought to reform teaching and to remake understandings of teaching as a profession, it was certainly not the first time that interest in what teachers should know has been related to their claim for a professional identity. Ken Jones, for example, notes a 'radical shift' in England between 1968 and 1974 during which departments of teacher education '... were affected by, and themselves generated, movements of protest and attempts to develop new kinds of knowledge and new sorts of social identity' (Jones 2003: 87–8).

Bullough (2001) has written about how the 'professionalizing' instinct of late nineteenth-century teacher educators in the US – as they moved from the normal schools to the university sector – also made special, epistemological claims. So although an interest in what kinds of knowledge teachers should have (and that teacher education should develop) has been of long-standing interest, what the 1990s did bring was an attempt to mould this interest around a new managerialist (Sachs 2003) professional identity.

Teaching as a profession

Hoyle and John offer what they refer to as a 'classical conception' of a profession: an occupational group that bases its practice on a body of specialist knowledge, that is able to work autonomously, and of whom there are high expectations of responsibility. With reference to the 'body of specialist or technical knowledge' of a profession, they identify two parts: '... first, it has been tested by scientific method, thereby acquiring validity; second, it is supported by a variety of theoretical models and case descriptions which allow the knowledge to be applied to specific aspects of practice' (1995: 46–7).

Hoyle and John suggest that the application of this 'medical model' of professional knowledge to teaching is problematic because of the long-standing distinction between the technical and practical elements of knowledge (after Oakshott 1962): the practical knowledge of teachers, 'expressed in the act of practice and through reflection on those acts' (*ibid.*: 46), appears to resist the codification required for high-status theoretical knowledge and doesn't claim to have the always-and-wherever, positivistic validity sought by 'scientific method'. Although it may appear that Hoyle and John are suggesting that teaching's claim to professional status is unfounded, in fact their argument is that *profession* itself 'is an essentially contested concept' (*ibid.*: 1).

Calderhead (1987: 1–3) offered an influential rationale for considering teaching as a profession in which practical and theoretical knowledge are key elements. The rationale identified four characteristics of professional activity: the first, again, is the possession of a 'body of specialised knowledge acquired through training and experience' – it is the blend of theoretical and practical knowledge realized through *praxis* that is important in this definition; the second characteristic is that the knowledge-in-use is 'goal-oriented in relation to [...] clients', although he recognizes that in the case of education the specification of a clientele can be problematic; the third characteristic is that professionals use their expert knowledge to 'analyse and interpret' problems that are 'complex and ambiguous', making 'judgements and decisions as they formulate a course of action intended to benefit their client'; finally, this leads to the fourth characteristic of professional activity identified by Calderhead: 'skilful action that is adapted to its context', '[t]hrough repeated practice, the professional has developed various specialist and "knowledgeable" skills' (*ibid.*: 3).

Acknowledging that 'skilful action' – although founded on principled or strategic practical and theoretical knowledge – will vary according to context, and that this allows for the generation and deployment of *new* practical and theoretical knowledge, again seems especially apposite when considering teaching as a professional activity.

As discussed in the previous chapter, Eraut also identified a category of knowledge termed 'professional' and suggested that the context of professional performance affects what '[professional] knowledge gets used and how' (1994: 20). Like Calderhead, Eraut maintained that this knowledge is contextual – or situated – and tacit; it is therefore of a different order to what Eraut called 'discipline-based knowledge' which appears to be in some sense *a priori* and always true, without depending on 'use value and relevance'. In this way, Calderhead and Eraut's contributions are paradoxical in that whilst proposing that teaching has a specialized body of knowledge unavailable to the lay person and thereby making the occupation deserving of professional status, professional knowledge is simultaneously differentiated as a tacit, relativistic, uncodifiable form of knowledge in comparison to what Eraut refers to as 'traditional disciplines' (*ibid.*). This understanding of professional knowledge accepts an objectivist epistemology insofar as it conceptualizes 'discipline-based knowledge' as 'not depending on the field of professional action' (*ibid.*: 43), divorcing knowledge from the communities of practice and activity systems in which it is developed. In this analysis, disciplinary knowledge is just 'out there' whilst professional knowledge is forever idiosyncratic.

Nevertheless, these considerations of teaching as a profession are interesting for my purposes here because of the importance they accord to teachers developing and possessing a body of specialist knowledge. The work of Calderhead, Eraut and others (arising out of McNamara and Desforges 1978, Tom 1984, Elbaz 1983, Leinhardt and Smith 1985, etc.) is indicative of attempts from within the profession to identify a specialist body of knowledge that will provide grounds for claims to professional status. As Labaree (1992: 123) points out, this move can also be seen as an 'extension of the effort by teacher educators to raise their own professional status' and to secure their own sometimes precarious position within universities by identifying an area of knowledge uniquely their own and over which they will have some control. Labaree's thesis falls within what Hoyle and John refer to as the 'ideological view' of the professions where professional status 'is seen as a function of the power which has accrued to a profession through its increasing control of the market' (1995: 7).

'High status, high standards': a very brief history of subject knowledge

Teachers' knowledge of the subjects they teach (as a dimension of their professional knowledge) has been a consistent feature in claims for the professional status of school teaching. Attempts in the 1980s from within the profession (particularly in the US) to identify and promote professional knowledge as a concept paid attention to teachers' subject knowledge. Elbaz (1983), for example, in her attempt to specify five categories of teachers' 'practical knowledge' included knowledge of the subject matter along with knowledge of the self, knowledge of the milieu of teaching, knowledge of the curriculum and knowledge of instruction. Leinhardt and Smith (1985) broke teachers' 'expert knowledge' into subject matter knowledge and knowledge of lesson structure.

But a view of teaching which emphasizes the importance of how much teachers know about the subjects they are teaching – and which makes the assumption that the more the teacher knows about this subject the better the attainment outcomes for their students – is not a new one. Periodic crises in schooling – whether referenced to what are perceived to be declining intellectual or moral standards or to a suspicion of a largely female workforce – have often seen the rise of high stakes tests for new teachers in their subjects or 'key skills' (see, for example, Hoffman 1981). Indeed, from the beginning of the system of formal training for elementary school teachers in England from the mid-nineteenth century to the inter-war period of the twentieth, training college curricula and, indeed, subject knowledge examinations were prescribed by central government (Gosden 1969: 195). With reference to what we now call English or literacy, these examinations included sections on:

...

Reading

To read (December 1855) with a distinct utterance, with due attention to the punctuation, and with a just expression, a passage from Mr Warren's 'Select Extracts from Blackstone's Commentaries.'

...

English Grammar

1. Its principles.

2. To parse (December 1855) a passage from the Chapter on 'The Doctrine of the Hereditary Right to the British Throne', and 'The History of the Succession of the British Monarch' in Warren's Extracts from Blackstone.

3. To paraphrase the same passage. (Report of the Committee of Council on Education for 1854–5: 17–21; cited in Gosden 1969: 196–7.)

In England, McNamara (1991) and Turner-Bissett (1999) trace a renewed interest by government in specifying what teachers should know about the subjects they teach to the 1983 White Paper, *Teaching Quality* (DES 1983) and the Circulars which established and reconstituted CATE (McNamara 1991: 114). Subsequently, Circular 14/93 (DfE 1993) laid down the number of hours prospective primary teachers should spend on English, mathematics and science and: '... set out strict new criteria which training courses must meet, focusing on the subject knowledge and teaching skills new teachers require to be effective in the classroom' (*ibid.*: 3).

The introduction of the pupils' National Curriculum as a result of the 1988 Education Reform Act also served to reinforce the position that initial teacher education was a preparation to teach the subject knowledge codified in the National Curriculum.[1]

Subject knowledge and the Initial Teacher Training National Curricula
Circular 4/98 (DfEE 1998a), the document that enforced the new ITTNCs, was significantly different, however.[2] Furlong *et al.* show how various 'contexts of influence' in the policy space shaped the formulation of this Circular, in particular the 'neo-conservative' voices who considered that:

> The primary task for initial teacher education ... is therefore to develop professionals who are themselves experts in their own subject area; ... the chief weakness of current approaches to initial training [according to the 'neo-conservative voices'] is that they are dominated by preparing students *how* to teach rather than *what* to teach. (2000: 11)

In responding to these voices, Circular 4/98 was a 'concerted attempt to use initial teacher education to define the nature of teaching in those subjects' (*ibid.*: 144) and to codify professional knowledge. Although there was some agreement about this codification among teacher educators of secondary mathematics and science, as Furlong *et al.* acknowledge, the ICT and, especially, the English curricula (Primary and Secondary) were seen as 'much more explicitly political and therefore much more controversial' (*ibid.*: 155).

The Secondary English ITTNC set out, for the first time, what government expected prospective English teachers *to be taught* and then what it expected them to *know, understand and be able to do* (in the formulation of the Circular) (DfES 1998a). In his introduction to the seven ITTNCs[3] contained within the Circular, there was a clear acknowledgement by Michael Bichard – then the Permanent Secretary at the Department for Education and Employment – that this specification of 'core knowledge' represented a major shift in the relationship between central government and the higher education sector that would lead to some aspects of existing courses being abandoned:

Effective implementation of the initial teacher training curricula may require considerable changes to courses for some providers. Providers implementing the primary training curricula in English and mathematics since September 1997 have found it easier to redesign their course around the required core, replacing some components, than trying to fit the new training curricula around existing provision. (DfEE 1998a: 3)

In the preamble to the Secondary English curriculum, this was reinforced with the warning that '[t]he ITT secondary English curriculum is intended to form the **core** of secondary English ITT courses, not to fit around existing provision' (*ibid.*: 89; emphasis in original).

The Secondary English ITTNC was 15 pages long and divided into three sections: *A) Pedagogical knowledge and understanding required by trainees to secure pupils' progress in English; B) Effective teaching and assessment methods; C) Trainees' knowledge and understanding of English.* After a preamble of three and a half pages, the first two sections (A and B) consisted of eight and a half pages and the third (C – the section focused on 'trainees' subject knowledge') ran to three. The longest individual section (B) specified in 20 numbered subsections (containing 81 bullet points) what were considered to be the most 'effective teaching and assessment methods'. These requirements were highly specified, even to the level of classroom activities; for example:

Section B ...
15: Trainees must be taught how to teach grammar, including how to:
[...]
e. set pupils activities which demonstrate the way that grammar works and the factors which influence grammatical choices, *e.g. changing a first person account into the third person changes the focus of attention and the level of formality.* (*ibid.*: 96; emphasis in original)

Section C began by outlining the requirements for entry to Secondary English courses in terms of appropriate qualifications for admission to first degree courses (such as the BA with QTS) and, for PGCE courses, the statement that the graduate's degree should provide 'the necessary foundation for work as a teacher of English' (*ibid.*: 99). It then went on to cite variation in PGCE students' under-graduate qualifications – in terms of 'coverage' of English – as a reason for requiring initial teacher education courses to 'audit' the subject knowledge of their 'trainees' to ensure that there were no 'gaps':

... where gaps in trainees' subject knowledge are identified, providers of ITT must make arrangements to ensure that trainees gain that knowledge during the course and that, *by the end of the course*, they are competent in using their subject knowledge in their teaching. (*ibid.*; emphasis in the original)

Following a separate section on the requirements to audit (26a–c), the document laid out what 'all trainees must know and understand' about English (*ibid.*: 99–101). In order of their appearance in the curriculum, the following list represents the areas identified as the subject knowledge necessary to 'teach English effectively' in the secondary school:

- *Technical terms*
  These were not specified and the explanation is vague, just that they are '*in addition* to those in the National Curriculum English order' (*ibid.*: 99; my emphasis).
- *The nature and role of standard English*
  The claim here that standard English is the 'general, public English used to communicate within the United Kingdom and throughout the English-speaking world' (*ibid.*) would seem to go against the grain of generally accepted understandings of language variation and change and the development of world Englishes (see, for example, Crystal 2004).

There was then a long section which specified knowledge that was said to be necessary to give 'trainees a more explicit insight into their own writing' and to 'analyse and evaluate others' writing' – including (almost as an afterthought) 'pupils' writing' (*ibid.*: 100). It is claimed that what follows will give 'trainees the terminology [once again] and concepts to understand processes such as language acquisition' and to 'study research evidence on language' (*ibid.*). It begins with:

- *Lexis, including morphology and semantics, phonology and graphology*
- *The grammar of spoken and written English, to include word classes, word order and cohesion, sentence types and clause structure, coordinaton and subordination*
- *Punctuation*
- *Textual cohesion*
- *A broad understanding of language as a social, cultural and historical phenomenon*

and, finally:

- *Knowledge about texts and critical approaches to them.*

The final subsection offered general and non-statutory guidance about what new teachers should know in order to teach A-level syllabuses.

As a list of items intended to represent the subject knowledge of English that secondary teachers need in order to teach effectively, it would be an understatement, I think, to describe it as eclectic. The order in which these items are presented (are we to assume that they are in an order of priority?), the predominance of linguistic terminology and the lesser status accorded to texts, together represents a rather different body of knowledge to the one English teachers and teacher educators had been used to working on and with. And that, of course, was the point.

Overall, as Furlong *et al.* suggest of the history of central government interventions in the field of English teaching, a key focus in the document was on the 'uses of standard English in contemporary schools' (Furlong *et al.* 2000: 155). To this we might add a heavy emphasis – first and foremost – on an unspecified 'terminology' and on aspects of linguistics such as morphology, syntax and cohesion, another bugbear of the neo-conservative voices with their enduring preoccupation with the explicit teaching of grammar. The view of teaching implicit throughout is inevitably mechanistic and teacher-centred: it would be difficult to envisage any document with this purpose being anything but. As such, it exemplifies the kind of objectivist epistemology – with all its limitations – I discussed in the previous chapter.

The reaction from the teacher education and research communities was, predictably, extremely critical. It is interesting to note, however, that the overwhelming majority of direct responses published in books or journals were to the proposed ITTNC for Primary English when it was first released in Circular 10/97 (DfEE 1997); only one article was identified that took as its main focus an analysis of the Secondary English ITTNC. This was by Peter Daw, the HMI at the time in charge of teacher education inspections in English at Ofsted (Daw 2000) and will be discussed later. One can only speculate that, as the Secondary ITTNCs came into force in September 1998, a large part of the teacher education community was focused on planning for and enduring the associated inspections by Ofsted, inspections on the basis of which funding decisions were to be made by the TTA. It may also be that the earlier publication of the primary curriculum had 'softened-up' secondary teacher educators and their surprise and anger wasn't as great. Nevertheless, many criticisms of the Primary English ITTNC could also apply to the Secondary English document.

It was anger that characterized Judith Graham's response to the Primary English ITTNC. She criticized the 'unnecessary' document for its marginalization of speaking and listening, the complete absence of drama and storytelling. Indeed, the 'effective teaching and assessment' section of the Secondary English document devotes just two out of twenty sections to speaking and listening and one to drama. Graham also felt the ITTNC bore little resemblance to the pupils' National Curriculum, a document that Graham claimed was used to structure teacher education courses anyway and ensured a close relationship with pupils' learning. This is certainly true of the relationship between the Secondary English ITTNC and the pupils' National Curriculum. Graham also, importantly, maintained that the ITTNCs were an attack on the academic freedom of teacher educators. But it is the language of Graham's response that is most memorable:

The most appropriate key words that spring to mind for this document are: redundant, repetitive, inapplicable, ill-written, narrow-minded, mean-spirited, atheoretical, partial, unbalanced, unworkable, research-innocent, unimaginative, restrictive and an unwarranted incursion on academic freedom. This is an unnecessary document. A core that we do not need. Like an apple core, it needs to be thrown away. (Graham 1997: 249)

Blackledge also criticized what he saw as the focus on 'individual skills' inherent in the Primary English document and the neglect of the 'cultural practices' paradigm of literacy (Blackledge 1998). The main focus of Blackledge's argument, however, is the lack of attention to issues of language diversity and preparation to teach pupils with English as an Additional Language (EAL). The ITTNC, for Blackledge, represented a missed opportunity to improve educational opportunities for English language learners. In his view, the curriculum 'pathologises developing bilingualism as a problem' (*ibid.*: 57) and 'ignores social justice' (*ibid.*: 63). His response was stark:

Those pupils whose home culture matches the environment of the school will continue to do well, while those pupils for whom there is discontinuity between home and school are more likely to fail. In short, the revised requirements for literacy teaching constitutes [*sic*] a process of cultural hegemony. (*ibid.*: 56)

Graham's article (and that of Marshall (1998)) is notable for the hostility of the criticism levelled at the ITTNCs. Interestingly, there appeared to be no direct criticism of the requirement to 'audit' subject knowledge at the beginning and end of the course. Indeed, with the notable exception of Blackledge, there is sometimes the feeling that it is the assault on teacher educators' autonomy (and *their* right to specify subject knowledge content) that is most at stake for the authors and none of the articles note that a critical interest in primary student teachers' subject knowledge was established within the teacher education and research community prior to the ITTNCs. This is an important point: there appears to have been no published criticism of the objectivism promoted by these documents.

Poulson, however, links contemporaneous educational research about primary teachers' subject knowledge to the formation of policy generally and the introduction of Circular 4/98 and the ITTNCs in particular:

A conclusion drawn in much of this work [from 1989 to 1997] was that apparently low levels of subject knowledge were problematic: teachers could not teach what they did not know; therefore subject knowledge in initial training, professional development and in-service courses should be enhanced and prioritised. (Poulson 2001: 44)[4]

Explicitly presented as a challenge to the 'ideological dominance' of the importance of subject knowledge in the primary teacher's repertoire, Poulson's article is important as it draws attention to the rise of the concept from within the profession in England rather than simply presenting it as a concept imposed by governments in attempts to regulate and reform teaching and teacher education. It also identifies the emphasis on subject knowledge in initial teacher education and development with the move to establish a 'scientific basis for teaching' (*ibid.*: 49).

In the next section of this chapter, I focus on the research into the development of teachers' subject knowledge and attempt to trace both the evolution of the concept and its rise in importance from within the education research community itself.

Traditions of researching teachers' subject knowledge: professionalizing typologies

In my earlier discussion of the identification of a specialist category of teacher knowledge in pursuit of claims for professional status (on behalf of the profession in general and teacher educators in particular), I referred to research from the 1980s that proposed the importance of teachers' subject knowledge in various conceptualizations of professional knowledge (for example, Elbaz 1983, Leinhardt and Smith 1985). The most influential research in this field (in the US and, later, in the UK) grew out of the research programme of Lee Shulman at Stanford University.

The contribution of Lee Shulman: pedagogical content knowledge
By the beginning of the 1980s, there was a growing awareness in the US that the relationship between teachers' subject knowledge and the effectiveness (or otherwise) of their teaching was under-researched (Shulman 1984, Feiman-Nemser and Parker 1990). Alongside this renewed research interest in the importance of the subject content in teaching, there was a growing political interest in improving the quality of teacher education and the development of teaching standards based upon an agreed 'knowledge base' from within the teacher education community itself (Holmes Group 1986, Carnegie Task Force 1986). The advocates of these reforms of the profession gave a great deal of importance to the codification of a 'knowledge base for teaching', of which appropriate subject knowledge would be a part. This was seen as an important move from within the profession as teachers' knowledge base had come to be regarded as weak and teaching as a sub-professional activity.

Against this background, the research programme of Lee Shulman and others at Stanford University sought to identify the knowledge base for teaching and to give credibility and status to teachers' professional knowledge. Through the 1980s, Shulman's research was associated with the development of national standards for teachers by the US National Board for Professional Teaching Standards. It should also be noted that this was a large research programme, known as 'Knowledge Growth in Teaching', to which Shulman recruited a number of graduate students, several of whom have since published in this area (for example, Gudmunsdottir and Shulman 1987, Grossman 1990, Gudmunsdottir 1991, Wilson and Wineburg 1988, etc.).

The main part of the 'Knowledge Growth in Teaching' programme consisted of the development of a number of case studies of beginning secondary teachers taking a one-year postgraduate course of initial teacher education. The subjects taught by the group of beginning teachers in the study were English, mathematics, biology and social studies. Shulman's team first attempted to trace an 'intellectual biography' for each new teacher, identifying their sources of comprehension and understanding and significant networks of knowledge formation. In doing this, the team employed interviews that were structured by questions and the setting of 'clinical tasks'. The team felt that it was using a 'different' approach to measuring these teachers' subject knowledge in that they were not administering a standardized test. The researchers followed the new teachers through their teacher education course and into their first post.

Shulman's 1987 essay in the *Harvard Educational Review* is often seen as his seminal article on teachers' knowledge, especially the pedagogic dimensions of teachers' subject knowledge. Entitled 'Knowledge and teaching: foundations of the new reform', the link with teacher assessment, measures of effectiveness and the development of national teaching standards is explicit from the outset. Equally, however, Shulman makes clear that the relationship between his research and these initiatives from within the arena of policy is based upon a view of teaching and teacher development that regards the knowledge base as complex and multifaceted and suggests that new knowledge – in relation to the subject matter being taught – is generated during the course of the professional activity: 'Teaching ends with new comprehension by both the teacher and the student' (Shulman 1987: 7).

Here, he offers a full typology of the knowledge base for teaching. This, along with its explanation of 'pedagogical content knowledge' as a concept, provoked considerable interest:

Categories of the Knowledge Base
- content knowledge;
- general pedagogical knowledge, with special reference to those broad principles and strategies of classroom management and organization that appear to transcend subject matter;
- curriculum knowledge, with particular grasp of the materials and programs that serve as 'tools of the trade' for teachers;
- pedagogical content knowledge, that special amalgam of content and pedagogy that is uniquely the province of teachers, their own special form of professional understanding;

- knowledge of learners and their characteristics;
- knowledge of educational contexts, ranging from the workings of the group or classroom, the governance and financing of school districts, to the character of communities and cultures; and
- knowledge of educational ends, purposes, and values, and their philosophical and historical grounds. (*ibid.*: 8)

This categorization, especially the more detailed discussion of pedagogical content knowledge, aroused a great deal of interest and continues to do so (as I discuss later). It acknowledges the variety of sources of information, the knowledge of the subjects, learners, values and contexts, the modes of understanding and decision-making and routines of behaviour and action upon which a teacher might call. As a discrete categorization, it may appear to be definitive.

Critical responses to Shulman's project

There is another view that teachers' knowledge of the subject taught is relatively less important in teaching and learning than factors such as general pedagogical knowledge, teaching skills, contextual understanding and affirmation of values and ideals. In response to Shulman's 1987 article, Hugh Sockett allied himself to elements of this view but does so in the course of developing an argument about teachers' professionalism and educational reform. Shulman's strategy is flawed, according to Sockett, for three reasons:

> ... first, in the relative lack of attention to context, as opposed to content; second, in the inadequacy of its language of description of the moral framework of teaching; and third, in the lack of sophistication in its account of the relation between reason and action in teaching. Each of these weaknesses, it will be argued, arises from the fact that Shulman's analysis appears assessment-driven. (Sockett 1987: 208)

Acknowledging that, Shulman's work made a useful contribution to under-standings of subject knowledge in teaching, McEwan and Bull nevertheless assert that Shulman's distinction between content (subject) knowledge and pedagogical content knowledge was 'unnecessary' and that it led to research questions about the transformation from one kind of knowledge to another that were 'misconceived' (1991: 318). Instead, and drawing on the work of John Dewey, they suggest that Shulman's work was premised on an objectivist epistemology: they refer to his use of the phrase 'subject matter *per se*' and its presentation as *a priori* and essential; they also draw attention to his concern with 'the teachability of representations' (*ibid.*: 319) and the transmission model of teaching implicit in his focus on the use of analogies and explanations.[5] Moreover, they argue that there is no epistemological difference between content (subject) knowledge and pedagogical content knowledge. Both categories of knowledge – as knowledge – are developed in relation to 'webs of belief':

> Scholars must be concerned with the comprehensibility and teachability of their asser-
> tions, that is, with whether those 'representations' can find a meaningful place in
> others' webs of belief. In other words, the justification of scholarly knowledge is inher-
> ently a pedagogical task, and successful scholars must engage in the sort of pedagogical
> thinking supposed by Shulman to be a hallmark of pedagogic reasoning. (*ibid.*: 324)

McEwan and Bull's position here is clearly influenced by the kind of contextualist epistemology discussed in the previous chapter and, in proposing that 'ideas
are themselves intrinsically pedagogic' (*ibid.*: 332), they are also arguing that they
are developed in relation to a community of practice. McEwan and Bull's article
is important in that it shows how the early Shulman typology can be interpreted
as reductive.

But it is important to recognize that from the time of Shulman's work onwards,
successive US governments have argued for 'commonsense' solutions to what has
been perceived as the poor quality of the nation's teaching force. Teacher
educators are sometimes held to be part of this problem and policymakers have
argued for the 'dismantling of teacher education systems and the redefinition of
teacher qualifications to include little preparation for teaching' (Darling-
Hammond and Young 2002). Verbal ability and subject knowledge have been
proposed as 'the most important components of teacher effectiveness' (*ibid.*: 13)
and a good deal of research effort has gone into attempting to prove or disprove
this assertion (see Wilson *et al.* 2002 for a systematic review of the research).
Shulman's research programme (and the early research of many of his doctoral
students) attempted both to provide evidence of the effectiveness of university-
based ITE and to make the standards of the profession explicit and the profession
more accountable.

In England, the moves from within the initial teacher education community
were somewhat different. Alongside the interest in researching beginning teachers'
subject knowledge (referred to by Poulson (2001)) there was also a growing
interest in broader conceptions of teachers' professional knowledge and a focus
on practice. Nevertheless, as the 1990s drew to a close, research on teachers'
subject knowledge and Shulman's concept of pedagogical content knowledge grew
in influence in England both in teacher education research and in the arena of
policy. Indeed, at a TTA meeting I attended in April 2004 for those involved in
the development of induction materials for newly appointed teacher education
faculty, the agenda included a 30-minute lecture on the legacy of Lee Shulman
from the 1980s and the enduring importance of the concept of pedagogical
content knowledge. Again, the implication was that this was the special category
of knowledge belonging to teacher educators (and teacher training agencies) and

those newcomers who were making the transition from school- to university-based teacher education (teacher to lecturer) would need to name it and call it their own.

The work of Shulman and, indeed, the early research of Pamela Grossman (Grossman 1989, 1990; Grossman and Stodolsky 1995) are important for my own purposes here because of their emphasis on the school subject and the acknowledgement that teachers' values, beliefs and 'conceptions of purposes' for teaching a subject have an important role to play in the development of knowledge.

Research on teachers' subject knowledge after Shulman
Variations of Shulman's typology of teacher knowledge
There have been numerous attempts to produce a typology or model of teachers' professional knowledge (e.g. Elbaz 1983, Leinhardt and Smith 1985, Calderhead 1987, Hoyle and John 1995), some of which are discussed in detail in this chapter. The influence of Shulman's typology (1987) is pervasive, however, and more recent efforts often present their work either as a revision of Shulman (e.g. Banks *et al.* 1999) or as an elaboration that accepts the premises on which his typology was developed. Turner-Bissett's work (1999) is a significant example of the latter.

Turner-Bissett's typology grew out of her research with beginning teachers of History in primary schools and was developed in the context of the QTS Standards framework introduced by Circulars 10/97 (DfEE 1997) and 4/98 (DfEE 1998a). For Turner-Bissett, 'the model of knowledge essential for teaching [offered in these Circulars]. . . is impoverished' (Turner-Bissett 1999: 39). Instead, she develops a model of teachers' professional knowledge – presented as pedagogical content knowledge – that is 'more comprehensive' than that of Shulman and others (*ibid.*: 53). It is interesting to note that in Turner-Bissett's work, the conceptualization is of the elements that make up pedagogical content knowledge *as* teachers' professional knowledge rather than of a 'knowledge base for teaching' (Shulman 1987), of which pedagogical content knowledge is just one element.

Although Turner-Bissett makes claims for the comprehensiveness of her model, many of the elements in her representation of teacher knowledge (as pedagogical content knowledge) were present in Shulman's typology, including dimensions of subject knowledge, curriculum knowledge, general pedagogical content knowledge, knowledge of contexts, knowledge of learners and knowledge of ends and purposes, including values. The most obvious addition is knowledge of self, an awareness of one's own developing subjectivity in relation to other aspects of development. For Turner-Bissett, this kind of knowledge is an essential part of reflective practice. However, knowledge of self was a key feature of Elbaz's five categories of professional knowledge (Elbaz 1983) and is therefore not unique to Turner-Bissett's model. Turner-Bissett also elaborates on Shulman's 'knowledge of learners and their characteristics' (Shulman 1987) by splitting this into 'cognitive' (meaning teachers' mental models of how children – specific children – learn) and 'empirical' (meaning 'what children of a particular age are like; how they behave in classrooms and school' [Turner-Bissett 1999: 45]).

Turner-Bissett's model of the knowledge base for teaching seeks to be both more comprehensive than Shulman and less impoverished than that of the QTS Standards framework. She presents the model as an interacting set of categories of knowledge and suggests that the precise terms of the interaction will vary. Nevertheless, the categories are static and, as she herself acknowledges, somewhat 'stable' (*ibid*.: 53). In attempting to develop a more complex typology, she may have succeeded in making a more fragmented one.

Daw (2000), on the other hand, accepts the proposition that the QTS Standards framework, the ITTNCs and the requirement to audit subject knowledge will all inevitably lead to more effective teachers. He focuses on English teachers' subject knowledge and, as I have already mentioned, as a senior HMI at Ofsted in charge of inspections of initial teacher education in English, he draws on his experience of inspection in his article. There are no references to the work of Shulman in Daw's article (nor to other researchers) but the model of subject knowledge he developed uses many of the organising concepts present in earlier work: for example, the relationship between conceptions of the subject and 'past educational experience', the distinction between 'subject content' and 'conceptual frame-works', the development of curriculum knowledge and the interaction between these categories of knowledge and pedagogy.

Daw's article is interesting in that he implicitly criticises teacher education 'providers' (universities and schools) for exposing 'gaps' in student teachers' subject knowledge through the 'repeated application' of long, self-assessment checklists and he asserts that some of the criticism levelled against the ITTNC subject knowledge requirements by ITE tutors was due to their 'nagging doubts as to whether the process really captures the *essential subject knowledge* needed by teachers' (Daw 2000: 5; my emphasis). Daw noted that 'knowing what' and 'knowing how' were separated in the ITTNCs (*ibid*.: 4) and suggested that they should be integrated in the specifications for planning and teaching within an ideal of a 'specific English pedagogy' (*ibid*.: 11). Despite his protestations that subject knowledge shouldn't be isolated as a category, Daw nonetheless presents a codification of what all prospective English teachers should know about an essentialized and stable concept of 'progression in English'.[6]

Researching the importance of subject knowledge and pedagogical content knowledge in initial teacher education: some contrasting examples
Following the publication of the work of Shulman and his associates – and, in England, the introduction of the ITTNCs – there has been a growing interest in

investigating the effect of teacher education programmes in developing both teachers' subject knowledge and their pedagogical content knowledge. Betts and Frost, as one example, writing from a Canadian perspective, use rather reductive interpretations of Shulman's categories to propose that 'a greater emphasis on breadth as opposed to depth of subject knowledge is the best option for preparing teachers to effectively implement curricular requirements at all grades' (2000: 39).

In contrast, Burgess *et al.* (2000) undertook their work within the teacher education setting in England and explored how their beginning teachers of • English developed aspects of subject knowledge against the background of the ITTNC referred to earlier. Their particular focus was the 'transformation' of their student teachers' subject knowledge of grammar into pedagogical content knowledge, grammar being identified as the area in which most of those undertaking a postgraduate teacher education course need some support and development. This study is interesting for two reasons: first, Burgess *et al.* identify the student teachers' own understandings of language learning as the key to the development of pedagogical content knowledge (2000: 15); second, that the opportunities provided for student teachers to develop this aspect of their professional knowledge in schools varied enormously and highlighted a disjuncture in some schools between the existing, professionally validated formations of the subject and new (and for some schools, contentious) additional knowledge associated with the government's reforms of teacher education and teacher educators (*ibid.*: 16). For the researchers, this provoked questions about professional reconstruction. Their work implicitly foregrounds the importance of setting in the development of teacher knowledge.

Thornton (2003), however, from a US perspective, accepts the proposition that 'greater' subject knowledge available for transformation into pedagogical content knowledge will lead to more effective teaching and learning. The question for him is how to make time available for subject knowledge development in short, intensive, teacher education courses. This point is also addressed by Sanders and Morris (2000) in their research on primary student teachers in Wales. Sanders and Morris tested their own students on mathematical subject knowledge and found frequent 'gaps' in this knowledge. Interestingly, they found that most of their students found ways of explaining away their poor results – such as forgetfulness or not remembering the topic being covered when they were at school – and they described the way in which the students approached the requirement to 'fill' these gaps by dividing them into three groups: 'ostriches, nettle graspers or mañanas' (Sanders and Morris 2000: 404). What is remarkable about Sanders and Morris's article is not just their acceptance of the test as a valid proxy for the kind of knowledge effective mathematics teachers need but their suggestion that student teachers should be 'confronted' to address the gaps identified by the tests and that QTS could be withheld if they don't – even if they are in every other way identified as effective classroom teachers (*ibid.*: 407).

The use of standardized tests or questionnaires to assess student teachers' subject knowledge is also a common feature of research in this area. Halim and Meerah, for example, working with a small group of student teachers of science in Malaysia, devised a test that they felt would assess these teachers' pedagogical content knowledge of physics. The questionnaire posed the kind of questions about physics that lower secondary pupils were said to ask and the student teachers were meant to respond to the questions as if they were addressing these hypothetical pupils. The researchers believed this was a valid test of pedagogical content knowledge and was in preference to a test simply of subject knowledge. Their finding that student teachers pedagogical content knowledge of physics was limited is perhaps unsurprising (given that they were *student* teachers) but their assertion that it was the student teachers' poor subject knowledge of physics that was the cause (Halim and Meerah 2002: 223) cannot be supported from their data.

Halim and Meerah's work can be located within a research tradition by science teacher educators that investigates the process by which student teachers develop the 'broad and balanced' pedagogical content knowledge for physics, chemistry and biology teaching. Some of this work has taken place in England (and some in the context of Circular 4/98 and the ITTNC for Secondary Science) and has used pre- and post-test measures to assess the impact of PGCE courses on the development of student science teachers' subject knowledge (for example, Lenton and Turner 1999). This research tradition and the other research (with the notable exception of Burgess *et al.* (2000)) I have referred to in this section all assume that effective teachers must have good pedagogical content knowledge and this special category of teacher knowledge is a transformation of subject knowledge that takes place entirely *within the head* of the individual teacher. In order to have good pedagogical content knowledge, it is therefore necessary to have good subject knowledge. As I have already demonstrated, this has been the assumption behind government policy for initial teacher education in England for quite some time. So, given this assumption and the 'circularity' of English education policy (Wyse and Jones 2002), perhaps it was no surprise that the TTA commissioned research into the subject knowledge that effective teachers of literacy needed at the time of the development of the ITTNCs and the *National Literacy Strategy Framework for Teaching* (DfEE 1998b).

The Effective Teachers of Literacy project
Between December 1995 and February 1997, researchers at Exeter University and the College of St Mark and St John worked with a group of 228 experienced and 'effective' teachers in 13 local education authorities (LEAs) and in a number of grant-maintained and independent schools (Medwell *et al.* 1998). Their study had been commissioned by the Teacher Training Agency (TTA) 'to help the Teacher

Training Agency and teachers in England to understand more clearly how effective teachers help children to become literate' (Medwell *et al.* 1998: 3).

The findings about the nature of the teachers' subject knowledge were particularly interesting, however. Neither the effective teachers nor the validation sample did very well at all on aspects of a literacy quiz, particularly the part that tested their ability to identify language structures and to use linguistic terminology. Nevertheless, the effective teachers demonstrated a good understanding of some aspects of literacy content *in the classroom* about which they did poorly in the quiz (for example, phonemes) (*ibid.*: 15). One element of the quiz on which the effective teachers performed significantly better, however, was their knowledge of authors writing specifically for children (*ibid.*: 18). But it was the effective teachers' relatively poor scores on the linguistic aspects of the literacy quiz compared with their skilful demonstration of such linguistic knowledge in their teaching that led the researchers to speculate that the way in which the effective teachers knew this linguistic material was different:

> It did not seem to be the case that they knew a body of knowledge (content) and then selected appropriate ways to represent it to their children (pedagogy). Rather, they appeared to know the material in the way they taught it to the children ... The knowledge-base of these teachers thus *was* their pedagogical content knowledge. This is a rather different concept of pedagogical content knowledge from that of Shulman ... for whom this refers to knowledge of ways of transforming content in order to represent it for others. (*ibid.*: 24; emphasis in the original).

Medwell *et al.*'s reconceptualization of pedagogical content knowledge is important as it offers a view of subject knowledge as 'totally embedded in their pedagogical practices' (*ibid.*), as a form of knowledge developed in practice and achieving validation in a community of practice, like any other. It is a less stable and more situated concept than the usual interpretations of Shulman's original and presents pedagogical content knowledge as knowledge in its own right rather than as a by-product of the transformation of an objectivist concept of disciplinary knowledge.

Another key finding from the work of Medwell *et al.* was that the effective teachers of literacy were able to articulate 'strong and coherent personal philosophies about the teaching of literacy' (*ibid.*: 8) that focused on the construction of meaning in social contexts (so, for example, prioritising 'shared' reading). The effective teachers acknowledged the importance of the 'building blocks' of literacy but did so in a way that emphasised the end goal of 'purpose, communication and composition' (*ibid.*: 25). This was less true in the validation sample where teachers tended to emphasise technical knowledge and terminology; less effective teachers tended to foreground definitions of language structures whereas more effective teachers began with demonstrations of the language structures in use (*ibid.*: 77).

Medwell *et al.* acknowledge that any study of primary teachers' subject knowledge will inevitably differ in design from that of secondary teachers where, it could be said, the secondary subject (in this case, English) is more clearly bounded than the 'subject' of literacy. Nevertheless, the definition of literacy adopted by the research team – with its emphasis on books, specific genres such as fiction and poetry, the structure of narrative, literary concepts such as setting, character and plot, and even 'enjoyment' (*ibid.*: 3) – suggest a definition of literacy very close to more traditional understandings of the subject English. With this in mind, another relevant outcome from this research is that 'the content knowledge held by effective teachers of literacy cannot be readily separated from understanding of its use or from their beliefs about how it should be taught' (*ibid.*: 45).

The outcomes from Medwell *et al.*'s study were particularly relevant to my own research. In particular, identifying the importance of teachers' thinking about the subject knowledge and how this is informed by questions of value and belief is directly relevant.

Research on teachers' values and beliefs and their subject knowledge

In her case studies of four experienced and 'expert' high school history teachers, Gudmunsdottir found that 'the teachers' value orientations to their subject matter influenced their choice of content, their use of the textbook, pedagogical strategies, and their perceptions of students' instructional needs' (1991: 44). Gudmunsdottir distinguished between values and ideologies stating that values 'always imply a choice, a choice of principles ... they have penetrated the "core of one's definition of oneself"' (*ibid.*: 45; quoting McKinney 1980). In this analysis, school subjects – as taught by teachers in classrooms to young people – become texts infused with values; pupils are 'not just learning facts; they are acquiring a world view imbued with values' (*ibid.*: 47). In developing this analysis, Gudmunsdottir draws on the work of Schwab (1964) (whose substantive and syntactic structures are said to be 'value-laden organisations of knowledge' (*ibid.*: 46)) and that of her doctoral supervisor, Shulman. Gudmunsdottir suggests that the transformative process outlined by Shulman from content knowledge to pedagogical content knowledge is a 'reorganization' that 'revolves around teachers' personal values and those embedded in their specialisation' (*ibid.*: 47). Although there is an unsatisfactory exclusion of learners and setting in this conceptualization, Gudmunsdottir does suggest one way of accounting for the growth in expertise of the developing teacher:

> I want to suggest that one of the differences between novices and experts is that the novices' *values* do not seem to have achieved the influence in the reorganisation of their pedagogical content knowledge that characterises excellent, experienced teachers...
> (*ibid.*: 50; my emphasis)

Yaakobi and Sharan explored the value differences between teachers of different, secondary school subjects in a study of 142 teachers in Israel. Using Bernstein's (1972) distinction between those subjects organized by a 'collection code' and those by an 'integrative code',[7] the researchers developed a question-naire that would elicit the teachers' values related to their own subject area. They found that socialization into different academic subject areas appeared to 'exert differential effects on teachers' ideas about academic knowledge and about classroom instruction' (Yaakobi and Sharan 1985: 196). This view that teachers are socialized into sets of beliefs about the subject they teach and the nature of knowledge itself will be explored in the final section of this chapter, with reference to the subject English.

Wilson and Wineburg, in case studies of four beginning teachers of history, also noted that teachers of the *same* subject can hold very different conceptions of that subject (in this case, what they thought history was) and that these conceptions – developed out of their prior 'disciplinary backgrounds' – were a 'strong – and often decisive – influence on their instructional decision-making' (Wilson and Wineburg 1988: 526). This study points to the importance of beginning teachers' preconceptions and proposes that an important element of initial teacher education should be to encourage students to examine their 'previously held beliefs' (*ibid*.: 537). This study is also interesting for the emphasis it places on tracing the beginning teacher's intellectual biography as a way of uncovering the values underpinning their knowledge of the subject.

Hillocks' (1999) study of 19 teachers of writing in community colleges and high-school – published as *Ways of Thinking, Ways of Teaching* – gives particular emphasis to two dimensions of teachers' thinking 'their epistemological beliefs about what constitutes knowledge in their field, and their deeply held beliefs about the likelihood that their students will be successful in learning to understand what they teach' (Hillocks 1999: viii).

In exploring the relationship between what he termed 'epistemological stance' and attitude towards learners, Hillocks sought to go beyond the 'simple conge-niality of pedagogical content knowledge' in accounting for the wide range of differences among 'teachers of the same subject', 'I suspect that great differences in teaching may amount to differences in ways of thinking about the nature of knowledge, in epistemology' (*ibid*.: 6).

Hillocks distinguished between two epistemologies – objectivist and construc-tivist – and two sets of beliefs about the likelihood of learners being successful – optimistic and pessimistic. In his introduction to Hillocks' work, Shulman outlined the four quadrants developed in this analysis:

> Thus we can have *objectivist pessimists* (the knowledge is out there waiting to be learned, but the students are just not smart enough to get it), *constructivist optimists* (the knowledge is theirs to construct and, by golly, they are going to do it), *objectivist*

optimists, and *constructivist pessimists* (although there were no examples of this last category in Hillocks' study). (Hillocks 1999: viii–ix; emphasis in the original)

Although not a study into effective teaching practices *per se*, Hillocks' research nevertheless found important differences between the more effective (in his terms) teachers of writing in the sample (a minority, it has to be said, who were the *constructivist optimists*) and the less effective (by implication, the majority category of *objectivist pessimists*). His findings accord with those of Medwell *et al.* in suggesting that the more effective teachers of literacy (Hillocks' sample were specifically teachers of writing rather than English) had coherent systems of belief about literacy that focused on 'purpose, communication and composition' (Medwell *et al.* 1998: 25) rather than technical knowledge and terminology for its own sake.

Hillocks' research also offered a conceptualization of pedagogical content knowledge similar to that of Cochran *et al.* (1993):

> … pedagogical content knowledge appears not to be some body of pre-existing knowledge that teachers dip into, but *knowledge constructed by the teacher in light of the teachers' epistemological stance and conceptions of knowledge to be taught* (in this case rhetoric or writing), learning theory, and students. (Hillocks 1999: 120–1; my emphasis)

For Hillocks, the most important of these was epistemological stance. Although the binary categorization of objectivism and constructivism hardly seems an adequate account of either the complexity of cognition or pedagogy, the concept of epistemological stance was useful in my analysis of teachers' thinking in that *how* the beginning teachers conceptualized knowledge itself was an important factor in the analysis.

This concept and the importance of teachers' attitudes towards learners had been anticipated by Douglas Barnes more than 20 years earlier. In *From Communication to Curriculum* (1976), Barnes distinguished between two attitudes of teachers towards their pupils' written work: a *transmission* view of teaching and learning and an *interpretation* view (1976: 139–57):

> The Transmission teacher sees it as his task to transmit knowledge and to test whether the pupils have received it. To put it crudely, he [*sic* to end of quotation] sees language as a tube down which knowledge can be sent; if a pupil catches the knowledge he can send it back up the tube. Such a teacher does not see speech or writing as changing the way in which the knowledge is held. For the Interpretation teacher, however, the pupil's ability to reinterpret knowledge for himself is crucial to learning, and he sees this as depending on a productive dialogue between the pupil and himself. (*ibid.*: 142)

Barnes' distinction developed out of his previous work on language and learning, particularly the role of talk and writing in different school subjects. Hillocks' focus, however, is on explaining the differences amongst teachers of the same subject as a matter of epistemology. More recently, Banks *et al.* (1999, Leach and Moon 2000) have developed a model of teachers' professional knowledge which places teachers' values and beliefs at the centre.

The work of Banks, Leach and Moon: towards a situated model of professional knowledge

Against the background of the political context of initial teacher education in England in the late 1990s, Banks *et al.* explain their interest in modelling teachers' professional knowledge as an attempt to explore the links 'between a teachers' knowledge and the associated pedagogic strategies and practices [that] ensure successful learning' (1999: 89). They describe Shulman's work as 'informed by an essentially objectivist epistemology' and that it:

> … leans on a theory of cognition that views knowledge as a contained, fixed and external body of information … [and] a teacher-centred pedagogy which focuses primarily on the skills and knowledge that the teacher possesses, rather than the process of learning. (*ibid.*: 91)

Instead, they propose a 'more dynamic' model in which the 'personal constructs' of the teacher (including beliefs about the purposes of the subject, about learning, about what constitutes good teaching and aspects of the teacher's biography) 'underpins a teachers' professional knowledge' (*ibid.*: 95). Indeed, in their model, the personal construct of the teacher is the organizational core. However, whilst criticizing Shulman's work, they nevertheless build their model out of his categories of content knowledge, pedagogical content knowledge, curricular knowledge and general pedagogical knowledge. They acknowledge that their *school knowledge* 'subsumes' the curricular knowledge of Shulman but is 'an analytic category in its own right' (*ibid.*: 94). They further differentiate the category of school knowledge by using the work of Verret (1975) and Chevellard (1991) to describe a process – '*la transposition didactique*' (Chevellard) – by which subject knowledge is transposed to school knowledge. They argue (after Verret) that school knowledge is deserving of separate status as 'knowledge in general cannot be sequenced in the same way as school knowledge' and that school knowledge is 'inevitably codified, partial, formalised and ritualised' (*ibid.*: 93).

Although, in their 1999 article, Banks *et al.* say they dislike Shulman's metaphor of *transformation* (of content knowledge into pedagogical content knowledge) (*ibid.*: 91), their preferred metaphor of *transposition* doesn't seem to be significantly different: transposing still implies changing something into a different modality. Whilst acknowledging that Chevellard defined this as a process of 'restructuring', there is no acknowledgement of the similarities in the processes nor that Shulman himself proposed pedagogical content knowledge and curricular knowledge as separate analytic categories. Indeed, in their 2000 article about teachers' professional knowledge, Leach and Moon use the very word – transformation – that in 1999 they claimed was less appropriate than transposition. School knowledge, in the Banks *et al.* model, may perhaps be better described as an amalgam of Shulman's categories rather than a qualitatively different conceptualisation. One effect of this amalgamation is to make the distinction between subject knowledge and school knowledge unclear: why should the historical origins of subjects, their vocabularies and discourses be seen as a separate category, for example? This is particularly apparent in Banks *et al.*'s (1999) model of English teachers' professional knowledge.

In the 1999 model, whereas some aspects of school knowledge (English) might appear equally at home in subject knowledge (for example: 'knowledge about language'), others might come under Shulman's heading of curricular knowledge (for example: the 'status/nature of the English "coursework folder"') and others still under their own heading of pedagogic knowledge (for example: 'the reading process'). Another important question to ask of Banks *et al.*'s model is where are the pupils (the learners clearly present in Shulman's typology [1987])? And also, where is the setting in which the teacher's knowledge develops? They do acknowledge that the development of professional knowledge is 'brought into existence by the learning context itself' (*ibid.*: 96) and, later, that subject constructs might be collective as well as personal (*ibid.*: 105) – acknowledging the influence of the school subject department and the mentor – but these vitally important aspects of the development of teachers' knowledge are not elaborated and are omitted from the model itself.

Nevertheless, Banks, Leach and Moon – like Gudmunsdottir (1991), Grossman and Stodolsky (1995) and Hillocks (1999) – make an important contribution to our understanding of teachers' subject knowledge by emphasising the importance of the 'personal subject construct', a complex web of beliefs and values about the purposes of the subject, the nature of its knowledge and how it is learned. Additionally, Banks *et al.* also begin to foreground the importance of setting and community of practice in the development of teacher knowledge through their appropriation of the work of Lave (1988) and the concepts of arena and setting (see especially Leach and Moon [2000], discussed in the previous chapter). Their work is therefore useful in beginning to theorise the interaction between the 'concepts of arenas and settings and what is now understood about teacher knowledge' (Leach and Moon 2000: 396). In this respect, their work can be understood as an important contribution towards a more situated model of professional knowledge.

In the final section of this chapter, I explore the ways in which the formation and institutionalisation of English as a subject is related to questions of its subject knowledge content and how this, in turn, comes back to questions about the purposes of the subject and the goals of teaching as professional practice.

Professionalizing English

> What does his [*sic* – to end of quotation] knowledge mean to a teacher? It is his stock in trade, part of his claim to expertise. A secondary teacher during his specialist course at college or university will have learnt to identify himself more or less strongly both with the knowledge and skills of his subject and with the implicit styles of speech and ways of going about things which every subject depends on. For many secondary school teachers their self respect and hopes for promotion – indeed parts of their very identity – become bound up with their subject. (Barnes 1976: 152–3)

In his discussion of 'knowledge and the teacher', Barnes draws our attention to the importance of secondary teachers' relationships with their subject and their work towards – and *on* – a particular form of cultural identity. He emphasises the link between subject identity and personal or professional identity and – in his references to 'implicit styles of speech and ways of going about things' – notes that subjects offer particular genres and discourses that teachers and learners inhabit and shape. In the research on teachers' subject knowledge reviewed thus far, teachers' conceptions of the purposes or aims of their subject have been identified as an important aspect. Banks *et al.* (1999) referred to this as the 'personal subject construct'; Grossman (1990) as the 'conceptions of purposes for teaching subject matter' that provide an 'organising framework' for the development of pedagogical content knowledge; Grossman and Stodolsky (1995) suggest that the subject is part of the context of, and resources for, learning to teach, the subject being a 'conceptual context'. In this section, I review some of the research into the formation and constitution of school subjects, particularly in relation to the subject English. This area has seen a great deal of research and scholarship over the last 30 to 40 years, especially in the sociology of education, so I must organize my brief discussion here around the literature on school subjects and the constitution of school English as it relates to the activity of learning to teach.

Compartmentalizing knowledge: the formation of school subjects
In her eloquently critical discussion of US teacher education, *Practice Makes Practice* (1991, 2004), Britzman analyses the ways in which student teachers are confronted by the 'fragmentation of experience' in their initial courses. One important aspect of this fragmentation is the 'compartmentalisation of knowledge', a discourse that constrains and limits student teachers' understandings of learning and knowledge:

> 'School subjects' such as English, history, science, or math, organise more than the division of the school day, the movement of students, and the labor of teachers. They also authorise the classification, arrangement, and selection of forms of knowledge. That is, school subjects represent knowledge that has been compartmentalised. This form of knowledge serves as the basis for curricular organisation. (Britzman 1991: 35)

In predetermining the 'limits of relevancy' (*ibid.*), Britzman sees this inevitable process as one which 'abstracts knowledge from its socio-cultural roots ... and decontextualis[es] knowledge and skills from their practical existence' (*ibid.*). This is, if you like, an effect of, in terms of schooling, curricularization and, in terms of teachers, professionalization. For intending teachers, its practical consequence is 'accepting the rules and rites of specialisation, claiming and guarding a piece of academic territory, identifying with an academic department, and taking up a particular discourse and its accompanying practice' (*ibid.*: 37).

The process by which teachers – and especially new teachers – are socialized into subjects in secondary schools has been of interest to sociologists of education for some time (e.g. Lacey 1977, Ball 1981). A related effort, represented, perhaps, by Young (1971), has been concerned with an analysis of school knowledge as 'inevitably codified, partial, formalised and ritualised' (Banks *et al.* 1999: 93). An early and influential example of work that combines both perspectives is that of Esland (1971, Esland and Dale 1973). Esland's view of teachers of secondary subjects forming different 'epistemic communities' would appear to offer a socio-cultural and sociohistoric account of the development of knowledge. In 1971, for example, he proposed that:

> The knowledge which a teacher thinks 'fills up' his [*sic*] subject is held in common with members of a supporting community who collectively approach its paradigms and utility criteria, as they are legitimated in training courses and 'official statements'. (Esland 1971: 79)

In 1973, Esland and Dale re-emphasized the importance of the 'epistemic community' in the development and organisation of knowledge:

> Teachers, as spokesmen for subject communities are involved in an elaborate organisation of knowledge. The community has a history, and, through it, a body of respected knowledge. It has rules for recognising 'unwelcome' or 'spurious' matter, and ways of avoiding cognitive contamination. It will have a philosophy and a set of authorities, all of which give strong legitimation to the activities which are acceptable to the community. (Esland and Dale 1973: 70–1; quoted in Goodson *et al.* 1998: 6–7)

For Esland, it was in the course of activity and in the evaluations of a community that knowledge is developed and, of course, organized; the 'body of respected knowledge' is passed on historically through social practice. The problem for teachers and teaching, identified by Esland, was that teachers – as 'communities' – tend to be widely dispersed and so proportionately greater power to evaluate claims to knowledge fell into the hands of school inspectors, journal editors and professional associations. In its emphasis on journals and professional associations, Esland's work perhaps shows its age.

Research interest into secondary schools subjects as 'realms of knowledge' (Siskin 1994) has continued (see, for example, Goodson with Anstead and Mangan 1998). An important contribution to this work was made early on by Stephen Ball and Colin Lacey (1980) with their concepts of *subject paradigm* and *subject pedagogy*. Ball and Lacey took issue with Esland's concept of 'epistemic community' as they felt it didn't describe the 'extent of variation and subdivision within particular universes of knowledge' (Ball and Lacey 1980: 149). In their analysis, they give an important emphasis to the role of the subject department as 'a crucial mediating context in the translation of curriculum knowledge from the level of "subject communities" into the pupils' experience of "subjects" in the process of the classroom interaction' (*ibid.*: 150).

The secondary subject department is presented as 'an arena of competing paradigms and definitions' that 'confer[s] a sense of identity' upon its members (*ibid.*: 151). Ball and Lacey traced the extent to which the 'agreement and allegiance' (*ibid.*) could be discerned within four secondary English departments. On the basis of this investigation, they developed two concepts that would be useful in their analysis: *subject paradigm*, referring to 'view of English as a subject held by English teachers in terms of the appropriate content' (*ibid.*: 157); and *subject pedagogy*, referring to 'the system of ideas and procedures for the organisation of learning ... that is, appropriate method' (*ibid.*: 158).

Subject paradigms and the constitution of English

> *'English is a quicksilver among metals – mobile, living and elusive.'*
> *(Dixon 1975: 1)*
> *English is ' ... "a sack of snakes".'* (Wilson 1964: 86)

In England, the majority of student teachers of secondary English follow one year postgraduate PGCE courses and so bring with them understandings of the subject developed in the setting of their undergraduate (and sometimes postgraduate) English studies. As I mentioned in the first section of this chapter, the perceived variation in student teachers' subject backgrounds was one of the reasons given in Circular 4/98 (DfEE 1998a) for the introduction of the secondary ITTNC and the requirement to 'audit' subject knowledge. The variation amongst English degrees in particular has also been noted by teacher educators themselves over at least the last 15 years (for example, Hardman and Williamson 1993, Davies 1996, Marshall *et al.* 2001).[8]

This sense of variation and difference – if not the slippery or snake-like qualities attributed to English by Dixon (1967) and Wilson (1964) – is an effect of the subject's history and is not a new phenomenon. Histories of the subject English abound but in each of them it can be seen that debates about the constitution of the subject (in terms of the selection and organization of knowledge – its content) are inextricably linked with conceptions of the purposes for English. For example, Viswanathan (1989) traced the institutionalization of the study of English literature in India (in schools and universities) by the East India Company (under contract to the British Government) from 1813 onwards. The purpose of teaching English literature was, literally, to colonize and therefore 'civilize'. Eagleton

Creative/expressive	Grammarian	Sociological
Emphases Creative writing The self-expression of pupils	Functional use of language, communication and syntax	Personal relationships Children's own culture and free expression Opinions
Uses Poetry and literature	Coursebooks and exercises	Magazines and newspapers, etc.
Key words Stimulus and excitement	Basic skills	Pupils as individuals

Source: Ball and Lacey (1980: 174)

Table 3.1 *Subject paradigms of English*

(1983) described the 'rise of English' in the Mechanics' Institutes and extension colleges as an alternative force for social cohesion – 'beamed' to the working class – to an established religion that was seen to be in decline in the late-nineteenth century. Mathiesen presents the development of English in schools and universities in England as the triumph of a liberal and progressive move on the (elitist) study of classics and shows how it developed from 'the rudimentary skills of literacy into the humane centre of the curriculum' with 'high hopes invested in its activities and its teachers' (Mathiesen 1975: 223).

Mathiesen's account was controversial when it was first published as she argued that in order to reclaim its progressive purpose and radical edge, it needed to place greater store by direct instruction in literacy skills and connecting pupils with the cultural heritage. She described a 'contemporary shift of emphasis from knowledge and formality to feeling and freedom' (*ibid.*: 214). But, as Eagleton and Viswanathan have shown, disputes about the selection and status of the knowledge that constitutes English – indeed, whether it can make a claim to knowledge at all – were structuring devices present at the beginnings of the subject and devices inextricably linked to the new subject's social and political purpose. George Sampson, for example, the school inspector who wrote *English for the English* (1921) as a proposal for reform of the English curriculum, declared that English was 'the one school subject in which we have to fight, *not for a clear gain of knowledge*, but for a precarious margin of advantage over powerful forces of evil' (1921: 14; my emphasis).

From its earliest incarnations, therefore, that compartmentalization of knowledge known as English has been a basis for purposeful social action; its organization has been determined politically and its content reified historically. If we accept this as a fair description of the evolution of the subject, then it is misleading to suggest both that governments and bureaucrats *alone* have sought to shape the subject *and* that they have only sought to do so recently. Histories of the subject such as those by Eagleton, Viswanathan and (especially) Hunter (1988) show that the subject has always had a 'governmental' function and that English teachers have always been – at least in part – bureaucrats. In this way, the governmental function of the subject English is related to the bureaucratic identity of the English teacher, both aspects of the process that Parr (writing in 1888 – see Bullough (2001)) referred to as 'professionalizing subject matter'. Professionalization can be seen as an important dynamic at the core of school English and the formation of subject identity as a matter in which English teachers have been actively engaged.

Exploring subject paradigms of English in practice

In their early work on subject subcultures, Ball and Lacey (1980) identified three subject paradigms of English based on their empirical work.

Each of these subject paradigms makes a different claim to the constitution of English in terms of its subject knowledge. The creative/expressive paradigm, for example, 'uses' canonical or non-canonical (i.e. written specifically for young people) literature to stimulate pupils' language development. Literature is used here to develop better (that is, more 'creative') people. The grammarian paradigm emphasizes linguistic knowledge – codified in textbooks and exercises – to produce a more functionally literate person. And the sociological paradigm aims to develop pupils' interpersonal relationships through better communication fostered by reading 'relevant' and popular texts. Texts here are 'used' to develop better (adjusted) young people. The content of an English curriculum (in terms of subject knowledge) developed from within these different subject paradigms would look very different and would be differently motivated. Nevertheless, Ball and Lacey's point wasn't that these paradigms were the basis on which English departments became uniform and consensual epistemic communities. Rather, these paradigms, whilst forming a rationale for a department's group action as a 'performance team' (Goffman 1959; cited in Ball and Lacey) – for example, in talking to other departments or selecting new teachers – were also the grounds on which individual teachers came to their own understandings of the subject on the basis of consensus or dissensus with the paradigm. It is also important to note that Ball and Lacey's three paradigms were developed out of empirical work with a very small group of schools at a very particular moment in history. As they said, they offered an illustrative case rather than a model that could be generalized.

The *Versions of English* project (Barnes *et al.* 1984) was an attempt to describe the varieties of English taught to 15–17 year olds as they appeared to the observers. The authors interpreted their observations in relation to the different institutional contexts in which the versions of English were realised and – with reference to English in what is now Year 11 – developed a model of the variation they observed. This model is interesting in that its different dimensions (of what Ball referred to as subject paradigm) are related to varieties of subject pedagogy which in turn are related to teachers' perceptions of their pupils' likely success and their perspective on knowledge. In this way, Barnes' work once again can be seen to anticipate that of Hillocks (1999). For example, Barnes *et al.*'s *personal growth* and *basic skills* subject paradigms are both classified as 'restricted' versions of English in that they are modified for those pupils in the 'lower sets'. Literature in their *personal growth* paradigm is 'for pleasure and not for study' (Barnes *et al.* 1984: 247); literature in the *basic skills* paradigm 'occurs only as a source for ["comprehension"] exercises' (*ibid.*: 248).

Barnes *et al.*'s model is particularly interesting as it was developed out of a three-year study in six schools and four further education colleges. There are also interesting similarities with Barnes' earlier work (Barnes 1976) in that there is some attention paid to teachers' (to use Hillocks' term) epistemological stance: the versions they describe as *belles lettres* and *basic skills* might also be described as transmission versions based upon an objectivist epistemology whereas the *public rationality*, *cultural tradition* and *personal growth* versions might be described as interpretive and constructivist. This study also links these dimensions of pedagogy and epistemology to the classification and organization of knowledge in the version of the subject (whether it is restricted or extended) – even though this does seem to focus mainly (if not wholly) on the amount of literature studied.

It is obvious, I think, even from the highly selective account I have given here, that from its beginnings English has been a contestable subject, resulting in considerable diversity of subject knowledge content (subject paradigm) interpreted in a variety of different ways (subject pedagogy and epistemological stance). These debates have not simply been about the substantive and syntactic structures of the subject (Schwab 1964) – what to include and how it is organized – but about the values and beliefs that provide its organizing framework. Decisions about the 'necessary' subject knowledge are made on the basis of conceptions of the purposes of the subject, purposes that have much to do with the preparation of young people for society and for the kind of ideal society the teacher (as a part of a differentiated profession) would envisage. This very explicit political dimension has led to claims for a 'special status' for English that, as the following quotation demonstrates, would also extend to special epistemological status:

> [English is] nothing less than a different model of education: knowledge to be made, not given; knowledge promising more than can be discursively stated; learning as a diverse range of processes, including affective ones; educational processes to be embarked on with outcome unpredictable; students' perceptions, experiences, imaginings and unsystematically acquired knowledge admitted as legitimate curricular content. (Medway 1980; cited in Rosen 1981: 19)

Nevertheless, attempts to identify the 'knowledge-base' for English – of which Medway's above represents one, particularly liberal/progressive kind – have been consistent features of the institutionalization of the subject, whether in universities or in schools throughout its relatively short history. These efforts, combined with the parallel efforts also from the late-nineteenth century to professionalize teaching – have produced periodic crises of knowledge in which debates about what English teachers *should know, understand and be able to do* are paramount. One such periodic crisis, I have argued, reached a peak in England in the years following the publication of Circular 4/98 and the ITTNCs.

4

Culture, activity, agent: designing the research

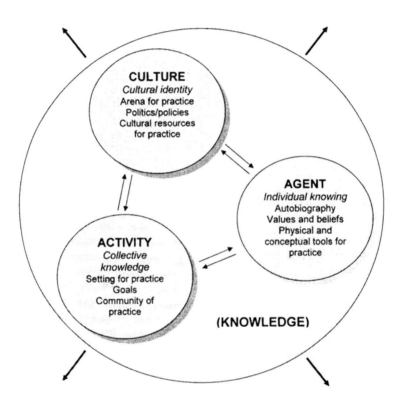

The previous chapter argued that attempts to develop a codification of teacher knowledge – and in doing so to emphasise the importance of subject knowledge – have been associated with internal and external efforts to reform the profession. Shulman's (1987) typology of professional knowledge has been shown to have been particularly influential and is in some senses prototypical of the profession-alising project's response to political pressure about poor standards of teaching whilst also attempting to secure the place of initial teacher education in the universities (Labareee 1992). Shulman's typology and other more overtly political attempts to reform teacher education have stimulated a widespread and worldwide interest in researching teachers' subject knowledge. Sometimes, however, this research has used a reductive interpretation of Shulman's work, particularly with regard to his attention to beginning teachers' 'general epistemic beliefs' (Shulman 1986) and the important dimension of conceptions of purposes for teaching the subject. Nevertheless, as Shulman himself has recently acknowledged, the concept of pedagogical content knowledge was 'strictly individual and cognitive' (Shulman and Shulman 2004: 258) and omitted the important dimensions of community and setting.

However, I believe that a theoretical framework that brings together the contextualist, sociocultural and ecological perspectives on knowledge and cognition (discussed in Chapter 2) with the research on subject knowledge and the constitution of school subjects that foregrounds values and purposes (discussed in Chapter 3), can be shown to be highly generative in analyses of teachers' thinking and teachers' knowledge. The framework can be premised on a theory of knowledge creation as occurring within a dynamic system.

Knowledge creation as a dynamic system: a theoretical framework

The dynamic and interactive nature of the systems in which knowledge is created can be represented in outline in diagrammatic form (see Fig. 4.1). Three layers[1] are seen to be interacting within a given bounded system or 'form of life' (Wittgenstein 1972). Knowledge is seen as an outcome of the interactions within this system and the proposition that knowledge changes over time and in relation to changes in social and cultural context is illustrated by the arrows emanating from the outer circle enclosing the interacting elements – indicating that the system itself is in motion. In other words, the conditions for knowledge and the grounds for its verification exist within the particular system but the system itself – and the conditions and rules for evaluation – may change over time and in different contexts.

Figure 4.1: Diagrammatic representation of knowledge creation as a dynamic system

Within the system, the interacting layers comprise:

- *Culture*
  This offers the arena for practice, defined by Lave as a 'physically, economically, and socially organised space-in-time … the product of social formation and political economy' (Lave 1988: 150–1). In the same way as Lave suggests that individual agency and the setting for activity are dialectically constituted, the arena for practice

is also dialectically constituted in relation to activity within settings. For example, the arena for practice in civil engineering – what we might refer to (using another spatial metaphor) as 'the field' – is dialectically constituted in relation to activity in the various settings in which civil engineers practice (laboratories, construction sites, universities, etc.). That is, practice determines the boundaries of the field and the rules by which the field as a whole validates knowledge. This is not to say that there is consensus about the boundaries and rules of the arena for practice but the reflexive nature of the interaction goes some way towards explaining the dynamic nature of the arena. The dimension of politics and policies is intended to indicate both that the arena for practice is formed in relation to political economy and that the arena provides the rules for the validation of new knowledge and for evaluation of the field as whole. Again, this is not to imply universal agreement within the arena but to suggest that it is subject to a dynamic process of change arising out of competing claims and contestation arising out of practice in different settings.

Also, the diagram suggests that resources for practice – physical and conceptual – exist at the cultural level (and are appropriated as *tools* by the individual agent in the course of activity). That is, under this definition, resources for practice include, for example, books and artefacts as well as concepts. Again, this aspect of culture is dialectically constituted in relation to activity in settings and the creativity of individual agents.

Finally, the layer of Culture within the system provides the grounds for the *cultural identity* of that system and of the activity and the agents within it (for example, civil engineering and civil engineers). In this way, the process of knowledge creation is connected to the development of a particular form of identity, a process in which legitimate peripheral participation in a community of practice is also a process of becoming.

- *Activity*

As I have already explained, activity in this analysis is defined as 'enduring, intellectually planned sequences of behaviour, directed toward particular objects and goals' (Yinger and Hendricks-Lee 1993: 103). The object-orientation is important and also reflects the personal commitments of individual agents towards certain forms of cultural identity. For this intentional activity to have systemic significance in the creation of knowledge, it must be situated in a community of practice, although this community does not have to exist co-temporally or co-spatially. Similarly, specifying a setting for practice does not necessarily mean that all members of that community are present at the same time: setting, under this definition, means a 'repeatedly experienced, personally ordered and edited version of the arena' (Lave 1988: 151); the concept of setting allows us to understand how individual knowing is instantiated in the world. Setting also allows us to understand more explicitly the relationship that exists between the individual agent and the culture.

The layer of activity therefore represents the means by which individual knowing can be validated as knowledge according to the rules operated by the community of practice. This is at the level of *collective knowledge* which can be distinguished from the level of individual knowing and cultural identity by its emphasis on social practice and 'rule-governed behaviour' (Edwards *et al.* 2002: 39).

• *Agent*
  This layer represents the individual learner and their potential for action or agency.

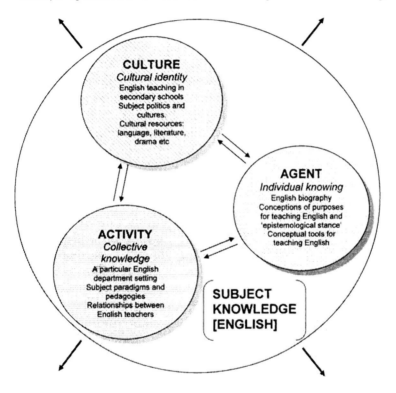

The dynamic nature of the system as whole is underlined by obvious interrelationships between the individual agent's perceptions and prior experience at the level of culture and activity, in particular their perceptions of and participation in the settings in which they are learning and their motivations for developing a particular form of cultural identity or becoming. This can be described as an aspect of autobiography. Also, with particular reference to motivation, the importance of the individual's values and beliefs should be stressed;[2] this can also be expressed as their conceptions of purposes for activity (why bother? what's important?). Again, acknowledging the interrelationship between layers is important when considering the issue of values and beliefs as these are in a reflexive relationship to the goals and conceptions of purposes for activity in the community and to the operation of the rules for evaluation and validation at the cultural level.

In this layer, the individual agent's appropriation of particular physical and conceptual resources for practice is represented by the concept *tool*. To refer to physical and conceptual tools for practice highlights the individual's agency in selecting the particular resource for a given purpose; the act of selection is behind the development from resources to tool (the resource not becoming a tool until it is selected by the individual for intentional activity within a particular setting and community).

The layer of agent suggests that *individual knowing* potentially consists of innovative interventions in a community and setting that leads to the creative displacement of usual practice and the development of new knowledge. Individual knowing can also be expressed more conservatively as the simple outcome of participation. In both cases, the interactions between agent, activity and culture are the core of this dynamic system in that the individual is not conceived of as 'prior to' or 'passing through' contexts but are rather *partly composed by* their interactions within them.

It is now necessary to apply this model to the specific focus of my research: the concept of subject knowledge and the development of beginning teachers' thinking. I am defining subject knowledge as that part of a teacher's knowledge that is directly related to school subjects and the curriculum. I am not using the term 'subject knowledge for teaching' as my interest was in the broader concept and in teachers' thinking about the constitution of the subject they teach and its informing purpose, etc., rather than how it might be 'used' in performance. My interest was not, therefore, in measuring teachers' subject knowledge and how this measure might figure in an assessment of their effectiveness as teachers. Rather, my intention was to explore how teachers' think about the subject knowledge of a school subject (English) and how this changes or develops as they learn to teach. Figure 2 provides a diagrammatic representation of subject knowledge within the dynamic system of knowledge creation I have presented.

Figure 4.2: Diagrammatic representation of English subject knowledge within a dynamic system

Once again, the dynamic and interactive nature of the system allows for the possibilities of difference and development as well as suggesting an interactive and reflexive relationship between individual agency, culture and activity. The subject knowledge of school English can be seen to be subject to contestation at the cultural level; it can vary from setting to setting; it allows for individual agency.

- *Culture*
  The cultural identity under study is that of English teaching; specifically, English teaching in secondary schools. At this cultural level, the subject policies, paradigms and pedagogies exist – both those 'rules' imposed upon the profession by government

and the profession's own culturally understood procedures for validating what counts as the subject knowledge of school English – as do the cultural resources for the constitution of English as a school subject. The latter will include the English language and literature written in English, aspects of drama and media study, and so on. This is the level at which the subject knowledge of school English becomes a cultural phenomenon. The specific example of English teaching clearly demonstrates that – at the cultural level – there is no assumption of consensus or uniformity.

- *Activity*
  In professional learning (the kind of learning that leads to socially purposeful, collective action), the setting for practice is obviously important. In England, beginning teachers spend most of their time learning in school departments, working alongside a group of teachers who, although they may not share the same identical set of values and beliefs, nevertheless coexist as a community of practice within which a form of collective knowledge is developed. There will be certain agreed parameters for group action even though the community will be internally differentiated on the basis of subject paradigms (what constitutes the subject and why) and subject pedagogies (how the subject should be taught and why) (Ball and Lacey 1980, Wilson and Wineburg 1988). These agreed parameters – arising out of a form of compromise over matters of subject paradigm and pedagogy – will nevertheless determine the goals of the community's activity and will do so also in relation to the arena for practice.

- *Agent*
  In this study, the individual learners were all graduates in English following a one-year course of initial teacher education leading to the PGCE. As such, they each had relatively long experience of studying English, observing English teaching and, as such, part of their *individual knowing* might be described as having an 'English biography' that is both concerned with the cultural resources of the subject and its pedagogy. They each brought a particular motivation for learning to teach that was related to their own conceptions of purpose for teaching English. Implicated in this was their own conceptions of knowledge – or 'epistemological stance' (Hillocks 1999) – and, implicitly, of how people learn. These conceptions in turn are one influence on the selection of physical and conceptual resources for practice from the cultural level that will be appropriated as tools in learning to teach English.

Returning to the questions guiding my research
In using these elaborations of *culture*, *activity* and *agent* to inform my research design, I hoped to avoid, firstly, making universal generalizations about the nature of English in schools; secondly, conceptualizing knowledge as an object to be acquired, commoditized and audited; and, thirdly, understanding development simply as a linear stage-scheme.

Given the theoretical framework presented above, it was also important to acknowledge that the two questions guiding my inquiry were *interconnected*:

1. What do the beginning teachers think about the subject knowledge of school English whilst learning to teach and does this thinking change or develop?
2. How can one account for this thinking about the subject knowledge of school English and how it develops? That is, how do the beginning teachers *come to know* the subject knowledge of school English?

'Ann'	'Grace'	'Liz'
Aged 23 at the beginning of her PGCE course at Parkton University, with a second-class honours degree in English. Ann had worked for the civil service and at a further education college for a short time before applying to PGCE courses.	Aged 22 at the beginning of her PGCE course at Newchester University, with a second-class honours degree in English and Management Studies. Grace had attended a number of schools and colleges and had initially dropped out of her A-level course.	Aged 22 at the beginning of the PGCE, course at Parkton University, with a second-class honours degree in English. Liz had resat her A-levels to gain admission to the BA at her preferred university (where she stayed for the PGCE).

Table 4.1: Outline biographical description of the three participants

The perspective I have elaborated would suggest that the 'what' of the first question should be seen to develop in relation to activity in settings that is culturally and historically nested. In other words, the 'what' is not a thing and not something that exists solely inside the head of the beginning teacher. The practical implication of this understanding for my research was that the investigation of what the beginning teachers (*agent[s]*) thought about the subject knowledge of English should involve the study of their accounts and perceptions of participation in object- and goal-oriented activity in settings (*activity*) in relation to a cultural arena and a particular form of identity (*culture*).

In the next section, I briefly describe the process of the research and show how this theoretical framework informed the research design and became the ground for a critical dialogue with the data that was generated.

The research process

Identifying the beginning teachers: a sample?

I decided early on that I did not wish to work with beginning teachers from within my own group of PGCE students. This was because I felt that my relationship with them as a researcher could be dominated by my relationship with them as their tutor and examiner. So I approached two colleagues at other universities and asked whether I could have access to their groups of PGCE English students. Although these colleagues taught at somewhat contrasting institutions, I did not intend to develop any kind of comparative analysis between them but simply thought that by working through two institutions, I could widen the pool of potential participants.

Both colleagues agreed to allow me access and I visited the two university departments of education early on in the academic year. As a result of my visits, six PGCE students emailed me and offered to take part in the research: four from the University of Newchester and two from the University of Parkton.[3] Two of the students from Newchester almost immediately withdrew as they experienced difficulties with managing their workload. One of these withdrew from the PGCE course very soon afterwards; the other withdrew from the course later in the second term. Another of the Newchester students participated in the first round of interviews but withdrew from the research shortly afterwards, saying that she felt that taking part would add significantly to her workload. This meant that three of the original six participated in the research for the duration of the project.

Introducing the beginning teachers

The three beginning teachers with whom I worked were similar in several ways. They were all young, white women from middle-class backgrounds who had good degrees in English from pre-1992 universities. In Table 2 below, I offer outline biographical descriptions of each participant at the starting point of the research.

As young women under 25 years of age, my participants came from the largest single category (28.40 per cent) of all PGCE completers in 2002 according to recent figures (National Statistics and DfES 2005). In addition, 84.40 per cent of all 2002 PGCE completers had a second-class honours degree (*ibid.*). To this very limited extent, my participants were not atypical of those who completed PGCE courses that year (but, to be clear: I am not claiming typicality).

It was necessary to conceal the identities of the two universities from which the beginning teachers were drawn for three reasons. First and foremost, I felt that it would be inappropriate to report anything the participants told me about their PGCE course directly. Second, it was not my intention to evaluate these universities' PGCE courses in any way or to identify the tutors. And third, I wanted to make it less likely that the beginning teachers themselves could be identified. I decided to conceal the identities of the PGCE and induction years' schools and the schools and universities the participants had themselves attended for similar reasons. Pseudonyms were chosen for these schools and universities that would make their identification difficult. I dealt with the issue of participant anonymity by asking the beginning teachers to choose their own pseudonyms at the end of the first interview. This also helped to preserve a sense of identity in the case studies.

Generating data

The methods I used to generate data are common in qualitative, interpretive research. The principal method was interviewing of a kind that could be described as somewhat ethnographic in that its object was to try to understand the participants' experience *in situ* over an extended period of time. However, the research design overall could not be described as ethnographic *per se* as, although I made several day-long visits to the three participants in their different schools and also observed them teaching during my first research visit (see below), I did not design a study that was focused around observation. This was because my interest was to describe, understand and theorize their thinking about the subject knowledge of English in situations outside of practice. This corresponded to the third tradition of research into teachers' thinking identified by Clark and Peterson (1986): teachers' theories and beliefs when not engaged in practice, a dimension of cognition Davis and Sumara (2000) described as 'individual knowing'. This is not, however, to say that my interest was focused on entirely 'inside the head' processes, as I have already explained. I was keen to include their perceptions of the settings in which they were learning and teaching and their reflections on and explanations over time of their thinking and development.

However, in order to enhance the credibility of my research and build a stronger argument, I decided to use multiple methods of generating data over an extended period of time. These included the drawing of maps, the writing of narratives, the collection of documents and the making of fieldnotes. My use of multiple methods was intended to provide a range of mediational means for the beginning teachers to work with (and on) and to engage with the questions guiding the research in a multifaceted way. There was no sense that by 'triangulating' the methods I was likely to come to a better understanding of identical phenomena.

Interviews

My conceptualization of the research interview was consistent with the theoretical orientation I have developed thus far. Mishler's classic critique of 'standardized' interview methodologies within a 'stimulus-response' tradition was influential on this conceptualization. Rather than viewing variation in the questioning of different respondents in different situations at different times as a methodological one that might be solved with highly structured interview protocols and training programmes, with the goal of a clinical class of objectivity, Mishler reinterpreted interviews as a particular form of contextually grounded speech events. Mishler's reconceptualization of the interview had four 'essential components':

> 1. Interviews are speech events; 2. The discourse of interviews is constructed jointly by interviewers and respondents; 3. Analysis and interpretation are based on a theory of discourse and meaning; 4. The meanings of questions and answers are contextually grounded. (Mishler 1986: ix)

This is not to argue against consistency of approach, however. In order to satisfy oneself that an effort is being made to understand the same phenomenon, it is necessary to identify roughly similar members of the same social group (beginning teachers of English in England) and then to design the research overall so as to contrive the same opportunities for all participants to jointly construct discourse with the researcher. (A table showing the progression of questioning foci across the three interview schedules is provided as Appendix A.) Equally important, given this understanding of interviews as speech events, was their audio-recording and subsequent careful transcription. (A note on transcription is provided as Appendix B.)

In developing the interview schedules, I found the early work of Grossman (1990) helpful, particularly in relation to tracing the beginning teachers' intellectual biographies. The interview transcripts were analysed using qualitative data analysis software and procedures adapted from the work of Miles and Huberman (1994) in an iterative process that brought emerging meanings into dialogue with the *culture*, *activity* and *agent* theoretical framework discussed earlier.

Narratives

Narrative has been an important concept in much research on teacher knowledge over the last 20 years (e.g. Clandinin and Connelly 2000, Connelly and Clandinin 1986, Carter 1993, 1994, Conle 2000, etc.). Sometimes narratives have been used as data upon which the researcher (in the research tradition of Shulman) seeks to generalise (e.g. Carter 1993, 1994) about teachers' 'pedagogical content knowledge'. From this perspective, learning to teach involves the acquisition of 'event-structured knowledge' (Carter 1994). Sometimes, on the other hand, claims have been made for 'narrative analysis' as an interpretive process that shifts 'from a researcher's interpretation' to a 'mutual researcher-participant reconstruction of meaning in action' (Connelly and Clandinin 1986: 296).

I decided to ask the beginning teachers to write narratives in the period between the first and second interview and to email or post them to me. I did so as I wanted to provide my research participants with another mediational tool to work with (and work on) in the process of exploring their thinking about the subject knowledge of English. I asked that they were narratives of teaching episodes in which subject knowledge as a concept had figured in some way and suggested a minimum of three (this turned out to be the number submitted by all participants). I also specified that they would be discussed at the second interview. As such, I was indicating that they would be partly interpreted within the broad framework of 'narrative analysis' rather than in the paradigmatic mode of 'analysis of narratives' (Polkinghorne 1995: 12–21). That is, the narratives were designed to become part of the research interview and would be a focus for the jointly constructed discourse. Therefore, my use of narratives as a method differs from Clandinin and Connelly's 'narrative inquiry' in that my end-purpose was not to arrive at a mutually agreeable interpretation and the interview itself was not conceptualised as a research/professional development hybrid. Rather, my use of narratives as method has some similarities with that of Doecke *et al.* who sought to 'reconceptualise narrative as discourse' foregrounding the 'narrative situation, including the purpose of the storyteller' (Doecke *et al.* 2000: 336).

Analysis of the narratives within the interview transcripts proved to be the most reliable as, on their own, they stood out (to the beginning teachers as well as to me) as rather 'hardened stories' (Conle 2000).

Maps of English subject knowledge

I also decided to use a mapping task in the interviews to offer participants another mediational means through which to work on their thinking about the subject knowledge of English. An important influence on my decision to include this task was, once again, the work of Grossman who had included a similar task in her interviews for *The Making of a Teacher: Teacher Knowledge and Teacher Education* (Grossman 1990). However, my use of the mapping task differed from Grossman's in several respects:

- The task was to draw a map of the areas of *English subject knowledge* and how they *might* be related.
- The mapping task was introduced in the course of a less overtly structured interview than was the case in Grossman's research and it was not conceptualized as a clinical task.
- The task was repeated during each of the interviews with the participants over the two-year period; my understanding is that Grossman used the task once only in the first interview.
- During subsequent interviews, I asked the participants to reflect on their previous maps after producing a new one and to consider the similarities and differences between them.
- The maps (and written narratives) were explored during the interviews using a form of 'narrative analysis' (Polkinghorne's (1995) definition).
- In Grossman's research, the maps are not dealt with explicitly and it is not apparent what part they played in the analysis of her data. The maps themselves were not published. In this study, I deal with the maps explicitly as part of the analysis.

I did not make the decision to use a mapping task in the research from any belief that it would provide me with more authentic or 'natural' insights into the participants' thinking than their spoken language. Whilst recognizing that some people might find drawing or producing a graphical representation a useful way of articulating complex or abstract ideas, others might be equally constrained by their graphical skills. My intention was simply to find another means of putting the ideas under examination and to explore the research questions in a multi-faceted way.

In developing a procedure for the analysis of these maps, I also drew on the research of Mavers *et al.* (2002) – and Pearson and Somekh (2003, 2000) – into pupils' conceptions of ICT as part of the British Government's ImpaCT2 evaluation of school ICT initiatives. However, my conceptualization of the mapping task also differs from that of Mavers *et al.* in two important respects:

1. I am not claiming that the maps produced by the participants are 'externalised representations' of their minds; that is, I do not believe there to be an absolute, one-to-one correspondence between what the participants drew and what they *really* thought (a claim to authenticity) nor that the map itself represents *everything* that they think about the subject (a claim for uniquely transparent attributes of drawing as an activity). This view is consistent with my position on language and thinking outlined earlier.

2. I do not make any claims about a correlation between a measure of a map's complexity and the sophistication of the participant's thinking; that is, that successful (i.e. highly skilled) graphical representation is neither an indicator of an individual's cognitive capacity nor the complexity or depth of their understanding of a phenomenon.

Nevertheless, I found Mavers *et al.*'s method of analysis very useful in attempting to take the visual images seriously *as* visual images. In particular, I adapted several of their strategies for describing the 'maps'. In view of the relatively rare use of visual images as a data-generation strategy in educational research, I now offer a more detailed account of my analytic procedures than I did for the analysis of the interview and narrative data.

In describing the maps *qualitatively*, I was interested in the map in terms of its construction as a visual image: the organization of the image, the use of icons or symbols, the concentration of detail in particular areas of the map and its perspective. I was also interested in the words that were used in the map and the ways in which they were given any sort of emphasis – for example, by graphical means (underlining, boxes, etc.) or by repetition. I attempted to get a sense of the map as a whole as well as of its constituent parts. I found Mavers *et al.*'s work useful in two respects here: first, in the categorization of 'organisational type' and, second, in the attention to '"levels" of conceptualisation' (Mavers *et al.* 2002: 192, Pearson and Somekh 2000).

1. *Organizational type*

   Organisational type refers to how the map is structured or organized; for example, one might be able to describe certain images as a flow chart or a family tree and others as a spider diagram. Mavers *et al.* proposed the following categories:

- *unconnected*: objects or elements ('nodes') with no links;
- *linear*: nodes linked to other nodes in sequential fashion;
- *one-centred*: 'with a clearly discernible central node from which links to other nodes radiate outward' (Mavers *et al.* 2002: 192);
- *several-centred*: 'two or more nodes acting as centres of interest' (*ibid.*);
- *spaghetti*: 'highly complex and multi-lined' (*ibid.*).

To these, I added two supplementary categories that best reflected the organization of the maps I had in front of me:

- *bounded*: the image or elements of the images are within a drawn boundary that may or may not include inter-linking lines;
- *unbounded*: the image is not enclosed by a drawn boundary but again the

Time	Data collected
September Year 1 *(near to start of PGCE course)*	• Preliminary conversations in groups at university base: simple biographical information • Subject knowledge audit and other course documents
January/February Year 1 *(near to start of first, five-day-a-week block of teaching experience)*	• Long interviews (75–90 minutes) • Completion of first mapping task • Lesson observations at PGCE school
February–June Year 1	• Beginning teachers wrote narratives about teaching episodes in which their subject knowledge was, in some way, a feature
June Year 1 *(near to end of PGCE course during five-day-a week block teaching experience in second school)*	• Long interviews (75–90 minutes), including discussion of narratives previously sent • Completion of second mapping task
July Year 2 *(near to end of Induction year in first appointment school)*	• Long interviews (75–90 minutes) • Completion of third mapping task
August–September Year 2	• Attempt to collect responses to and reflections on interview transcripts

Table 4.2 Timeline of data generation and type of data

These categories refer both to the organization of the image and to the way in which it might be framed. This is also a matter of perspective (the point of view from which the image is being presented). In making a description of any map, I would refer both to whether it was bounded/unbounded and whether it corresponded to any of the organizational types suggested by Mavers *et al.*.

2. *'Levels' of conceptualization*

In the ImpacT2 work, Mavers *et al.* also considered the possibility of 'looking for evidence of "levels" of conceptualisation' 'where some parts of the map became the focus for more detailed depiction than others (in the manner of a zoom lens honing in on one part of the map)' (*ibid.*).

I felt that this would be a useful category to use when describing the very much smaller set of images I was working with as it would enable me to reflect the greater level of detail given to elements (or groups of elements) in some of the maps.

Using a second approach – that I am loosely terming *numerical* – I was interested in developing codes that would allow me to use a common language of description across all the maps and that could lead to the presentation of the description in numerical form. I felt that this would be a useful and complementary approach to the more qualitative description, one that might allow for the identification of patterns related both to the content and organization. Again, I drew on the work of Mavers *et al.* in developing the following codes that would allow me to make some straightforward numerical descriptions (rather than any form of statistical analysis, as was the intention in ImpacT2):

3. *Nodes*

For my purposes, I defined nodes as the total number of elements or objects in the participants' maps. The participants were asked to draw a map which showed the different areas of English subject knowledge and how they might be related so, predictably, the nodes in their maps consisted of words or phrases which were either linked to or in relation to other words or phrases. To achieve consistency, I determined that a word or phrase would be counted as a node if it was connected to or in relation to another word or phrase but that I wouldn't count words or phrases as nodes if, for example, they could be interpreted as annotations on a previously counted node or if it was an annotation on a linking line. I decided not to count words or phrases that were used to annotate links and connections as I felt they were being used to describe the relationships between elements rather than identifying new elements. Nevertheless, I decided to account for this use of words and phrases separately.

4. *Links*

As in Mavers *et al.*, I counted the number of links between each node, with link being defined as a line with or without an arrowhead. To calculate the total, I counted the number of links emanating from each of the nodes.

5. *Linear connectivity*

I decided to conceptualize connectivity differently to Mavers *et al.* I felt that dividing the number of links by the number of nodes would only give me a measure of what I could refer to as 'linear connectivity', that is, connections represented by lines. One could argue that linear connectivity – with lines representing simple relationships between elements – is a relatively unsophisticated measure of complexity and that as understanding of the complexity of the relationships between elements develops it could become more difficult to represent them with lines. In other words, I accepted that a reduction in the measure of linear connectivity would not necessarily indicate a less sophisticated understanding of the phenomenon. In fact, it might simply indicate a *different* way of understanding it, focused on the relationships between its elements.

Two other codes were developed through the process of checking for points of comparison and contrast outlined earlier:

6. *National Curriculum Attainment Targets (NCats)*

   I checked whether the participants' maps referred to the three attainment targets of the pupils' National Curriculum for English: speaking and listening, reading and writing. I did not double-count references to the attainment targets so there was a maximum score of three. Given that the participants were learning to teach English as framed within a statutory order, I was interested to see whether references to the NCats figured in their representations of the subject.

7. *Areas of Subject Knowledge (ASK)*

   I counted the number of different areas of English subject knowledge referred to in each of the maps. I did not double-count references to the same element so, for example, if literature was mentioned three times, I counted this as the same element. The emphasis provided by the repetition was to be addressed in the qualitative description. I included in this number, any references to areas of subject knowledge usually associated with English as a school subject in England (including, for example, drama and media). I did not count references to other subject areas (e.g. history) nor did I count references to policy initiatives such as the Key Stage 3 English Framework (although, obviously, the Framework's emphasis on grammar might be reflected in the elements of subject knowledge mentioned) nor to examination arrangements (e.g. SATs).

   The qualitative and numerical description of each participants' maps is presented in the relevant case study. The discourse in which the production of the maps was embedded was analysed as part of the interview data and then combined in the relevant subsection of each case study. Changes in the maps within and between the three participants are analysed in Chapter 8.

Timeline of data generation

Table 4.2 provides a timeline of the data generation, noting the type of data generated at each stage:

Cases as prototypes: an argument for signicance and theoretical generalizability

There are many definitions of 'case study' within the qualitative research literature. Bassey (1999) and Merriam (1988) discuss this range in their methodological reviews and many of the definitions seem to be complementary, suggesting that there is a 'bounded' focus on individuals, institutions or events. Stark and Torrance assert that it is 'an "approach" to research' (rather than a single method) that stresses the 'social interaction and social construction of meaning *in situ*' and that 'what is common to all approaches is the emphasis on study-in-depth' (Stark and Torrance 2005: 33).

However, according to Brown and Dowling, 'there is ... no such thing as the "case study approach"' (Brown and Dowling 1998: 167). Instead, they see the use of the term as an effect of the 'mythologisation' of research and a 'fetishising' of method. Whilst their argument might at least in part be interpreted as resistance to methodological orthodoxies, they do make a point highly relevant to my own research: the analytic focus on a 'single actor, a single institution, a single enterprise' under 'natural conditions' as a 'bounded system' is an illusion. Actors, institutions and enterprises are not, as they point out, 'mutually independent (bounded) systems' that are 'transparently knowable' to the researcher (*ibid.*: 166).

This view of the situatedness and ecological character of the object of research is consistent with the epistemological position I have developed thus far. An important dimension of the research presented here is that the development of the beginning teachers' thinking can only be traced with reference to their participation in communities and settings rather than asserting that either their thinking or their development is somehow contained within the head of the single actor. My use of the terms 'case study' and 'case study approach', therefore, builds on this epistemological position and is consistent with the methodological definition provided by Stark and Torrance:

> ... case study seeks to engage with and report the complexity of social activity in order to represent the meanings that individual social actors bring to those settings and manufacture in them. Case study assumes that 'social reality' is created through social interaction, albeit situated in particular contexts and histories, and seeks to identify and describe before trying to analyse and theorise. (2005: 33)

The case studies that follow in Chapters 5, 6 and 7 seek to understand the complexity of the beginning English teachers' thinking by tracing development over a two-year period as they learn to teach. Another important 'social reality' in this research is the research setting itself and the beginning teachers' social interactions with me as a researcher. In other words, I became part of my participants' social realities and therefore part of the research. This is not presented as a problem for which some sort of methodological adjustments can be made but to acknowledge, as I discussed earlier, that my analysis of their thinking and its development is underpinned by the Vygotskian understanding that there is a reciprocal relationship between thinking and language and that the data under study here is principally their spoken language generated in the research setting rather than everything that they ever thought everywhere. Although I do not accept Stark and Torrance's apparently clear distinction between description and analysis, Chapters 5, 6 and 7 identify and describe what the beginning teachers think about the subject knowledge of English before Chapter 8 explicitly theorizes the process of development.

I have said that I chose to adopt the case study approach in designing the research as I wanted to understand and represent the richness and particularity of beginning teachers' thinking about subject knowledge, something I had come to feel from my own work as a teacher educator was much more complex and affective than the simple accumulation of fragments in a linear progression or the transformation of something from one box into another. However, even though I did not intend to make empirical generalizations to the population of beginning teachers in England (something that would have necessitated first and foremost a fundamentally different epistemological position), it was still necessary to be clear about the potential significance of my research to the field.

My principal argument with reference to the significance and generalizability of my research is concerned with *prototypicality*. The case studies may be regarded as *prototypical* (rather than typical) and the individual cases as *prototypes* (rather than as a sample) (Langemeyer and Nissen 2005). This view arises out of the sociocultural understanding that an examination of 'higher mental functions' (Vygotsky 1986) is made possible by creating them in the research situation. A prototype is, therefore, 'different from a sample in that it is something new' (Langemeyer and Nissen 2005: 189) that has been co-created in the research setting. The case studies might also be regarded as prototypical in that they act as a valid pattern for other cases that might be co-created by other researchers in other settings. And, as I have already stated, this might provide the grounds for a claim to theoretical generalizability in terms of my conceptualization of the development of beginning teachers' thinking about subject knowledge. Although this involves a consideration of common dimensions to development across the case studies and the generation of new concepts, there is no attempt to identify variables in the way that the term 'cross-case analysis' might imply. Given the epistemological position informing this research, it would be rather odd if I wanted both to capture the particularity, richness and complexity of each case and then obliterate it in pursuit of empirical generalizations.

Writing the analysis/writing as analysis
The moves from guiding questions to interviews to transcriptions to networks of codes and quotations to the construction of three extended case studies is consti-

tuted by another level of interpretation intrinsic to the process of writing. In referring to systematic, analytic procedures in educational research, a scientistic aura can sometimes be created. This is why I think it is also necessary to draw attention to the textual status of the case studies and the way in which judgements and choices made in the course of writing are also interpretive moves. Britzman refers to this as the way the research text 'intends to translate, even as it is meant to stand in for, social life' (Britzman 2004: 244). The challenge for the researcher is to resist the 'desire to construct good stories filled with the stuff of rising and falling action, plots, themes and denouement' and to 'abandon the impossible desire to portray the study's subjects as they would portray themselves' (*ibid.*: 248). Doecke *et al.* (2000) and others propose that there must be resistance to 'narrative unity' and a commitment to drawing out contradictions and silences. The alternative is the sentimentalization of both researcher and participants.

In writing these case studies, I used the results of systematic analytic procedures – the lists of codes and quotations and frequencies, and so on – to build an argument that had to embrace contradictions in the data. The organization of each case study was directly informed by subdivisions of my guiding questions. This is apparent in the use of subheadings: *Settings for learning to teach*, *English biography*, *Auditing subject knowledge*, *Constituting the subject*, *The purposes of English teaching*, *Epistemological stance* and *Reflections on development*. But I also made aesthetic choices about how to choose a representative quotation, how to edit it, how to situate it within a paragraph of description and, fundamentally, how to tell the story – not as a simple story, but as a rather complex one with neither a beginning nor an end. I deliberately foregrounded inconsistencies and contradictions and my own role in jointly constructing the research in order to, as Britzman put it, 'narrate development as a creepy detour' (Britzman 2000: 248).

5

Ann: thinking about the subject knowledge of English

Ann was 23 when she began her PGCE course at Parkton University. She was brought up in the English Midlands and attended the local comprehensive school. After graduating from Riverbank University with an upper second class honours degree in English, she worked for a short time at a local office of the Benefits Agency before joining the IT department of a further education college as a student adviser. In both of these posts, Ann began to consider applying to PGCE courses, an option previously suggested to her by family, friends and former teachers but one she had consistently rejected up to this time.

There were many reasons why Ann said she changed her mind. One was her desire to help people to help themselves by teaching basic skills:

… working at the Benefits Agency which is a big eye opener and seeing people who, you know, who are filling application forms who couldn't write their name, you know, who couldn't even sign their name, you know, and couldn't understand forms is really saddening and really, sort of, you know, hit me thinking, 'you can do something, perhaps you can go out there … and help these people'. (Ann 1)[1]

Another was her belief that she *could* teach: her time as a student adviser in a further education college also exposed her to what she felt were some poor examples of teaching: 'looking at these people teaching and thinking "I could do it so much better" ((laughter)), "you're doing it terrible!"' (*ibid.*)

Ann also admitted that the government training bursary had influenced her decision to apply to PGCE courses. Having become a salaried employee, she was reluctant to return to a student's lifestyle and debts. And she also said that she had always enjoyed and been interested in English as a subject. Her motivations for entering teaching were, as so often it seems, quite complex.

Settings for learning to teach

Ann enjoyed her PGCE course at Parkton University and spoke enthusiastically about some memorable sessions. One such session was focused on different literary critical approaches in the post-16 English classroom and made use of young children's picture books. She regarded this as a 'bit of an eye opener' (Ann 2) in that what she had previously understood to be so difficult (literary theory) could be the focus of teaching in secondary schools. Another memorable session was on 'poetry from other cultures and traditions' and involved researching the biographies and social/historical contexts of poets whose work is featured in the GCSE English Literature anthology. Ann also recalled sessions on sentence grammar and the AS and A2 assessment objectives that were taught by visiting tutors from local schools.

Another session, taught by the course tutor, was also particularly memorable: this focused on 'developing a rationale' for English teaching and a critical analysis of the pupils' National Curriculum for English:

> … it just, um, slots into your idea of why you're being an English teacher and what it is to be an English teacher and that's still something that we, I go back sometimes to the handouts that we got (and sort of) it inspires me and when you're feeling down, you, you think, yeah, this is why I'm doing it, to try and sort of keep going. (Ann 2)

It is clear from what she says here that there is a form of sustenance and nourishment to be found in a consideration of the philosophical dimensions to practise even when, practically, the going is tough.

The PGCE course at Parkton includes two school placements, one relatively short, early on, composed of serial days as well as a block placement and a later, extended, full-time block in another school. The first time that Ann gave me her impressions of her first placement school, Peak Down County High, was shortly after beginning her second placement and so these impressions are filtered through her limited experience of the second and, of course, the PGCE course. Ann thought that Peak Down County High was fairly traditional in its approach to English and perhaps rather similar to her own experience of English in schools. The classes were set from Year 7 and she found pupils' attitudes towards English and towards learning quite polarized; top sets were enthusiastic and chatty, bottom sets were demotivated and lessons went by slowly. It seemed that Ann wasn't very comfortable teaching English at this school and related this in part to her experience of teaching the top set in Year 9: 'I didn't sense that there was that much kind of … I don't know, enjoyment, or sort of passion, but there again maybe they just felt "oh", and getting on with it so it's difficult to judge' (Ann 1).

In her third interview towards the end of her NQT year, Ann also commented on the uniformity of the English curriculum at Peak Down and did so negatively, implying that this had constrained teachers' creativity or ability to respond flexibly to pupils' needs:

> They'd done their … plans, units and schemes of work … it was lesson one, things, aims to do, what you'd do and equipment you needed and you'd go to the cupboard and

you'd find that. So the teachers were all teaching the same and it didn't really feel like you could vary that really. (Ann 3)

Ann's second placement school was a specialist media studies college in the city centre of Parkton, St Helen's Community College. St Helen's was a small, well-resourced, 11–16 school where English groups were organized on a mixed-ability basis. Ann taught a wide range of classes here, including some focused on practical media production. In fact, Ann had indicated an interest in developing this area in conversations with her PGCE tutor and speculated that this was why she had been placed here. The groups were more prone to shouting out than at Peak Down but Ann preferred the classes here.

Later, Ann recalled that the English department at St Helen's had 'a lot of money to spend on computer equipment' (Ann 3) and consequently came in for some envious comments from other departments in the school. Unsurprisingly, she noted that English at St Helen's was 'saturated' (*ibid.*) with video and 'focused on media' (*ibid.*). An unexpected effect of this for Ann was that showing a video to a class was no longer a treat: 'It's a video', 'Oh, do we have to?' (*ibid.*). She felt that unless the pupils were 'doing critical literacy' (*ibid.*) with video, they weren't responsive. Another unexpected effect of this emphasis on moving image media in Ann's eyes was that the class readers at St Helen's (she gave Anne Fine's *Goggle Eyes* as an example) seemed 'dull' and 'ordinary' (*ibid.*) in comparison.

Ann took up a first post at Abbotts, a large Beacon school in Essex with technology college status. It was an oversubscribed, 11–18 comprehensive school serving a mainly affluent community (although Ann also identified a council estate as being part of its catchment area) and had recently been featured in the local press as having the best A-level results in the county. All subjects at the school were taught in setted groups from Year 7. Ann felt that the parents and carers were generally keen for their children to do well and supported the school with its tough line on rules and uniform. She said she enjoyed teaching there although said she disagreed with some aspects of school policy. For example, referring to Year 9 and GCSE options choices:

> … the bottom 45 in the year, umm, are not allowed to take the options that they want. They have to take things like GNVQs and vocational qualifications so our school statistics are better in the A* to C range so we can go up to 100% rather than just looking at 70% or whatever we are now. (Ann 3)

Ann felt that this was 'pigeon holing [pupils] at the age of 14 which seems wrong somehow' (*ibid.*). This was an example of the school's 'inflexibility' for her, an inflexibility she also saw in some teaching colleagues' attitudes towards some pupils in her tutor group whom they had difficulty managing in lessons.

For Ann, English at Abbotts had a 'strong emphasis on the classroom reader' (*ibid.*) which she felt, as she felt about Peak Down, was quite 'traditional' (*ibid.*). Unlike Peak Down, however, she felt that the organization of the English curriculum at Abbotts was quite flexible in that there were choices of texts and, as long as certain assessment outcomes were achieved, 'you can do it any way you wish' (*ibid.*). In her comments about English at Abbotts, Ann once again made comparisons based on her previous experience at Peak Down and St Helen's. The most frequent points of contrast were drawn with St Helen's, Ann characterizing the differences with references to the use of group work, the emphasis on reading visual images and the relative importance of the class reader and literature:

> … things were more creative at St Helen's, using images, umm, using pictures, using media, using television shows, that kind of idea to get ideas across was more prominent … (*ibid.*)

> … at St Helen's there was more kind of critical theory and analysis of media type images and pictures, whereas at Abbotts, things tend to be more passive … (*ibid.*)

> … Abbotts concentrates more on class reader, and literature. … (*ibid.*)

Ann did not present these comparisons between settings to me as polarizations, however, and noted that 'all the elements of Abbotts are there at St Helen's but just at different degrees' (*ibid.*) and that teaching English at both schools to an extent marginalized the study of (spoken and written) language: 'in both … language is the least aspect of it, linguistics, so it's literature and media that's the main focus' (*ibid.*). However, although Ann was generally positive in her comments on teaching and teaching English at Abbotts, her comparisons with St Helen's do not always appear to be favourable to her current school.

Nevertheless, Ann felt Abbotts school took her professional development seriously and, when she successfully applied (independently) through open competition to join NATE's delegation to the 2003 Melbourne conference of the International Federation for the Teaching of English (IFTE), they released her from teaching for just over a week and offered her some financial support. Ann attended conference workshops in the 'twenty-first-century literacies' strand (where there was an emphasis on the 'impact' of ICTs on literacy) and also attended the plenary sessions (where there was a focus on issues of social justice and globalization). My third interview with Ann took place at the end of her induction year and after her return from the IFTE conference. In this interview, she identified the conference as one of two highlights of the year (the other being her involvement in the school production of *Bugsy Malone*) and, in her comments on the interview transcripts, Ann noted that 'the IFTE conference has really affected my thinking' (Ann's comments on transcripts). The impact of the IFTE conference is perhaps most apparent in Ann's comments on the political opinions of her pupils and their families:

> … I am so aware that children are so white, middle class that, you know, things like, they all believe that asylum seekers are coming into the country and taking their jobs, you know, they seriously believe that. (Ann 3)

This comment arose out of her discussion of the opening presentation in which the speaker described September 11th as an occasion that 'halted the march of capitalism' (Luke 2003; quoted by Ann 3) after which it was time to rethink why, for what purpose, we teach literacy and English. In what followed, it was clear that the IFTE conference, for Ann, had 'opened a window to think' (*ibid.*) about English and why she was teaching it.

Ann's English biography

In the third interview, Ann described the English teaching at her own comprehensive school as 'traditional'. For her, this meant a focus on 'class readers' in which the teacher would orchestrate readings of the novels around the class in a methodical if rather boring fashion:

> … I remember being about two chapters ahead of where we actually were because I was reading on … I remember being bored stiff at school and just ploughed through a class reader, just reading and reading and reading. (Ann 3)

My second interview with her took place at St Helen's, an English department associated in her own mind with the use of group work. Here, she told me that most of the English work she was assigned as a pupil was to be completed on an individual basis with very little group work, as she remembered it, and a strong emphasis on the recall of plot. The best teacher she could remember was an older man she characterized as 'enthusiastic' who varied the learning activities and moved pupils towards analysis (Ann 2). Variation of learning activities was again something she associated with St Helen's (*ibid.*).

The most memorable school experience of English for Ann was her A-level work on Ayckbourn's *The Norman Conquests*. A class reading of the play was focused around understanding how its comic effects were realized and the class was also taken to see a performance of the play. Over the three interviews, however, Ann's comments on her school experience of English portray an overwhelmingly dull and formulaic subject, and detached in that she recalled very little effort to open up what was being read for analysis so that readers' own experiences could be elicited in interpretation:

… we never looked at media, I think we did a newspaper, I don't think I was ever taught how to set out a newspaper, the difference between broadsheet and tabloid journalism. And so, yeah, the whole media, I mean there wasn't anything on language, it was very literature based, it was read a book, answer your comprehension questions, do a character study, write the essay. And that was just a repeated and repeated and repeated formula. (Ann 3)

Once again, Ann appears to be drawing on her experiences of St Helen's and Abbotts in her reflections on the English teaching she herself experienced at school, noting the omission of Media Education from her own school English and a similar lack of attention to language to that she noticed in both St Helen's and Abbotts. The distaste for repetitive, formulaic and detached approaches to English she expressed about Peak Down County High also seems to be present here.

It is interesting to note that Ann doesn't refer to statutory orders or government curriculum initiatives in her comments and comparisons. Ann is young enough to have experienced the pupils' National Curriculum for English throughout her schooling and so is likely to have been exposed to some semblance of the curriculum coverage required by that document, including Media Education and some attention to the structures and varieties of written and spoken language. Yet she comments more often on the general subject paradigms and subject pedagogies of the departments in which she has been taught or teaches and sometimes – unprompted – to the individual teachers who she believes have been particularly influential in the formation of these paradigms and pedagogies.

Nevertheless, there is an interesting potential contradiction in Ann's comments on her experience of English at school that surfaced in her first interview with me at Peak Down County High. Talking about the focus on reading a literary text around the class in her own schooling, she admits:

… we just went through the text sort of reading and analysing, which even, I know now … moving away from it, it's a kind of method but I still enjoyed it (laughter) in the same way that I think, you know, oh, you sort of feel guilty almost now, it just feels such, just taking the kids through the text and say 'hey, you know, look at this, this is great', I've always felt guilty for doing it ((whispers)) 'we should be doing something more exciting than this surely'. (Ann 1)

This focus on the enjoyment of teacher-centred reading with a class doesn't recur in Ann's comments and neither does the expression of guilt at not 'doing something more exciting'. What does occur, again quite often, however, is an enjoyment of analysis – of trying to understand why things are read in the way that they are, how certain aesthetic effects are experienced, etc. – whether this is in relation to her experience of being taught an Ayckbourn play at school or learning to teach media texts at St Helen's.

After school, Ann studied for an English degree at the University of Riverbank. Her understanding of the nature of this English degree in relation to other English degrees from other universities – an understanding developed by talking to other English graduates on the PGCE course and in schools – is shown in her third interview with me, when she notes:

> When I speak to other people, umm, they may not, who have done English courses, at different universities, they often say that they haven't studied it in a linear fashion, or they, the university selects a period which they study. I feel I have a comprehensive overview. (Ann 3)

Literary theory also had 'quite a prominent part' (Ann 3) in the Riverbank degree as a core component of the course. Ann said that she enjoyed this aspect of her degree even though she had found it difficult initially. It was difficult at first but I suppose it comes back to this basic 'I like analysing the text', so really enjoyed that and looking for different interpretations in text … (Ann 1).

Later, in her third interview, Ann felt that the literary theory element of her degree had 'moved me on in my analysis and interpretation of texts' (Ann 3).

Auditing subject knowledge

The Parkton PGCE English course complied with the requirement to audit student teachers' subject knowledge by issuing them with a self-assessment checklist that would form the basis of a meeting with the course tutor. The checklist was divided into ten sections starting with 'Speaking and Listening' and ending with 'Post-16'. These sections were in turn broken down into 69 bullet points (e.g. 'poetry from different cultures and traditions', 'discourse structure', 'language and gender', etc.) and PGCE students invited to rate their confidence about their knowledge against each of these bullet points on a 'fairly' or 'not very' basis. There was also space for written comments about action taken by the student in each of the three PGCE terms. Information from this subject knowledge audit was carried over to a more general profile and action plan that became a key course document for every student.

In response to my first question about the audit of subject knowledge, however, Ann didn't immediately refer to the checklist but to a more general level of awareness that there were some things she needed to learn about some aspects of English as a school subject. The main areas for development she described initially as 'language and linguistics' and then as 'grammar'. When I asked her how she found out that she needed to learn some 'grammar', she replied:

> Because I suppose I recognize it, I suppose it was talking to [course tutor] and then as the course started it became apparent that it would be … literacy strategies, that it

wouldn't be something that you'd be able to push to the side and sort of, you know, look it up when the time came, it was something that was fundamental to your teaching ... (Ann 1)

Rather than an objective gap in a checklist of subject knowledge, Ann's more general level of awareness seemed to recognize and accept the variation in subject paradigms and subject pedagogies for English. This was reinforced for

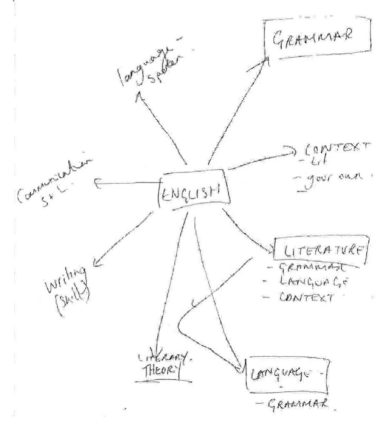

Figure 5.1: Ann's Map 1

her when she came to teach A-level English Language in a sixth-form college for a short period as part of her first school experience and she found herself needing to learn terminology to express her tacit understanding of language structures with these older students:

I had to learn all sorts of new terms, things I already know but it's just sort of not knowing the term for it ... you still have to go back to basics with them, they're not language gurus there you know, at the end of the day they still not that sure, but when

I first went I was 'oh gosh' I was really nervous. (*ibid.*)

Nevertheless, later in the first interview, Ann did recall completing the audit checklist, ticking boxes to indicate whether she had a good knowledge of a particular area or not:

… you had to make little ticks and my language section was 'I don't know' because I didn't know a lot of the terms but then I felt quite confident because I knew quite a lot of all the others. (*ibid.*)

The aspect of subject knowledge identified in the completion of the checklist that Ann felt she most needed to learn she termed 'grammar' or 'linguistics' and, at the time of this first interview, she seemed quite confident that this 'gap' in her knowledge was simply due to the fact that she had studied English literature at university (*ibid.*: 858) and that this could be easily remedied. She identified several ways in which she was developing what she perceived to be the necessary knowledge: first, independent study; and second, talking to other members of her PGCE group:

… I feel like I rely on them, 'cause they've sort of done their degrees in linguistics and things so I feel like I've got some back-up behind me if I really don't know where to go, and asking people … [visiting tutors] 'oh, you know, what should I read, where should I go for this?' and sort of tapping in to them. (Ann 2)

In her second interview with me, however, Ann admitted that the experience of discovering a 'grammar gap' and working to fill it had been a cause for concern:

… I was very concerned about the whole grammar thing.
… I was uncomfortable and not confident because it had been highlighted in the audit that I couldn't do anything on the list. (*ibid.*)

Notwithstanding this earlier anxiety, by the time of this second interview (near to the end of the PGCE year) Ann told me that she was feeling much more confident about grammar and that her memories of the audit were now 'very vague' (*ibid.*):

I'm more confident with [grammar] so it's not such a big deal any more. It's like, well, we can do a little bit of it here, you can do a little bit of it there, that's OK, I don't need to be the guru, I don't need to know everything but I know enough now to be confident about it, to sort of train you, so it's sprinkled around now rather than, 'Oh my God, grammar'. (*ibid.*)

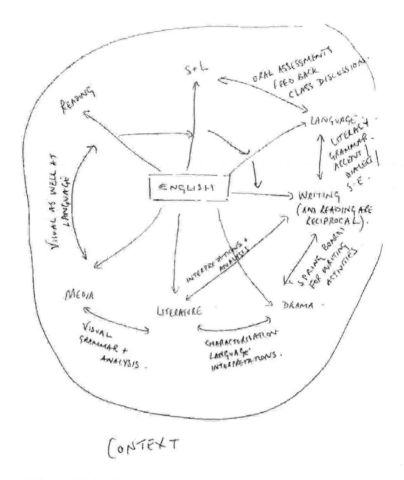

Figure 5.2: Ann's Map 2

This comment, coming as it does towards the end of the PGCE, would seem to indicate that Ann had developed a different understanding of subject knowledge and auditing in the process of learning to teach, different to the objectivist understanding inscribed in the audit checklist, an objectivism that had caused her anxiety and concern at the time, even if she had decided not to tell me this then. This understanding of subject knowledge seems similar to that general level of awareness Ann said she had developed at the beginning of the course: that there were some new things she needed to learn that would be 'fundamental' but not an exclusive indicator of her success as an English teacher. This more sensitive understanding at the level of awareness seems to have been challenged – albeit temporarily – by the application of the audit checklist. To understand that she didn't need to be the 'guru', that the teacher doesn't need to know everything, seems to be an important and insightful realization for any beginning teacher but perhaps especially for one who has been made to feel there is a large gap that shall be known as 'Oh my God, grammar'.

Constituting the subject

In the first map of English that Ann drew (see Fig. 5.1), she began by boxing in the word *English* at the centre of the page and then drawing in spokes at the ends (or nodes) of which she placed other words. As she drew, she spoke about what she was doing 'So, if I, kind of, put English there and have branches coming out. … So if I say grammar … and context … literature …' (Ann 1).

In this last comment, Ann describes in order the first three nodes she drew; these were closely followed by *language* and the comment, 'I suppose language … is related to sort of grammar.' *Grammar*, *language* and *literature* were then boxed in. The node *language* was followed by *literary theory, communication* (with the additional *S + L* to indicate speaking and listening), *language (spoken)* and *writing* (with the word *skills* written in beneath later). Just after writing in *communication* (and describing it as 'a skill I suppose of English' [*ibid.*]), Ann said:

Gosh, it's just so, it's sort of so vast, I mean, English. (*ibid.*)

In the discussion that followed the drawing, Ann speculated that the reason she had written in *grammar* first might have been that we had just been talking about it in the context of the required auditing of subject knowledge. (The same may also be true for 'literary theory' as we had discussed this earlier in relation to her degree.) She also suggested that grammar may have been the first node drawn as she was 'not as confident at it as in other areas' (*ibid.*). Ann explained why *context* was also important but not boxed in:

Context, yeah … but then I suppose it's literature context and then it's your own as well, it's what you bring … and then what the text brings … I suppose, and then the age that you live in, and that's why literature is timeless in a sense. (*ibid.*)

In this comment, Ann appears to be alluding to at least three important strands in literary theory: reader response (e.g. Rosenblatt 1978), with its focus on the transaction between the reader and the text; cultural materialism/new historicism (e.g. Gallagher and Greenblatt 2001), with its emphasis on text and (con)text; and an appeal to timelessness that is associated with more traditional and aesthetic-appreciative approaches to literature. However, rather than merely being recalled in a previous discussion of her degree, it may be that literary theory for Ann does have a significant impact on her thinking here (although it is worth noting, too, that Ann had had to revise the social and historical context of texts for her teaching at the sixth-form college).

Although the words *grammar* and *language* appear three times each on this map (and *literature* only once), Ann explains that her 'main focus would be literature and not language. I would teach probably language through literature' (*ibid.*) and, with that, she drew a line from the node *literature* down to *language*. This comment illustrates the connections she is making between the constitution of the subject in terms of areas of knowledge and her teaching of it.

When drawing the second map, Ann was silent for much of the time. The map itself bears some similarities to the first with English boxed in at the centre and with various spokes and nodes. The major differences are that there are many more interconnections between the spokes and nodes, these are enclosed within a circular boundary and the word context (appearing only once) is situated outside this boundary (see Fig. 5.2).

Ann explains the use of *context* in this map as follows:

> I just think that, kind of, everything that you do in English sort of has a context, what you bring to a subject, umm, what the subject brings it brings in itself, kind of the background and texts and things like that. And then, how it is in kind of the social construction in our society today. (Ann 2)

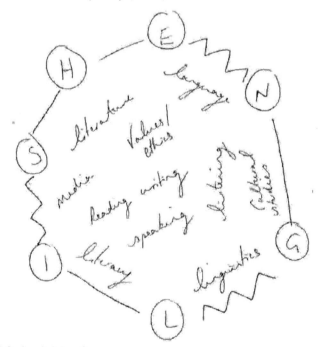

Figure 5.3: Ann's Map 3

In this comment, Ann appears to be adding a social semiotic dimension to the literary theoretical perspectives on context apparent in her discussion of the first map, the additionality of this dimension reflected in the use of 'And then'. There are important new emphases in this second map, completed towards the end of the PGCE and her time at St Helen's Community College. *Media* now becomes a node but, more than that, there is a new emphasis on the 'visual' and the connections between the visual and the verbal. This area of interest appears to be combined with a new attention to *analysis* and *interpretations*. Indeed, *visual grammar* now becomes a feature in its own right and verbal grammar (now mentioned only once) is situated between *literacy* and *accent* and *dialect*.

In her comments on the second map as a whole, Ann identifies 'writing, literature and media' as 'sort of the main themes that I always think ... of encompassing English ... the main components of it' (*ibid.*) and notes the 'reciprocal' nature of the relationship between these areas. Writing is no longer seen as a 'skill' that is 'tag[ged] on at the end' (*ibid.*) but as an integral part of the learning activity (*ibid.*). Interestingly, Ann associates this more 'focused' and 'integral' conceptualization of writing with attention to 'text types', ... 'we'll do some writing, but really focused writing, so what we're talking about before, looking at text types, looking a specific types of writing, not just vague ...' (*ibid.*).

(Verbal) grammar is defined as 'learning how to use punctuation or apostrophes or, you know, the basic components' (*ibid.*) and literacy as 'sort of encompassing all of that, to do with kind of literature as well, so not just looking at the bare facts and doing little exercises' (*ibid.*).

But it is context rather than literacy that has assumed a greater importance in the second map, as Ann acknowledges (*ibid.*). She describes this as:

> ... sort of like a diagram ... context of your own and that overlaps with society, with the school, with everything. I suppose everybody lives within their own context, their own ideology anyway, and I think English is a great subverter of that and can just ... tap into so many sort of issues relating to that because of its context. (*ibid.*)

In this comment, Ann seems to be developing a politics for English teaching that goes beyond questions of the subject's constitution *per se*. It is certainly a view of the social purpose of English teaching and is associated in what Ann says with feminist approaches to literature:

> But if you can say, you know, can you see what you are reading, English can sort of turn it on its head and subvert us and say, is this what you should be annotating here? Is the women always the victim and you're always rescuing her? (*ibid.*)

The reference to annotation here is perhaps connected to a questioning approach to the teaching of the GCSE English literature anthologies and a rejection of the noting of bits of information on them rather than possible ways of reading and interpreting. Nevertheless, Ann's emphasis on theorizing reading and foregrounding interpretation could be seen to accord with her earlier emphasis on literary theory.

Ann commented thoughtfully on the differences between the first map and the one she had just completed. She felt that she was able to account for some of the changes and that these were associated with her development as a teacher. Grammar, for example, was no longer such a significant feature of her thinking about the subject knowledge of English as she was more confident with it and felt she could use her knowledge of it when appropriate in her teaching (*ibid.*). She felt that her conceptualisation of writing was less skill-based (*ibid.*). Literacy (not mentioned specifically in the first map) is presented here as an aspect of the relationship between language and writing. When talking about the different situation of 'context' in the second map, Ann explained why this change may have come about:

> ... I think the more I do the job and I've been an English teacher, you can see ... what the theory is and what it should be and what it means in life and things like that, the bigger picture, not just what you're teaching in class. (*ibid.*)

This is a particularly interesting observation in that Ann is expressing a different understanding of theory in relation to practice than the usual dichotomy. Theory is seen as being in a reflexive relationship with practice – not just that theory is modified in the 'light' of practice but that practice itself generates theoretical understandings that provide access to the 'bigger picture'.

When I met Ann for the third interview, she told me that she had been thinking a lot about the drawings she had done, that she could remember the shapes but that since her return from the IFTE conference, she wasn't sure she could do another drawing about the subject knowledge content of English, 'it encompasses so much that it virtually, it virtually has no meaning because there is so much' (Ann 3).

She associated the difficulty in representing this understanding of English with her participation in the conference and, particularly, the opening speech of the IFTE conference that had 'opened a window to think' 'what are we actually

	Ann Map 1	Ann Map2	Ann Map 3
NCats	2	3	3
ASK	6	10	4
Nodes	9	8	(11)
Links	9	31	0
Linear connectivity	1	3.87	0

Table 5.1: Numerical description of Ann's Maps

teaching and should we be teaching things like ethics and values and social morality, or should we be teaching so that this student can answer, can get a grade B at GCSE?' (*ibid.*).

Ann took relatively less time drawing the third map than the second (see Fig. 5.3). She'd already told me that she had been thinking about this activity and her previous maps.

In her comments on the map, Ann suggested that English is perhaps just a useful organizing definition for something that is actually more diffuse and wide-ranging, blending substantive areas of knowledge with skills and values:

> English is encompassing all of these and (it's, it's) a definition that's just about hauling them all in. I've got things like literature, language, media, skills in English … like, reading, writing, speaking and listening, literacy, linguistics, um, and I've got more abstract concepts like values and ethics … (*ibid.*)

Ann explained that the zigzag lines that form the boundary around the terms (the boundary being named as English) were meant to indicate where 'definitions are slightly breaking down' (*ibid.*). The terms adjacent to the boundary (language, cultural studies, linguistics, literacy, media and literature) she described as the 'main strands of what we teach' (*ibid.*); speaking, listening, reading and writing she described as the skills; and values and ethics, 'these are kind of almost like the philosophy' (*ibid.*). The third map and Ann's comments on it appear to form a quite coherent representation of the subject knowledge of English at this moment in time. In her comments, however, and particularly in her references to the IFTE conference, it is clear that Ann's views about the constitution of the subject are enmeshed with her views about its purposes. In her comments on the interview transcripts and her set of three maps, Ann recognized that by not, for example, 'containing English within a boundary', she was 'question[ing] the very concepts which create the complex question of what English *does* and what it *should incorporate*' (Ann's comments on transcripts; my emphasis).

Describing the maps
Qualitative

In terms of organizational type, Ann's three maps are significantly different. The first is one-centred and unbounded; the second is also one-centred (although with more complex relationships indicated between nodes) but now bounded; the third is also bounded (although the nature of the boundaries is differentiated by straight and zigzag lines) but the elements are now unconnected. These changes represent significantly different ways of structuring and organizing the visual images over time.

Ann's first map is notable for the repetition of certain words: *grammar* (mentioned three times), *language* (also three times) and *context* (twice) (see Fig. 5.1). Repetition of words is also a feature of the second map: *language* continues to be mentioned three times and *grammar* is now mentioned twice (see Fig. 5.2). Significantly, both language and grammar are now mentioned with reference to both visual and written language. The words *visual*, *analysis*, *reading* and *interpretations* are also mentioned twice in the second map and the word *context* is now mentioned only once but in a prominent position in the space outside the boundary. In the third map, no words are repeated but three distinctively different items now appear for the first time: *values/ethics*, *linguistics* and *cultural studies* (see Fig. 5.3). The word *English*, previously used to denote the central organizing node is now dispersed letter-by-letter along the boundary. It is interesting to note in Ann's maps how the repetition of a few key words – and the emphasis this gives them – in the first map is more diffuse in the second and this strategy is not present at all in the third. It is also interesting to note the similarity between the first and second maps in that *language* and *grammar* are given emphasis, although, in the second, *grammar* is mentioned in relation to visual as well as written language. Other than references to all or some of the National Curriculum attainment targets, *literature* and *language* are the only words in common across the three maps.

In all three maps, various levels of conceptualization are discernible. In other words, some parts of the map are more detailed than others. In the first map, the nodes of *literature* and *language* are depicted in more detail – these are the only nodes that are inter-linked and both have at least one additional level of depiction underneath. In the case of *literature*, there are three additional levels of depiction. Also in the first map, *context* has two additional levels ('lit' and 'your own') and there is a line to indicate a possible third level. Although *context* is not linked by a line to *literature*, the word nevertheless appears underneath at a third level.

In the second map, the number of nodes, the links between them and, especially, annotations on the links identify a more detailed area of depiction around *language, writing, drama* and *literature*. There are four annotated links in this area which suggest the ways in which the various elements might be linked; for example, between *literature* and *drama* the annotations focus on 'characterization, language, interpretations'. This area also contains the only link to cut across three nodes. Although there are annotations on links between *reading, media* and *literature*, the links and the annotations are not as detailed as in the other area. Indeed, if one measure of detail is the number of links emanating from a node, then it is *writing* and *literature* that are the most detailed, with four links emanating from each. All of the others have three. Although Ann talked about the increasing importance of media education and visual analysis at this point, a more complex level of conceptualization is present around writing and literature in the map.

In the third map, there are no links between the items in the map and they sit within a boundary that is named as *English*. The three National Curriculum attainment targets (speaking and listening, reading and writing) appear relatively close to each other near the centre of this map, along with *values/ethics*. *Language, cultural studies, linguistics, literacy, media* and *literature* sit near to the boundary lines of this seven-sided shape but it is the boundary itself that is depicted with a greater level of detail in a number of ways. First, as a regular, organizing structure, it stands in contrast to the unconnected elements within it; second, the word *English* is dispersed around the points of the shape, capital letter by capital letter; third, the nature of the boundary lines is differentiated with straight or zigzag lines. It is interesting to note that a greater level of detail or conceptualization is given to the nature of the boundary in the third map rather than to the relationship between the elements within it, as in the previous two.

Numerical

It proved to be relatively straightforward to use the procedures outlined in Chapter 4 to make a numerical description of Ann's three maps. The only difficulty arose in dealing with the third map when deciding whether the words that appear within the boundary could be classified as nodes as it was not clear whether they stood apart as separate elements or were to be counted as one. In the end, I decided to count them as separate elements but to indicate the alternative possibility by placing this number in brackets.

In Ann's maps, we see that the National Curriculum attainment targets are all mentioned eventually (see Table 5.1). It is also apparent that the number of different areas of subject knowledge mentioned increases in the second map before decreasing again in the third to a figure below that of the first. The measure of linear connectivity also decreases (from 1 to zero) after an increase in the second although, as I argued earlier, this does not reflect the other ways in which relationships between the various elements might be being represented here.

The purposes of English teaching

At the time of the first interview, Ann articulated two purposes for teaching English, both connected to her own motivations for becoming a teacher. The first is strongly associated with literature and the second with social justice. She talked of the 'timeless' qualities of literature, how it can 'relate to you in your life' (Ann 1) and 'opens up so many doors' (*ibid.*). She wanted her students to 'get interest and enthusiasm number one for what they were looking at' (*ibid.*). Ann's comments seem to draw on both a personal growth and, to a lesser extent, a cultural heritage tradition. Combined with this, however, is a commitment to a 'basic sort of literacy skills' (*ibid.*) and the teachers' role in developing all students' literacy. She related this to her previous experience working for the Benefits Agency where she encountered for the first time adults who were unable to fill in a form or sign their name. Although she stressed that this wasn't some sort of 'marathon outreach', she commented: 'it just felt kind of personal to me' (*ibid.*). When asked about the relationship between literature and literacy in teaching English, she stated that her 'main focus would be literature' (*ibid.*).

This focus on literature and the purposes of teaching English is sustained in the second interview. In recalling a PGCE seminar on rationales for English and how looking at the handouts could still 'inspire' and revive her when she was tired, she emphasized the importance of literature in her subject paradigm of English and how this connected to her own conceptions of the purposes of English. The representation of literature as a medicine with an unpleasant taste in this comment is quite striking:

> ... because you do love literature and you feel that it has got a lot to give students and even if they're not grateful for it while they're doing it, it is important for them to learn and you are doing a worthwhile thing, you're trying to get these things across even if

they are unreceptive to it. (Ann 2)

Nevertheless, the impetus to teach young people about language was still strong in Ann's comments and had become couched in language such as 'empower[ment of] students', 'produc[tion of] text types' and 'deconstruct[ion]' (*ibid.*). Ann was aware how she had started to use this sort of language to describe her English teaching: she commented that she had learned it primarily in school – St Helen's Community College – and that she had found it difficult to use at first. She felt that even at this point, the teachers at the school 'say, in better terms, what I'm actually doing' when they gave her feedback on her lessons: 'I think, oh yeah, that is what I'm doing but I haven't recognised that' (*ibid.*).

These references to empowerment and deconstruction relate to a new emphasis in Ann's sense of purpose for teaching English around the time of the second interview, an emphasis that might be characterized as critical literacy (Muspratt and Luke 1997). Often this is associated with attention to contexts – personal and institutional – as well as in relation to texts. One of the purposes of English teaching might become a critique of gender stereotyping ('Is the woman always the victim?' [*ibid.*]) or to understand the ideological position of texts ('the bigger picture, not just what you're teaching in class' [*ibid.*]). There was also a critical edge to her discussion of the importance of genre in that she said she didn't want her students to become 'enslaved' by it (*ibid.*).[2]

At the time of the third interview, Ann had recently returned from the IFTE conference and she had clearly been thinking a great deal about the keynote presentations and workshops she had attended. For example, she had started to feel that English as a globalized language was having a 'crushing effect' (Ann 3) on cultural and linguistic diversity. Moreover, she had become particularly interested in the relationship between the aims and values inscribed in English as a subject and the credentialing function of schooling:

> … what are we actually teaching and should we be teaching things like ethics and values and social morality, or should we be teaching so that this student can answer, can get a grade B at GCSE? And indeed, is it the English teacher's job to do that? (*ibid.*)

In her comments, she considered the politicized nature of English teaching – a 'good thing' (*ibid.*) for her – and whether English teachers should foreground the critical literacy dimensions of their work by 'making children aware … of the kind of ideology in which they live', in an effort to correct their misconceptions about, for example, asylum seekers and homosexuals (*ibid.*). She recalled teaching an English lesson in which she challenged some of her students' 'bigoted views' (*ibid.*) and then caught herself thinking 'gosh, this is almost like PSE not English' (*ibid.*). This led her to think – and it's interesting to note that this is at the end of the Induction year – about the differences between university English and school

English and how her own subject paradigm had been influenced by an idea of the university subject:

> And I can define English from university ... what's English? Well we look at books and we look for interpretation and analysis and we critic and argue amongst ourselves. What's English at school? Well, it's something completely different because we don't do that. And I feel I have such a narrow view of what English was from university and it's so much more, so much more than that at school and it kind of needs to be as well. (*ibid.*)

The catalyst for this reconsideration of the subject seems to have been the foregrounding of aims and values for the subject and her own thinking about the purposes of teaching English. The dilemma at this stage for Ann was that expanding the boundaries of English and prioritising shared educational questions of politics, ethics, ideology and culture appeared to decentre the subject, to make it more interdisciplinary and less essential:

> You know, I don't want to be a kind of service of other subjects, I want a subject of my own, and it's all these things which are difficult to kind of grasp but are sort of contained within English. (*ibid.*)

Epistemological stance

Near to the beginning of her first block PGCE placement, Ann had a relatively objectivist understanding of the subject knowledge of school English. She defined expertise in English in relation to what she herself didn't know: 'I'd expect them to do all the things I couldn't' (Ann 1). She mentioned grammatical terminology, literary historical periods and a chronology of Shakespeare plays. Even 'creative writing' became classified as a skill (*ibid.*).

Towards the end of the PGCE year, objectivism was still influential in her attention to terminology, this time concerned with media studies ('teach[ing] them the ... grammar of films' [Ann 2]) as well as literacy. This was now associated with the 'empowerment' of her students and this is well illustrated in her description of the lesson that focused on teaching the conventions of email and text messages so that the students weren't 'enslaved to the genre' (*ibid.*). Ann didn't consider the possibility that her students could be well versed in these conventions from their own, unschooled literacy practices but believed instead that a fragmentation of the conventions in school would 'empower' them.

Nevertheless, it was also at this point in her development that a more – in Hillocks' terms – constructivist epistemological stance was suggested by her discussion of a Year 9 unit on horror films. Ann didn't like horror films herself and hadn't watched many. She discovered that many of her class knew rather a lot about horror films and this fueled anxiety about having to teach something about which her students already had some expertise. In her third narrative (discussed at the second interview), Ann noted that the relationship with her students was different to that she had with other classes and she attributed this to the differential between her own knowledge and that of her students (Ann's third narrative):

> So it's not me standing at the front of the class saying 'this is what it is all about' ((laugh)) ... I think it's not sort of, as formal in the sense, not that I let them get away with loads ... I'm almost stricter sometimes in that lesson to get them to focus, but, ... we do a lot more oral work. (Ann 2)

This stance is also partly implicit in Ann's comments on teaching literature, particularly in her narrative about teaching a soliloquy from *Macbeth* and suddenly becoming confused over its metrical pattern, 'I begin to doubt what I knew about Shakespeare, under pressure now. "Why don't it add up, miss?" "It doesn't work does it?"' (Ann Narrative 1: 23–4).

Ann panicked but managed to 'mutter some excuse (or truth)' (*ibid.*: 26) about changes in pronunciation since Shakespeare's time and she felt reassured and affirmed when she found students working with the concepts of iambic pentameter and changing stress patterns in their coursework essays. However, although in her narrative and in the interview discussion Ann implicitly understood that this was, in fact, a successful lesson in which concepts had been developed and worked on jointly, it is interesting to note the use of the words 'panic' and 'excuse'.

By the time of the third interview at the end of the Induction year, Ann was more secure in the understanding that she didn't have to be the expert in the classroom. For example, when her A-level Literature students refer to concepts and terminology from their A-level Language course, taught by a colleague, she simply asked them to explain: 'tell us what it means, OK, so we all understand that context' (Ann 3).

Ann also showed she was aware of the potential of peer learning among students in her comments on situations where her teacherly explanations weren't as successful as those of students for cultural and epistemological reasons (*ibid.*). However, Ann was also aware of the constraints imposed on her by her department's focus on the Key Stage 3 English Framework. An engaging and relevant set of teaching ideas might be possible, for example, only 'if I said, my assessment piece is going to be this booklet and I'm going to test these things from the literacy strategy' (*ibid.*).

Ann's reflections on her development

Over the course of the research, it was clear from Ann's comments in the interview situation and, later, in her reflections on the transcripts, that she had insight into her own development. She understood, for example, at the time of the second interview that her subject knowledge was developed in the practice of teaching and through the 'dynamics of the classroom and a class' (Ann 2). Following the IFTE conference, she also identified the importance of aims and values in determining the constitution of the subject. In her comments on the transcripts, she realised that, over the course of the two years, 'although more articulate, I'm still considering the big questions and my own viewpoints' (Ann's comments on transcripts) and that although her representations of subject knowledge were 'being broken down or [were] evolving', that was 'not necessarily a negative thing' (*ibid.*). Finally, as she took on a PGCE mentoring role herself, she had reached the understanding that she 'still [didn't] have the answers to all questions (my own or my pupils) but that [was] alright' (*ibid.*).

6

Grace: thinking about the subject knowledge of English

Grace was 22 when she began the PGCE course at Newchester University. She had spent most of her early childhood as part of an expatriate family in the Middle East, returning to England when she was 14. Between the ages of 14 and 16 she attended two schools, both private: first, a co-educational boarding school and then a single-sex day school. But Grace said that she didn't go to school much during her GCSE course and didn't do that well. Nevertheless, she started sixth form straight after GCSEs. She changed colleges but quickly dropped out. When she came back – after a year – to take three A-levels at a Roman Catholic sixth-form college, she chose English, Theology and Business Studies.

Grace's main reason for applying to Cookley University was that her boyfriend at the time lived nearby and it was also an easy journey home. She liked Cookley, found it 'cosmopolitan', and enjoyed her degree course in English and Management Studies. In Years 2 and 3 of her degree, she took an Education Studies module and this led her into secondary schools as a volunteer. On graduation, she knew she was going to apply for a PGCE course and had two unsuccessful interviews. She disliked one of her interviewers and told me how he had positioned himself with his back to the sun so that it shone straight into her eyes and then bombarded her with what she felt were hostile questions. But she stopped this story abruptly, embarrassed, saying, 'he's probably a friend of yours' (Grace 1). After a third interview, she secured a place on the course at Newchester.

When I asked her why she had wanted to become a teacher, Grace looked at me quizzically and said, 'you want the honest answer presumably, not the one you give at interviews?' (*ibid.*). Her 'honest answer' was 'Because I like working with kids' (*ibid.*). Later, however, she told me that she had also been 'inspired' by some 'bad teachers': she too thought she could do better (Grace 3).

Settings for learning to teach

Grace recalled a varied selection of sessions on the PGCE course, ranging from English as an Additional Language to Behaviour Management to Inclusion. The session on Inclusion was especially memorable for Grace as it was led by a Local Education Authority adviser who she described as a 'very ranty lady'

(Grace 2). One of the other PGCE students 'behav[ed] very badly' in this session and was told '"if you don't want to be here, you can get out"' (Grace 1). Grace laughed as she told this story; Grace laughed quite a lot during the first two interviews. She also recalled sessions on language acquisition and syntax taught by a visiting lecturer and optional sessions on Chaucer and teenage fiction taught by the course tutor.

The course tutor's optional sessions were related to the subject auditing procedure. Grace had attended a few of these but on a fairly *ad hoc* basis:

> … they were like if you wanted to do them. Because I did an ICT course on a Tuesday, I might (as well sort of) go to them before I go to my ICT course … they didn't really teach me anything I didn't already know ((laugh)) but then again I don't think I went to ones that would have been, you know, really helpful … I went to ones I could make. (Grace 2)

When I asked Grace later on about the English-specific content of her PGCE, she replied:

> We didn't really study much English. What we did was get given a topic … we got given a couple of ideas and just practised doing lessons really. (Grace 3)

The Newchester PGCE course organizes the two school placements for its student teachers by effectively nominating a principal school. The student teachers join this first school early on in the course for serial days and then begin a block school experience there at the start of the second term. Towards the end of this term, they transfer to another, sometimes contrasting school for a four-to-five week period before returning to their principal school until near to the end of the course.

Grace's principal school was Park Girls' School, an inner-city, single-sex comprehensive working with children from predominantly British Asian backgrounds. The school organized its teaching groups quite rigorously in sets – the bottom sets containing children who 'need the extra help and the extra time and the extra support … that include[s] a lot of dyslexics' (Grace 1) – and seemed to pride itself on a fairly traditional ethos exemplified by rules and uniform requirements. Results were among the best in the small (unitary) local education authority and the headteacher had recently been honoured for services to education. In Grace's third interview with me, at the end of her Induction year, she also realized that the school had been comparatively well-resourced and well-maintained.

Many of the girls were from Muslim families and, looking back on her time there in her third interview, Grace realized that there was a good deal of support from parents ('lots of push, you know, you will succeed, you will do well' [Grace 3]) and a sometimes quite competitive edge among the girls in top sets who would be 'cutting [each other's] throats' – even in Year 7 – to achieve top grades (*ibid.*). Bottom sets were hard work not just because of the students' specific learning difficulties but because of poor behaviour that Grace characterized early on as 'rudeness, absolute rudeness' (Grace 1). Nevertheless, even at this stage in her development, she was aware of the risks of defensive teaching for students like these:

> I do tend to, keep them on a tight leash and maybe I shouldn't so I'm trying to give them a bit more independence this lesson and see what they come up with rather than me giving it to them. (*ibid.*)

This 'tight leash' was also partly associated with the English department's tightly structured schemes of work that Grace characterized as 'compartmentalized, this is why you're doing it, this is what you're going to achieve' (*ibid.*). Grace saw this as the head of department's influence and found it 'quite hard work' (*ibid.*).

However, at the end of her Induction year, Grace looked back on Park Girls' School as somewhere where the English teaching *lacked* explicitness: teachers didn't always write objectives up on the board, 'didn't explain it expressly to the kids', didn't follow the multipart lesson structure recommended by the Key Stage 3 English Framework, and didn't *need to* break down the requirements for written tasks bit by bit: 'at Park Girls' [all] you need to say [is] "right, you need to include a quote"' (Grace 3).

Grace's second school placement on the PGCE was Duke of Wellington School, a recently built Private Finance Initiative school in the relatively affluent outer suburbs of the city. This was a short, four-week placement and Grace was to return to Park Girls' School straightaway afterwards. In her second interview with me – after she had returned to Park Girls – Duke of Wellington School became the focus of unfavourable comparisons and Grace was eager to tell me that it was Park Girls that had provided her with the 'best training that anyone could possibly hope for' (Grace 2). By the time of the third interview, the focus for these unfavourable comparisons was almost entirely personal and Grace described a 'very incestuous staffroom … snide comments, everybody was sleeping with everybody else' (Grace 3). She also commented on the middle-class nature of the students (*ibid.*) and the surprise that teaching boys for the first time had been. It simply wasn't her 'cup of tea at all' (*ibid.*). Nevertheless, Grace did recognize that the Head of English at Duke of Wellington School was 'very good', 'interesting to watch' and was someone 'to learn off' (*ibid.*). It is also possible to see in what Grace said about this second school placement (and her obvious loyalty to Park Girls, a loyalty that had been developing since September) that, at four weeks in length and in the knowledge that she would return to Park Girls, there was in fact little incentive to become part of the school and the English department setting at Duke of Wellington.

Grace took up her first teaching post at Green Road Community School, an 11–16 comprehensive situated in the middle of a council estate in one of the most socio-economically disadvantaged areas of Newchester. Grace had been encouraged to apply by the head of department at Park Girls' School and she knew that it would be hard work. The school had failed an Ofsted inspection in the recent past and had just come out of special measures. Grace had already been told that the school would be inspected again during her Induction year.

In the interview towards the end of her Induction year, Grace drew many comparisons between Green Road and Park Girls' School. An important focus of these comparisons was assessment and Grace knew that at Green Road the English teaching was much more assessment-driven, 'we are much more geared to the exam criteria and the Literacy Strategy and the optional tests than we were at Park Girls' (Grace 3).

Grace thought that this meant that there was 'less independent learning' (*ibid.*) but explained that, because the school had a 'reputation, an undeserved reputation' (*ibid.*) 'if we don't get those results, it's in the papers' (*ibid.*). Anxiety about failing the students at Green Road – and being seen to fail them – was an important theme in Grace's third interview. This anxiety was compounded by pressure from Grace's head of department who Grace knew, in turn, came under pressure from the headteacher (*ibid.*).

Grace connected the drive to improve exam results and to work for the students' success with an almost overwhelming emphasis on objectives-led teaching. She spent some time explaining this in terms of a comparison with Park Girls:

> We are much more tightly focused, much more tightly structured. The objectives are much clearer, they are made clearer to the kids, the kids know why they are doing everything. (*ibid.*)

She also associated this focus on objectives with a more restrictive approach to classroom management and said that she was much more reluctant to allow students out of their seats at Green Road (*ibid.*). Grace found working at Green Road very stressful and was often upset during her Induction year. The reason for this was the students' behaviour:

> There's been lots of times when I've gone home and cried my eyes out and gone, 'why the hell am I doing this?' Um, it's not an easy school, you get some very personal comments and you've got to try very hard not to take it personally. And we've got a 10% hardcore beasts, they are beasts. (*ibid.*)

Another reason was the constant pressure to deliver results and a feeling of lost creativity:

… some of the creativity has gone out of English, it's very prescribed now, with the Literacy Strategy and the exam criteria ((coughs)) excuse me. So we don't have room to play with it as much, we can't say we'll have a one-off lesson and do this. (*ibid.*)

Grace laughed less during the third interview and she appeared to be struggling with a cold. She told me that she had thought about leaving teaching at one point because of 'the amount of pressure on you' (*ibid.*). When I asked her what the highlight of her Induction year had been, she said: 'Not failing Ofsted' (*ibid.*).

Grace's English biography

Grace's memories of English at school were rather fragmentary. She focused mostly on her A-level course at her (final) Roman Catholic sixth-form college. She didn't refer much to previous schools and colleges she had attended, other than to mention her dislike of an English teacher in the Middle East.

Grace took a combined A-level course in English Language and Literature. She remembered studying some Chaucer ('The Wife of Bath's Tale'), Austen's *Sense and Sensibility*, *Othello*, *The Tempest* and a selection of poetry by Ted Hughes. Overall, she 'absolutely loved it' (Grace 1). In the second interview, it seemed that part of her enjoyment came from having the 'best English teacher I ever had' (Grace 2), a nun called Sister Veronica, who 'gave me sort of degree-level knowledge' (*ibid.*). Grace felt that, although formal in teaching style, Sister Veronica's 'in-depth knowledge of the text' had made all the difference for her as a young woman returning to education after a year out (*ibid.*).

It was interesting to hear Grace talk about media studies as part of English during the first and third interviews, the first taking place as she was starting to teach some media lessons at Park Girls. She didn't recall studying the media at all in school herself even though she said that she 'must have done it' (Grace 3). She didn't like teaching media studies and struggled with concepts such as representation – 'what's representation? Not handy' (Grace 1) – but she recognized that her students might have a different perspective to her own and associated this with aspects of her biography:

… well, I think all modern kids have more access to TV than we did. Especially in the Middle East where we had two channels and one of them only showed *Little House on the Prairie*. (Grace 3)

Following A-levels, Cookley University allowed Grace a good deal of flexibility in choosing options on a modularized degree programme. In the first year, she had combined English and Management Studies with Classical Studies modules and studied some Greek Literature (*ibid.*). Although the majority of her degree modules were in English, she had taken Management Studies modules in

Organizational Behaviour and 'something else which I can't remember' (Grace 1) in Year 1; Accountancy, 'Quantitative Markets' and Marketing in Year 2; and Employment Law in Year 3. In the third year, she had also taken an Education Studies module (that took her into school) and a TEFL module. When I asked Grace whether the Management Studies modules had been useful in her development as a teacher, she mentioned Maslow's Hierarchy of Needs (recalled from the Organizational Behaviour module) and the importance of maintaining a good environment and having the right priorities (Grace 1). But she didn't pursue any connections beyond that.

In her selection of English modules, Grace had focused on her favourites: 'Old English, Viking sagas, heroic periods of literature' (*ibid.*). She said that these appealed to her as 'a bit of escapism' (*ibid.*). She had also continued with the

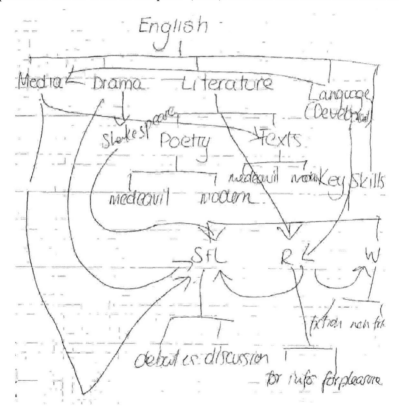

study of Chaucer and had followed this up with 'Langland and the Gawain poet' (*ibid.*). Grace chose not to study any Shakespeare during her degree and only came to the eighteenth century and 'modern literature' (T.S. Eliot, Virginia Woolf) in the third year (*ibid.*). She felt that the best thing she had done throughout her time at Cookley was an assignment on folk tales from an anthropological perspective: 'I got an 83 for it' (Grace 1).

In the second interview, Grace said that she thought not studying Shakespeare at university had been to her detriment (Grace 2) and in her second narrative she related this to the anxiety of being required to teach unfamiliar plays for the end of Key Stage 3 tests. By the time of the third interview, towards the end of the Induction year, however, Grace felt that the problem was more general:

> I don't think I got as well-rounded an English degree education as I might otherwise have done. I mean, if you look at the things I chose, they were all around the medieval period, Anglo-Saxon, they are not much out of that. (Grace 3)

During the second interview, Grace referred to the kind of knowledge she had developed during her degree as 'very compartmentalized' (Grace 2) and commented on the differences between this kind of knowledge and the kind of knowledge developed in secondary school where 'everything links into everything else' (*ibid.*). This will be discussed further on. But it is interesting to note at this point that the relative 'compartmentalization' of knowledge is an important issue in questions about her own English biography.

In the third interview, Grace stressed an antipathy towards poetry that was already present in the first interview while she was at Park Girls. At that time, although she felt she was 'pretty good' at most aspects of English and had no

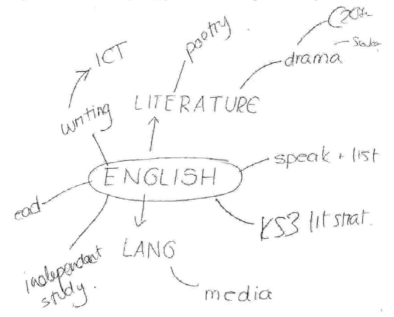

'major gaps', she didn't like or enjoy the poetry of Carol Ann Duffy, a poet often taught in secondary schools: 'Can't, don't get her. Can't stand her' (Grace 1).

Although in the third interview, she was much more aware of the relatively narrow range of her own subject background, her attitude to poetry had become hardened through her experience of having to teach the GCSE anthology:

> Why should half the exam be poetry? The kids are never going to use it again. They are not going to read it in their spare time. Wouldn't it be much more productive to teach them, you know, more media skills, they are going to come across more often, or you know, more drama skills, more communication skills, but no. (Grace 3)

Auditing subject knowledge

At Newchester University, the PGCE English course complied with the requirement to audit student teachers' subject knowledge by issuing them with a 'Subject Audit' form covering one side of A4. Student teachers were asked to provide the title of their degree and to provide a breakdown of modules taken or areas covered. Below this, there were six areas delineated: Shakespeare's plays, pre-twentieth-century literature, twentieth-century literature, contemporary literature, knowledge about language and children's literature. Next to these areas, students were asked to tick whether they felt their knowledge was 'good', 'fair' or 'no experience'. They were also asked to think of other areas for development in relation to the National Curriculum for English and to write in a box any 'areas of expertise/strengths' that they could 'share with others'. In this space, Grace wrote: '*The Tempest*, Chaucer, Old English' (Grace Subject Audit).

The subject audit had a high profile early in the course at Newchester. It was the focus of the second, full session in the first week and was returned to in the sixth session in week two. Grace felt that it was a priority for the course tutor, 'Because [course tutor]'s so high, here is your subject audit, these are things you need to know. I went, umm' (Grace 1).

On the audit and in interview, Grace identified as strengths the Shakespeare plays she had studied at A-level, Chaucer and Old English and, specifically in interview, 'the development of the English language' (*ibid.*). Areas for development were identified on the audit as 'Shakespeare, C20th drama, contemporary poetry, brush up on grammar?' (Grace Subject Audit). In interview, some three months after the first audit, she focused on media and *Julius Caesar* – Julius Caesar 'because I'm bad at it' (Grace 1) and media because 'I just don't understand it, I'm having real difficulties' (*ibid.*). At this stage in her development, after a term of serial school experience, she was developing a different kind of awareness of subject knowledge in relation to teaching:

> I know what I could teach and what I'm going to have difficulty with, because of my own subject knowledge but I think as long as you know up to Act 4, as long as you know

a little more than the pupils then you're alright ((laughs)). (*ibid.*)

Grace didn't found the audit process useful. She said that 'you just know what you know and what you don't know' and, when prompted as to how she knew how to assess her own knowledge during those very early days of the course, she referred to the time she had spent in secondary school classrooms as part of her undergraduate Education Studies module and to her two unsuccessful PGCE interviews (*ibid.*).

In the second interview, Grace discussed the optional sessions arranged by the course tutor. These were associated with the subject audit process and the tutor offered short lectures and seminars on the areas of subject knowledge itemized on the audit form. Students were encouraged to attend those that they felt would be most useful. Grace thought that the ones she had attended were quite enjoyable – 'an interesting perspective at degree level', 'but not really anything that I've managed to transfer into the classroom' (Grace 2). She did, however, acknowledge that she only attended those that happened on the same day as her ICT course rather than those she might have 'needed' (*ibid.*).

Grace did attend an optional session on grammar, specifically syntax, and spoke about how this didn't necessarily address what she saw as one of her own areas for development:

> It's improved my own knowledge of technical vocabulary in English and given me a slightly better idea about how things are ordered but the problem is, I mean, I've used it to try and teach simple and complex sentences, but teaching complex sentences is not as easy as it sounds. (*ibid.*)

On one level, while Grace appeared to be implicitly criticizing the classroom relevance of this session, she was also recognizing the complex nature of learning to teach and how 'subject knowledge' – in the way the audit-related, optional sessions used that term – figured in this process.

Towards the end of her Induction year, Grace indicated that although she didn't think her 'knowledge of English' had developed, she thought her 'ability to relay it to kids ha[d]' (Grace 3). Sometimes this is associated with her improved familiarity with aspects of linguistic terminology such as 'discourse markers' and her use of this terminology with students (*ibid.*: 947–60). She also felt that she still had terminology to learn – 'we teach them all the terminology' (*ibid.*) – this time about theatrical conventions in drama for Year 7 scheme of work. This was a cause of anxiety, something she felt 'a bit shaky on' (*ibid.*). She also complained that students – even 'top sets' – quickly forgot this terminology as soon as they moved on to a different scheme of work.

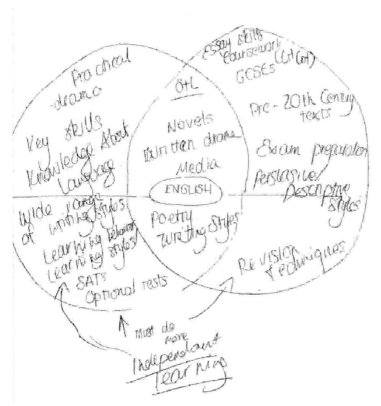

Figure 6.3: Grace's Map 3

Constituting the subject

In the first map of English that Grace drew (see Fig. 6.1), she began at the top of the page with the word *English* and then silently drew a series of lines underneath in the style of a family tree. The first word that came underneath was *Literature* and when I later asked her why, she said 'That's probably because that's my area of expertise, that's what I associate most with teaching English' (Grace 1).

Grace then drew in *Language* with *Development* in brackets. Earlier on in the interview, she had said this was one of her strengths (*ibid.*). She then drew in *Media* and *Drama*. Interestingly, she had also earlier explained that she was having difficulties with learning about and teaching the media (*ibid.*).

Figure 6.1: Grace's Map 1

She then worked downwards from *Literature* and later told me how she had wanted to separate this into *Poetry* and other *Texts* and also into historical periods (*medeavil* [sic] and *modern*). A later addition at this level in the diagram was *Key Skills* and a line was drawn down to this from the end of the top line next to *Language (Development)*. From *Key Skills*, Grace linked to the three National Curriculum Attainment Targets (*S + L*, *R* and *W*) and then broke these down into two parts – *debates/discussion, for info/for pleasure* and *fiction/non-fiction*. Grace then began to make interconnections between the various elements in the diagram, notably linking *Drama* to *Poetry* to *S + L* with the word *Shakespeare*.

Grace questioned the proposition that it was possible to be an expert in English: there were 'too many facets to it' (*ibid.*), she said; it was 'too wide-ranging' (*ibid.*). If someone was an expert in Language she would expect this person to know a great deal about 'grammar, spelling, dialect, spoken, differences between spoken and written, especially the history of English' but this was different to being 'an English literature expert' or a 'media expert' (*ibid.*).

In the second map (see Fig. 6.2), Grace again wrote *English* first and then, above this, *Literature*. Below *English* she wrote *Lang* and both *Literature* and *Lang* were capitalized. She then drew links from *Literature* (drama subdivided into C20th and Shakespeare), added in the National Curriculum Attainment Targets for English, added *media* and *ICT* as further links from *Lang* and *Writing* respectively. *Independent study* came next and *KS3 lit strat* at the end.

Figure 6.2: Grace's Map 2

Grace said that Literature was still the 'most important' (Grace 2) area of English subject knowledge to her as she 'use[d] it for teaching everything else' (*ibid.*).

When I asked her why she had put *KS3 lit strat* last, she replied,

> Well, that's because there are ways and means of teaching key skills and I don't think that the literacy strategy, it's wonderful as a track list but I think its starters are terrible. (*ibid.*)

This dislike of aspects of the Key Stage 3 Strategy recommended approach to teaching English – specifically the reference to 'starters' in a multi-part lesson structure is interesting to note when considering Grace's comments at the end of her Induction year.

In response to a question about why ICT had appeared on this map, Grace referred to her use of overhead projectors in her teaching and described using them with students as 'it's instant and because it's provisional' (*ibid.*). Overhead projectors were acceptable examples of teachers using ICT in the International Teacher Training National Curricula (ITTNC) for the Use of ICT (DfEE 1998a) and ICT was associated with 'provisionality' in this document. When I asked Grace whether this was why she had used it, she replied, 'That's probably why I've used it ((laughs)). It's gone into my subconscious now, the standards!' (*ibid.*)

Grace stressed the importance of *Literature* subject knowledge in her English teaching and we discussed the three narratives she had sent me in this context. For Grace, each of the narratives showed the way in which she focused on the teaching of literature and 'used' literature for 'teaching everything else': in the first, she wrote about a sequence of lessons in which the *Beowulf* poem and Rosemary Sutcliffe's *Dragon Slayer* were used to teach homophones and 'different grammatical concepts'; in the second, she described focusing on 'small sections' of *Twelfth Night* as end of Key Stage 3 test preparation (so as 'to avoid mis-informing pupils with shaky knowledge of the play' [Grace's second narrative]); and in the third, she recalled a Year 8 lesson in which she taught various literary terms and concepts with reference to Tennyson's 'The Lady of Shallott'. For Grace, these were examples of connecting literary study with language study (Grace 2), of her 'habit of using literature to teach the literacy strategy skills' (*ibid.*).

When I then asked Grace to compare the recently completed second 'map of English subject knowledge' with the first map she had produced some four months earlier, Grace's first comment was: 'I think I've got a better under-standing about what comes under what now really' (*ibid.*). She saw that *Literature* and *Lang* were 'my two "biggies" obviously, with the capital letters' that she had to 'trade off', but she did recognize that things had changed: 'I do have a different approach now, I've had to balance things and practise things' (*ibid.*). Referring to her first map, she felt that it was:

> … more compartmentalized, the way it would be at degree level, you are learning this, you will learn this, this is what you are learning today. They are very discrete topics,

aren't they? You don't do that at secondary school, everything links into everything else and the more links you make, the more relevant the pupils see it, the more likely they are to keep it in. (*ibid.*)

It is interesting to note Grace's interpretation of compartmentalization at this stage in her development and her view that 'discrete topics' within a very objectives-led approach are not straightforwardly associated with 'pupils … keep[ing] it in'. This is especially interesting when considering what Grace later says about this issue at the end of her Induction year at Green Road but also when considering how Grace described 'decompartmentalization' in her comments immediately

	Grace Map 1	Grace Map2	Grace Map 3
NCats	3	3	1
ASK	16	9	9
Nodes	22	14	(5)
Links	50	23	(6)
Linear connectivity	2.27	1.64	(1)

after those I have quoted above:

I've written fiction and non-fiction there [in Map 1]. If I do that now and decompartmentalize the bits of writing, it'd probably be writing to persuade, writing to describe, writing to argue … (*ibid.*)

It is not clear from what Grace says here why she interpreted this as decompartmentalization rather than, say, further compartmentalization.

When I asked Grace to attempt her third map (see Fig. 6.3) in the interview towards the end of her Induction year, she said: 'This is actually harder now I'm afraid' (Grace 3). She took longer than she had over the first two maps and often paused. For example, 'I'd like them to do more for themselves … I'm sure I'm missing bits on this side. I can't think' (*ibid.*).

After circling the word *English*, she started by drawing a line horizontally across the middle: 'I'm going to change it' (*ibid.*). This was going to represent the distinction between Key Stage 3 and Key Stage 4 but instead she decided to represent the age-related phases with two circles in the manner of a Venn diagram. She labelled the circle nearest the margin of the page 'KS3' and although she didn't label the right-hand circle, she said that she had just put the Key Stages 'in numerical order' (*ibid.*).

An important issue in the drawing of this map was the issue of independent learning. Early on in the process, referring to Key Stage 3, Grace had asked 'what goes on here?' (*ibid.*: 1256) and she had written down *learning behaviour/learning styles* whilst talking about independent learning: 'not as much as I'd like to. I'd like them to do more for themselves' (*ibid.*). At this point, she drew in *independent learning* at the bottom of the map, connected this to both circles with arrowed lines and also wrote another comment above it, *Must do more*.

When I asked Grace why she had found drawing this third map so difficult, she replied:

I think I've got more of a practical overview now, I mean, this is less subject-based and even when I'm writing [*sic*] novels, I'm thinking the skills involved in novels, like the analysis of a whole text as opposed to, oh, just doing books. So this is much more skill based than topic based which is fundamentally what I'm trying to teach now. (Grace 3)

Key Stage 3, for Grace, was centrally to do with *Key Skills* (*ibid.*) and Key Stage 4 built on this with a 'specified exam' (*ibid.*): 'it's taking the individual texts apart. Hopefully with some skills we've got from Key Stage 3' (*ibid.*). Grace had earlier complained about the emphasis on poetry in the GCSE English exam and arguing for more attention to 'skills' related to media, drama and communication (*ibid.*).

Nevertheless, when I asked her about some current teaching that she was enjoying, she described a scheme of work she had written with a colleague that had rather a different emphasis to the skills-based paradigm for the subject she had elaborated in the context of the discussion about her maps:

… a very good narrative scheme of work which will engage the kids, has lots of exciting resources, and is back to my own knowledge ((laugh)). It's alternative fairy tales. But there's loads of, umm, ways of playing with language, playing with the structure of stories, looking at different perspectives, looking at twists in the tale, looking at openings and endings and how to change them … And it will just let the kids have a real degree of independence over their own writing. It's not going to be writing frames. They're going to own that piece. (*ibid.*)

The vitality and detail of Grace's answer was noticeable and in great contrast to the tone of the rest of the interview. This was a different way of thinking about what 'made up' English and one that she associated with her 'own knowledge'. The emphasis on play, imagination and independence formed a striking contrast to her earlier comments about 'subject-based' versus skills-based approaches to English teaching.

Nevertheless, looking at all three maps and comparing the two earlier drawings with the one she had just completed, Grace maintained that what was apparent was something akin to the process of decompartmentalization she had discussed earlier. She noticed some things she didn't understand ('how I ever thought media came from language I'm not entirely sure') and remarked that 'It's not cut and dried this stuff' (*ibid.*). But beginning with the first map, she said:

When I started off, I'd obviously taken it apart and thought, well you take modules at university, right, I'll take this module, this module and this module and that will make an English course. So that is what that looks like to me. The second one I think I've got a slightly more holistic view in that everything is kind of linked. Umm, but it's still very subject-based with the odd bits in there. Umm, independent study, see? Still a key issue, I haven't changed that much. But it's still separated into isolated skills, may have different links. Umm, whereas this, even where I'd written things like novels or drama, I'm talking about the text, I'm talking about what they need to do to deconstruct the text. So this [the third map] is much more skill based, those are much more subject based. (*ibid.*)

Describing the maps
Qualitative
In terms of organizational type, the three maps differ significantly. Grace's first map is hierarchical (in that English is the first node form from which other nodes derive in a sequential and linear fashion) and unbounded. On first impressions, this map resembles a tree diagram. The second map is also unbounded and one-centred but more like a traditional concept map. Grace's third map is bounded and with several centres of interest. This map uses the conventions of the Venn diagram; that is, overlapping circles create (in this case) three distinct areas: the left circle, the right circle and the overlapping, common area in the middle.

The first map is notable for its apparently hierarchical design with *English* at the top and the progressive subdivision of elements at different levels. The National Curriculum attainment targets are near the bottom of this diagram and are prefigured by general areas of English as a school subject – *Media, Drama, Literature, Language (Development)* and *Key Skills* – and then by a focus on literary/dramatic text, including the division of *poetry* and *texts* into two, broad, historical periods. The National Curriculum attainment targets are then split further into two social or generic categories (e.g. *reading* into *for info* and *for pleasure*). In the second map, English is no longer at the top but in the centre and within an oval shape. The three attainment targets are repeated as are the words *literature, drama, media, Shakespeare* and *poetry*. The historical referent *C20th* is included once in relation to *drama* and in a binary split with *Shakespeare*. Three new terms appear: *ICT, independent study* and *KS3 lit strat*. In her third map, Grace only refers to one of the National Curriculum attainment targets and introduces many new terms into the three distinct areas of this map. Some of these terms (such as *knowledge about language, novels,* etc.) relate to elements of English subject knowledge whereas others (such as *GCSEs, exam preparation, SATs, learning styles,* etc) refer to aspects of the current assessment regime in schools or to general pedagogical issues. There are slightly more terms relating to English on this map than to general pedagogical issues. It may be that the left circle in the diagram is to be associated with Key Stage 3 as this annotation appears at the top of the page on the left. Although there is no annotation on the right-hand side, the implication may be that the right circle is to be associated with Key Stage 4 (this seems reasonable given the contents of the circle) and that the overlapping area in the middle represents the common ground: *speaking and listening, novels, written drama, media, poetry, writing styles*. Outside the diagram, at the bottom, there are two annotation linked by arrows to the left-hand and right-hand circle: *must do more* at the top and, beneath it, underlined, *Independent learning*.

There are some different levels of conceptualization discernible in at least two of the three maps, represented by greater detail in their depiction. In the first map, the area around the three National Curriculum attainment targets (*S+L, R* and *W*) is relatively more detailed in that each of the nodes/attainment targets has a greater number of links emanating from it (7, 5 and 4 respectively), indicating the interrelationships between the various elements on the map and these nodes. Although the map is headed by *English* and would imply a hierarchy, it is the attainment targets that act as an integrative device across the different levels of the hierarchy. In the second map, there is relatively more detail around the *literature* node, which is linked to *poetry* and *drama*, broken into to *C20th* drama and *Shakespeare* – although it is fair to note that this is a relatively sparse map compared with the first. At first glance, in the third map there does not appear to be any specific area of the map that is depicted in greater detail: the left-hand circle and the right-hand circle contain approximately the same number of items; there isn't one circle or annotation that is depicted in greater detail. Perhaps what is noticeable, however, is that the overlapping area is given relatively less space, there are fewer terms within it and it is unaffected by both of the annotations from outside the diagram. It is possible to say that this area of the map is depicted in less detail and that this indicates a different level of conceptualization.

Numerical
Once again, it proved relatively straightforward to use the procedures outlined in Chapter 4 to make a numerical description of Grace's maps. It was not always possible to use the categories positively but this, in itself, is meaningful.

Table 6.1: Numerical description of Grace's maps

In Grace's maps, we see that the National Curriculum attainment targets are consistent features of the first two but that, in the third, only one is mentioned explicitly. It is also apparent that the number of different areas of subject knowledge mentioned decreases from first to third map (with the total in the third map slightly higher than in the second). The measure of linear connectivity gradually decreases over the three maps, from 2.27 to 1.64 to (1). Indeed, with the possible exception of the annotations on the Venn diagram in the third map, there are no links or connections represented by straight lines.

The purposes of English teaching

Grace said that she had come into teaching because she 'liked kids,' 'they are so funny, they come out with some absolutely brilliant things … they're very entertaining' (Grace 1).

When I asked her during the first interview what she wanted her students to 'take from English', she responded:

> Key skills. I want them to be able to read, write. I know we've got a couple of girls whose parents are illiterate and how they are coping on a day to day basis I don't know. (*ibid.*)

Grace seemed to be drawing on her experience at Park Girls' School and referred to specific students and lessons when developing her comments about the purposes of English teaching:

> I'd like them to, in an ideal world, enjoy it and I'd like them to explore sort of social issues, life issues that you can do with a text, like we had one recently, umm, *Jane Eyre*, arranged marriages, we've got two of the Bengali girls who are going to have arranged marriages at some point in the future and it will, you know, give them a modern perspective on a historical thing and get to explore some opinions and backing up those opinions. (*ibid.*)

There is the sense in her comments that she is grounding her developing conceptions of the purposes for English teaching in the young people with whom she is working and with a more generalized idea about young people also. She presented media study as an important part of English and, even though she herself lacked confidence and experience in this area, said that although some of her students 'might not have a single book in the house', 'you can guarantee that they've got a telly' (*ibid.*). With reference to the exploration of 'issues', Grace also felt that drama was 'an important tool', especially for 'low ability children, who may have difficulty verbalizing or writing things down' (*ibid.*).

In the second interview, Grace returned to the importance of key skills in her conceptions of purposes for English teaching. She related her own efforts to develop a 'key skills strategy' (Grace 2) for her students with the 'track list' of the Key Stage 3 English Framework. Grace said that she was trying to 'contextualize the literacy skills that the strategy are telling us we must teach ... in isolation' (*ibid.*). She linked her efforts to contextualize skills with the concept of relevance – students must be able to relate in some way to what is being taught and must be aware of a purpose, 'They can see the relevance, it's doing something, it's creating something, there's a point to it, we're not just doing random exercises' (*ibid.*).

By the time of the third interview towards the end of her Induction year, Grace was aware that there was perhaps a more instrumental purpose to her English teaching at Green Road. She described her English teaching there as being more 'skills-based' and prioritized a socio-economic rationale for 'skills-based' English over the personal or intellectual: 'they may have the love of English by the end of it but they need the GCSE. To get a job' (Grace 3). In practice, this meant:

> We can't afford not to teach to the exam because no matter what else I'd like to teach them, and this is part of what's getting lost, because we are teaching to the exam there is less independent learning going on because if we don't get those results, it's in the papers. (*ibid.*)

Again, Grace showed an awareness of how her conceptions of purposes for teaching English were developing and how this was related to her situation at Green Road. A significant feature of this way of working at the school was that the whole English department '[taught] the same thing' so that test and exam results could be compared among the sets so that 'we kn[e]w where it [had] gone wrong' (*ibid.*).

Grace believed there was too much poetry in English generally by this stage, particularly in the GCSE English examination. It was described as something that students like those at Green Road would never read again outside school and was contrasted with what she said were useful 'skills'. Grace had already said that developing a 'love' of English in her students wasn't a priority for her but she also acknowledged a striking lack of pleasure in what she and her students were doing:

> Well I've sometimes, I've gone home and had a bit of a weep, which is a bit wimpy, but everyone I've talked to said they're overdoing it, they're tired. I've just had a year that's, I've had it up to here with it, the kids are up to here with it. (*ibid.*)

In the midst of this frustration and, indeed, unhappiness, Grace seemed to be putting the aims of her teaching at some distance in the future. An important purpose for teaching English was for her students to be able to survive in adult life and to become critical and (economically) independent:

> I'm not trying to teach them so that they have a wonderful understanding and knowledge of a text. I'm trying to teach them so that they can use the skills that I've taught them, to pick apart texts on their own. So it's the application of umm, what they've learned. (*ibid.*)

Grace's willingness to cope with the frustration and unhappiness of the present moment for an idea of some greater good for her students in the future was a notable theme in the third interview.

Epistemological stance

In the first interview, Grace explained that the concept of expertise in English is problematic as 'there's so many different facets to it' (Grace 1). She distinguished, in particular, between a 'language expert' and an expert in literature. She also suggested that 'knowing why language is how it is' and knowing 'influences ... like Shakespeare on everyday saying[s]' (*ibid.*) is important. English can be difficult for school-age students because 'you have to be able to organize your sentence structure, your words, you have to follow patterns' (*ibid.*).

It was in the second interview that Grace introduced her understanding of 'compartmentalization'. Referring to the first map of English that she had drawn, she described it as 'compartmentalized' and 'the way it would be at degree level' (Grace 2). She seemed to gently parody an explicit, objectives-led pedagogy: 'you are learning this, you will learn this, this is what we are learning today' (Grace 2). Grace thought there were good reasons why this wasn't necessarily effective in schools:

> You don't do that at secondary school, everything links into everything else and the more links you make, the more relevant the pupils see it, and the more they see it, the more likely they are to keep it in. So, I think I just see it as being less, and I've just got a better idea of the curriculum now. (*ibid.*)

Grace appeared to be arguing for a more integrated and culturally relevant way of teaching English and conceptualising knowledge in these comments. She also linked this understanding to her 'better idea of the curriculum', this idea being that a curriculum is made in relation to a specific group of learners. However, as previously mentioned, Grace's explanation of how she 'decompartmentalized' knowledge seems to run counter to this:

> ... so writing, see, I've written fiction and non-fiction there, if I do that now and decompartmentalize the bits of writing, it'd probably be writing to persuade, writing to describe, writing to argue, writing to ... (*ibid.*)

– although it could be that Grace was using 'decompartmentalize' in the sense of 'making explicit' or simply attempting to explain and represent the meanings of a very broad term.

However, when Grace explained her preferred way of working with poetry at this point, she still seemed to be operating within an objectivist epistemology that prioritizes what might appear to be 'facts' and terminology:

> ... I'd give them a title, the genre, and you would say, umm, what you do think this poem is about in the first few lines? What's it about? What genre is it in? What style is it in? What's going to happen? Who are the characters? That sort of thing. (*ibid.*)

Grace's attention to terminology was a theme in this interview and in the narratives she had written previously but were discussed at this time. In the third narrative, she wrote about wishing to 'develop and extend pupils existing knowledge' by 'teaching some of the terminology and approaches I personally use to critical analysis' [*sic*] (Grace's third narrative). For students Grace classified as 'less able', she provided a 'simpler writing frame with fewer technical terms and a much tighter structure' (*ibid.*).

Nevertheless, Grace did talk about wanting more independent tasks for her students and to move away from so much 'direct teaching' but found that:

> … unfortunately, because they are spoon fed these days, because there is so much emphasis on their SATS results, on their GCSEs results, a lot of them really struggle with independent work. (Grace 2)

The influence of the assessment system – and policy-recommended approaches to English teaching – on Grace's thinking became even more apparent in the third interview, which took place almost a year later towards the end of her Induction year. She talked about planning units of work that include 'visual, auditory, kinaesthetic learning, the strategy numbers' (Grace 3). She said that it was important that 'everyone [in her department] is teaching the same thing' so that results could be compared and 'where it's gone wrong' could be identified (*ibid.*). There had to be a 'tight focus' on skills so that her students could 'get a job' (*ibid.*), the economic rationale for her teaching being consistently foregrounded. English now and here, she said, is 'much more skill-based than topic based' … 'I'm not trying to teach them so that they have a wonderful knowledge of a text' (*ibid.*).

The emphasis on terminology was also still apparent – lack of terminology in her students being construed as a significant problem:

> … just assuming that they had this vocabulary at their fingertips. I mean they made a sterling effort, bless their cottons, but we had to take it back a step further and say, right, this is the terminology, this is how you use it, this is how you apply it. (*ibid.*)

Nevertheless, it is interesting to note that when Grace said she didn't have full responsibility for teaching a class – for example, if she took them for a weekly 'literacy group' – she was likely to be more flexible:

> You know, and I'm not scared to go off on a different tangent. If the kids say, miss, can we go do this next? If I'm not taking them regularly, like I've got a literacy group that I only take once a week, oh yeah, whatever, we'll do this, we'll do that. (Grace 3)

The flexibility with which Grace approached her own teaching and her students' learning seemed to be in relation to the responsibility (and, indeed, pressure) she felt for students' success in the assessment system and the school's success in Ofsted inspections.

Grace's reflections on her development

At the time of the second interview, Grace felt that she learned 'through practice, what works and what doesn't' (Grace 2). She also recognized that her own voice in the narratives belonged to a particular moment and that the narratives were almost frozen – or, to use Conle's description, 'hardened' (Conle 2000) – in a particular genre. Unfortunately she saw this as a flaw in herself: 'I'm really pompous, aren't I?' (*ibid.*) rather than as an effect of what I had asked her to do. She recognized her own 'steep learning curve' but also that if she hadn't changed and developed over the course of the PGCE year, 'that would have been pointless' (*ibid.*). And in the third interview, towards the end of the Induction year, Grace was clearly interested in how far the changes and development she had experienced were as a result of 'my own personal opinions and my own personal development and how much I've picked up by osmosis' (Grace 3):

> I'm aware of being influenced by other members of staff and other members of the team because what they say often makes sense but I'm not sure how deeply embedded that is. I'd like to think some of the ideas are my own, but I wouldn't bank on it. (*ibid.*)

7

Liz: thinking about the subject knowledge of English

Liz was 22 when she began the PGCE course at Parkton University. She had grown up in the west of England and had attended a single-sex, state, boarding school from the ages of 11 to 18. During the sixth form, she had been encouraged to apply to Parkton University. She studied for A-levels in English, Psychology and French and received extra examination coaching from her school with Parkton entry in mind. Unfortunately, her results didn't meet the conditional offer that Parkton had made and she chose to resit two A-levels in a private sixth-form college the following year; this time, she chose Classics and Philosophy. At the second attempt, she was admitted to study for a degree in English at Parkton.

Liz enjoyed her degree but didn't much enjoy the Parkton undergraduate experience overall. She said that she had only applied to Parkton 'because a teacher suggested it and I was very flattered by the suggestion' (Liz 1) and that she had become 'hooked' on it as an idea (*ibid.*). Once there, though, she found it very 'pressurized' (*ibid.*) and

> … very difficult to go from being the absolute top of the pile in school to the bottom of the pile in Parkton where people are coming from amazing places, you know. (*ibid.*)

Nevertheless, Liz had been the founding literary editor of a new student newspaper at Parkton and had enjoyed meeting authors and interviewing them. Indeed, she also chose to apply to Parkton for her PGCE and was successful at the first attempt. She said that she had also considered doing a Masters degree but had 'just had enough of sitting in libraries and struggling with essays and listening to lecturers' (Liz 3). Instead, she decided to become a teacher and gave two reasons for this: first, that she wanted a job that would allow her to exploit her 'love of communicating with people', contrasting this with the perceived isolation of 'sitting in an office' (Liz 1); second, and specifically why a teacher of English, because:

> I just have a passion for the subject and want to communicate that passion onto other people and also those skills that will enable people to continue in life. (*ibid.*)

However, as she articulated these reasons in my first interview with her, she also acknowledged that her 'choice wasn't as conscious as this' (*ibid.*).

Settings for learning to teach

Liz recalled enjoying several sessions on her PGCE course. She felt that the 'one that sticks most in [her] mind' was on poetry and led by a visiting tutor who had encouraged the use of visual images in poetry teaching, for example, by using an overhead projector and also lowering the lights while reading (Liz 2). To this, she quickly added sessions on Shakespeare and ways of teaching drama, some of which were taught by the course tutor. She said that she thought she remembered these most of all because:

> ... they were active sessions where we were almost participating in the role of the students so we understood how all of the methods taught to us worked. (*ibid.*)

Liz associated certain aspects of the PGCE English programme with particular visiting tutors (*ibid.*) but, overall, in the first term, felt that the emphasis was on planning lessons in a uniform way:

> ... we'd been so encouraged to, right, let's have your standard plan, you must put how much time you're going to allocate and try to stick to that because you, so you can get through everything. (*ibid.*)

The concept of 'modelling learning' was also associated with a PGCE session that had involved discussion of some research into family and community learning. Liz recalled this session as she talked about showing her own students how to work independently (and saw this as important) (*ibid.*).

Nevertheless, even by the time of the third interview (towards the end of her NQT year) Liz still vividly recalled the visiting tutor's poetry session and, even if her recall of the tutor herself seems less strong, the impact is still apparent over a year later:

> ... we had a particularly good poetry session with, I think it was [visiting tutor], who gave us lots of inspiring ideas, and just in a one-day session. And I have used quite a lot of those since, I mean like, listening to someone else reading the poem and kind of drawing the landscape, drawing the image that comes into your mind. (Liz 3)

Liz's first, short, PGCE placement was at St Benedict's School, a boys' 11–18 comprehensive. This school, she felt towards the end of her Induction year, had been a 'very sporting rugby school' (Liz 3) and it was 'expected' that the boys would do well at sport. It had also been moderately strict in its attention to 'rules and regulations' (*ibid.*). The English department had been fairly consistent in its approach to the Key Stage 3 English Framework:

> … they were all going out on 'this is the new literacy framework', and so they were, in Year 7 especially, doing the whole individual white board, flashing up answers, you know, let's find another word that's like this one, using the new government guidelines. (*ibid.*)

In terms of students, though, Liz thought that boys 'tend to be less interested' than girls (Liz 1). She wasn't sure why this was but felt that:

> … boys just tend to love non-fiction, they love facts, but the majority of them are not starting really interested in the world of fiction. Maybe they will be at some point in the future but they're not and I don't know why that is. (*ibid.*)

For her second PGCE placement, Liz went to Peak Down County High School, the school that Ann had been to for her first placement. Liz taught a very wide range of classes here, something that was possible because she didn't take responsibility for every lesson. She seemed to accept the setting arrangements in English and commented on some differences between them and her attitudes towards them: her Year 9 group was 'very able but also quite lazy' (Liz 1) whereas both her Year 10 groups were 'bottom' sets, 'very low but incredibly enjoyable actually almost because of this' (*ibid.*). Indeed, Liz said that she enjoyed working with students categorized as 'school action' or 'school action plus' on the school's Register of Special Educational Needs, and mentioned one Year 10 boy being reintegrated into the school from a special unit – and with whom she felt she had 'struck quite a rapport' (*ibid.*) – and a Year 8 boy who 'slam[med] his bag around' confrontationally:

> … to be honest that situation just amuses me, and I have to try hard not to laugh, and, I'm saying 'that's very inappropriate', you know ((laughs)), my teacher act, but inside I'm thinking 'how ridiculous', he's just a twelve-year-old. (*ibid.*)

Reflecting on this placement during our third interview at her Induction year school, Liz said that Peak Down's Learning Support department was very large and very successful and that this factor – combined with an early morning, breakfast-time Literacy Club – made it very popular with parents (Liz 3). Liz had previously commented on the uniformity of the English teaching at Peak Down and the use of common and highly specified schemes of work:

> Because in the department, there is a sense of, you need to stick to the schemes of work because if you don't we don't know what the students have done … this is what the classes are doing and they get the same experience. (Liz 2)

It was also a large school with over 2,000 students and Liz felt that the size made it difficult for departments to talk to each other. Again, looking back from her Induction year school, she felt that the school's size had an impact on the way in which the English department worked:

> … there were 13, 14 teachers all teaching English. So it was much more kind of, they had centralized schemes of work, centralized banks of information, so you would be teaching the same thing at the same time as everyone else, or staggering it within the term and following the same pattern of lessons, although you could vary it for your class. (Liz 3)

But Liz enjoyed learning to teach here and said she 'preferred the atmosphere' to that of her Induction year school; she mentioned the 'buzz and energy' of the 'rugby scrum' lunch queue and also the mixed ability Year 7 classes she had taught (*ibid.*). Boys in this school weren't 'afraid to say the wrong thing, so they shout out answers, even if it's wrong, they don't care and so the girls have a debate' (*ibid.*).

Liz began her first teaching job at Kiplings, a private boarding school for girls. Liz felt that the school was characterized by an ethos of academic and sporting achievement and she also noted the strong motivation of the girls to succeed and the way in which they silently engaged with learning activities to the extent that she sometimes felt she was 'twiddling [her] thumbs' (*ibid.*) at the front of the class.

Classes at Kiplings were mixed ability in Years 7 and 8 and set from the equivalent of Year 9 onwards (the school had its own names for year groups, Year 9 being the Lower Fourth). Liz noted that the 'bottom sets' often comprised of students with English as an Additional Language as 'we have a huge number of girls who are not English' (*ibid.*). She also described how the pressure for good examination results was experienced by her students and herself. She recalled how the new head of the Lower Fourth spoke to the students as they were about to choose GCSE options. Having been led to believe that this would be a general talk about GCSE and an invitation to come forward with any problems, Liz was shocked by what the year head actually said:

> And she proceeded to say, 'well of course, if you are having a really bad day, you'll get a B'. And I was so outraged that a B is terrible and you only get a B if you're having a really awful day, and my students told me later they could tell I was thinking that ((laugh)) (*ibid.*)

In addition to the 'extremely pressurized atmosphere' (*ibid.*) some girls experienced, Liz also felt that the pressure was affecting her teaching. It's important to note, though, that Liz connected this to the newly qualified teacher's responsibilities within the assessment and examination systems more widely as well as to the particular pressures at Kiplings:

But I think when you actually get into teaching, you realize that you are actually very pressured for time in terms of the number of lessons you have with pupils in which to teach *Macbeth* or *Lord of the Flies*, to write an essay for their coursework. So, I feel like in a way, my teaching in terms of solid methods has improved, but my teaching in terms of creativity has taken a step backwards. (*ibid.*)

The problem of 'time constraint' – not having time enough to 'talk it through or do anything creative' (*ibid.*) recurred later in the interview, even though Liz thought that her students usually produced work of a very high standard anyway.

Liz thought that English at Kiplings was broader in its 'coverage' than Peak Down and less influenced by the end of Key Stage 3 tests (tests that Kiplings – in the private sector – chose not to use). The Lower Fourth (Year 9) was effectively a 'foundation GCSE year' in which whole texts (novels, plays, poetry) were studied rather than extracts. In retrospect, Liz thought that Peak Down's 'freedom was limited in that sense' (*ibid.*). She also thought that at Peak Down, English had been 'topic based' whereas the focus at Kiplings was more on texts and she said that she enjoyed this (*ibid.*). She characterized English teaching here as freer:

… you're free to choose your own texts apart from the first one you do, and you're free to follow your style at your own pace. Whereas there [at Peak Down] it was like, you're at lesson eleven, you should be teaching this ballad today. (*ibid.*)

Liz also enjoyed the pastoral side of her role – her work as a form tutor and assisting in a boarding house. She talked about the house plays and house musical events in which she'd been involved and the educational visit to Derbyshire she had accompanied. She felt she'd been 'like a kind of mum in the school' (*ibid.*). She'd also enjoyed two in-service courses, the first on multiple intelligences and learning styles, and the second on teaching gifted and talented students. Liz felt that she would carry on teaching English here for the time being but said that she'd 'like to do more creative things' at some point (*ibid.*). Before teaching, she had briefly worked in museums education and felt that she might either move into this 'fulfilling and exciting' area (*ibid.*) or – subject to the 'SATS system chang[ing] slightly' (*ibid.*) – into primary teaching where she would enjoy:

… the creative, energetic challenges of younger children … I suppose it's some, an area that's a lot more free and creative and not constrained by a syllabus, working towards an exam. (*ibid.*)

Liz's English biography

In the first interview, Liz recalled that she had studied two plays by Shakespeare before GCSE and then another two for GCSE and A-level. She thought that doing two plays before GCSE 'is a fantastic thing to do, I realize now' (Liz 1). She also recalled studying novels – she specifically mentioned Pearce's *Roll of Thunder,*

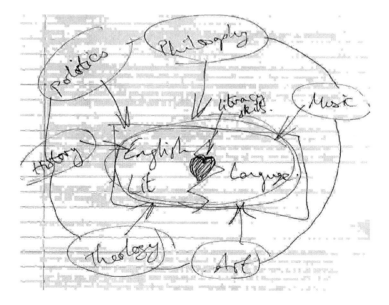

Hear My Cry – that she described as 'issues-based fiction' 'which I really could hate and now still loathe with a passion because they're quite transparent' (*ibid.*) – and contrasted this with *Jane Eyre* (' a more interesting text') that she'd wanted to read (*ibid.*).

Indeed, Liz described a 'recurrent pattern' in her own school experience of English:

> … almost every novel we were given was some kind of issue-based fiction … if only we'd had *Roll of Thunder* it probably would have been amazing and wonderful and life-changing but because it came at the end of this re-occurring pattern 'oh let's read this book because it's about people who suffer' ((laughs)) I was just crying out for something a bit different. (*ibid.*)

Poetry workshops were an important feature of her own schooling and she recalled 'quite a few' with local poets. Liz felt that these were 'quite important in pushing me in the direction of the subject' and said that it helped her to realize that English 'could be incredibly fun, you can take control of it, playing with it yourself' (*ibid.*). Indeed, Liz saw herself now as someone who was 'very playful with text and language' and felt that was 'integral to my strengths as a teacher' and in her approaches to literature (*ibid.*).

Liz said that she had enjoyed 'active things' at school and Shakespeare and creative writing lessons – along with the poetry workshops she mentioned – were examples of these. Liz said that she had been 'very into drama, not so much now' (*ibid.*).

In the second interview, Liz spoke about her favourite teacher, a woman who was about to retire, who had taught her during the first year of her A-level course. Liz found her 'very inspiring' and enjoyed the breadth and interest of her lessons:

> She was one of these people who wouldn't just stick to the exam syllabus, she would introduce you to other poets, other writers, anything she thought you would find fruitful. She would kind of treat you as an individual and take you aside and say, I think you should read this. (Liz 2)

Liz also described her as 'one of these very motherly types who just wants to look after everybody' (*ibid.*). For Liz, the combination of 'huge subject knowledge' and 'caring about you as an individual' was inspiring (*ibid.*).

The aspects of her school experience of English that Liz didn't enjoy she felt were those that 'tend to put everybody off doing English and hating English lessons' (Liz 1). She recalled a particular lesson in which she had been asked to underline examples of alliteration in Coleridge's *Rime of the Ancient Mariner*:

> It's really breaking, the idea of kind of breaking literature into its component parts and not looking at the whole … I remember vividly doing that, and since then have not wanted to touch Coleridge since, because the poem ended up not meaning anything, because we weren't reading it as a whole and so 'oh gosh, what does that mean? Isn't that amazing?' We were going 'oh, look, there's repetition in line three' and, you know, just dull and taking all the magic and spontaneity out of literature. (*ibid.*)

The second example she gave was when teachers adopted a 'prescriptive approach to literature … so your teacher says "this is what it means and if you think there isn't anything else you're wrong"' (*ibid.*).

Liz said that she had been 'very rebellious' in her approach to English at school. Her best piece of work had been a sixth-form assignment for which she had chosen the topic 'what is the difference between pornography and erotic literature?' (*ibid.*) and she said that her reason for choosing this was she had 'wanted to do some subject which requires embarrassing other people' (*ibid.*). In the third interview, Liz noted that her own 'relaxed' and 'exploratory' approach to A-level study was very different to what was required of her own sixth-form students, 'mainly because of the exam structure' (Liz 3).

Liz characterized her English course at Parkton as a 'chronological study from about 1350 to the present day' (*ibid.*). She chose to study Anglo-Saxon as an option and thought this helped 'in fitting together my view of English' (*ibid.*). Liz enjoyed studying Anglo-Saxon and Middle English and wrote her two dissertations on authors from these periods. She said that she 'loved … myths and

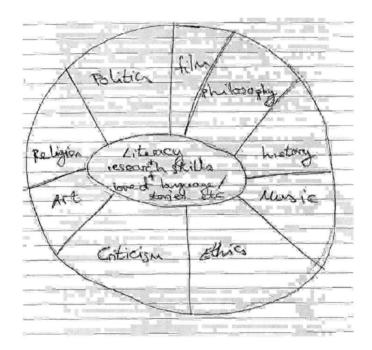

Figure 7.2: Liz's Map 2

legends ... the fairy tale elements of literature, folk tales ... allegorical stories'
(*ibid.*). Reflecting on her time at Parkton, Liz said that she had most enjoyed the
lectures on Anglo-Saxon through to the Renaissance. She said that the
Shakespeare lecturer 'couldn't be faulted' (Liz 1) but contrasted these lectures with
'some of the more modern stuff' that she described as 'a bit kind of wispy, airy
fairy' (*ibid.*). Overall, she felt that her degree was 'very heavily weighted on the
side of literature' (Liz 3) and said that:

> ... it might have been useful to be able to spend that time doing a chronological study
> of the English Language alongside English Literature. (*ibid.*)

She enjoyed all aspects of the literature studied with two exceptions: she disliked
revenge tragedy and 'very political allegorical poetry like Donne, Dryden' (Liz 1).
However, she said that she had found 'practical criticism' difficult throughout her
degree:

> ... which seems ridiculous because it's the life blood of literature really, is to be able to
> read something and make an opinion but I think, I'm quite a ponderous reader and I
> like to be able to take my time with something. Somewhere like Parkton it's very
> much, you've only got a week so you've just got to read it once and skim it and make

an opinion, and I loathe that. (*ibid.*)

This apparent rush to interpretation was one aspect of why Liz 'didn't love Parkton' (*ibid.*). Another was a set of expectations about being 'clever' and confident, often – as she described in the second interview – 'being confronted in tutorials, in supervisions with, you know, what about this, what about that, and you're meant to know the answer' (Liz 2). Liz felt that this was one of the reasons why she was 'afraid of not knowing the answer ... from being in that system and being expected to be very clever' (*ibid.*). Nevertheless, in the third interview, she talked about how she had planned her own teaching of poetry at Kiplings partly in imitation of the Parkton system she had disliked:

> I've tried to emulate the Parkton structure of teaching when I've taught poetry for a term. And every week, we did a different form but also took a single lesson to go through chronologically ... . So that was really enjoyable for me to structure it in that way. And to have the knowledge to be able to teach them in a simplified pattern. (Liz 3)

And she was also aware that when she recalled what was 'lectured [about] well' at Parkton and 'the stuff that I'm really into now, there's an amazing correlation ((laugh))' (*ibid.*).

Auditing subject knowledge

Liz engaged with the same procedures as Ann for 'subject audit' during the Parkton PGCE course, completing a checklist and then making a 'subject knowledge action plan'. However, the practice of auditing did not figure prominently in the three interviews and Liz's responses to my questions about the audit were quite brief in comparison to her other answers. Nevertheless, Liz offered the opinion that the subject audit document was a 'negative subject audit' in that it became 'a list of things you can't see rather than a list of things you can' (Liz 1). She described herself as a 'self-critical person' anyway and that she knew 'in [her] mind which things I haven't worked hard on, or have found difficult or and hence brushed over' (*ibid.*). She gave 'language' and 'English literary history' as examples of these.

On the audit document, she had also identified media education, the poetry of Ted Hughes and Shakespeare's *The Tempest* as areas to develop. She said that she had worked on these in advance of teaching them at Peak Down in the wide variety of lessons that she taught there. This work had involved reading that department's 'fantastic schemes of work' (*ibid.*):

> ... things I am less confident with I can use the lessons and the scheme of work and then

as I look through it and ameliorate it, create worksheets and do more fun things. (*ibid.*)

Although described here as 'fantastic', Liz echoed her earlier criticisms of these schemes as 'centralized' and uniform in her comments on 'amelioration' and 'do[ing] more fun things'.

When the subject audit document had first been introduced, Liz remembered that 'the entire class of people in the PGCE completely panicked and everyone said "I don't know anything about grammar"' (*ibid.*). She said that the class had split up into smaller groups to research specific areas and then peer teach each other. As they did so, they realised that 'we knew a lot more than we thought we did' (*ibid.*) and she felt that this was an indication they had been 'over-compensatory'

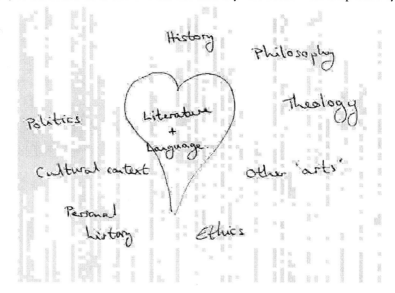

(*ibid.*). Liz was aware that 'there will still be things I'm not entirely confident with' but that wasn't necessarily a problem (*ibid.*). Indeed, there was a sense in some of what she said that she felt the audit could be misleading in its effect. One of her subject knowledge targets, for example, had been drama and, when asked to teach Russell's *Blood Brothers* at Peak Down, she had started to think she 'didn't have a clue on how to teach drama' (*ibid.*). She remembered her surprise that 'it went fine' (*ibid.*). This experience was repeated with her preparation to teach an unfamiliar poetry text; she came to the realization that 'it's something quite simple' (*ibid.*). It happened again in relation to 'literature from other cultures and traditions' – associated in the audit document with poetry by Caribbean authors writing in English, about which Liz felt she knew little. Liz realized soon after that 'America counts' as did 'Ibsen and Strindberg' (*ibid.*). She commented, 'I think intrinsically you think of the other cultures – black' (*ibid.*).

Overall, though, Liz felt that the practice of auditing had been 'effective, mainly effective', paradoxically not because it had identified genuine 'gaps' in subject knowledge but because 'it boost our confidence and made us realise that we knew far more than we thought we did' (*ibid.*). Perhaps the one area of English subject knowledge about which Liz felt less confident throughout the period of the research was grammar and, in the third interview, she described it as 'a huge missing part of my education' and, drawing on auditing's 'gap' metaphor, as an area 'which I'm starting to try to fill in now' (Liz 3).

Constituting the subject

In the first map of English that Liz drew (see Fig. 7.1), she began by writing the words *English Lit* first, followed to the immediate right by *Language*. She described them both as being 'integral' (Liz 1). Then, after boxing these in with a rectangle, she wrote a series of words in a circle around the centre starting with *Music*. As she wrote, she speculated 'I don't know if, more specific about ((laughs)) bits of English literature' (*ibid.*) – but she left it at that. The words around the *English Lit* and *Language* box were then circled and joined by a line so that the drawing came to resemble a constellation.
Figure 7.1: Liz's Map 1

Liz said that each of the areas at the periphery of the drawing – *music, philosophy, politics, history, theology* and *art* – were 'filtering into both' *English Lit* and *Language*. She drew an oval shape around the central rectangle and gave the following example of 'filtering':

> I mean even in politics you could even say that the entrance of French into the English language was political, because obviously it's just people of import who are using French and then it just fell down into the language of the country. (*ibid.*)

As we spoke about this map, I asked Liz where she might place literacy on it and she then drew a zigzag line between *English Lit* and *Language* over which she superimposed a heart image and added an arrow labelled *literacy skills*. She said, 'Well, I mean, I suppose, I mean you know it's going to be absolutely at the heart, isn't it? Of everything, because if a person doesn't have …' (*ibid.*). As her answer trailed off, I prompted her, asking 'have what?', 'If a person doesn't have those skills then they're unable to comprehend the rest of it to any depth' (*ibid.*).

My influence as researcher is apparent here in the way that my question about literacy imported a concept into the discussion of the subject knowledge map that Liz had not considered at first and which she took a little time to think about and subsequently include. I also asked her why, if *literacy skills* was 'at the heart', it hadn't come first in her drawing:

Because I don't think of, because I don't think of literacy skills as separate, I mean, literacy skills are here [pointing at the centre], you know. (*ibid.*)

In her answers, Liz connected *literacy skills*, at a 'very basic level' with independence and fluency in reading: 'if you can't read, how can you appreciate English literature' (*ibid.*). She also saw another dimension to language that she described as a 'deeper level, of a kind of metalanguage' (*ibid.*). For Liz, it was this 'deeper' dimension that distinguished English from literacy:

... to get terribly political about it for a moment, the government are using this word literacy a lot now almost as if is something that is completely separate from English and they're using it in such a way as they're almost trying to call English kind of literacy lessons, you know, 'this is the literacy hour' and then you move into secondary school and suddenly you've got this things called English ... but literacy smacks of something very basic, which everyone needs and is essential but is not what English in secondary school is, and is not what in primary school should be either, is so much more. (*ibid.*)

Expertise in English was a difficult concept for Liz as the subject appeared to draw on knowledge from 'so many other subjects':

... to be an expert in English and English in general is to be an expert also in British history, colonial history, philosophy, history of art, music ... I think that really to know about English is to know about other aspects of culture and society as well. (*ibid.*)

When she drew the second map (see Fig. 7.2), Liz started by drawing a circle. This, she said, was because she 'wanted a nice big area to fit everything in' (Liz 2). She then wrote *Literacy + research skills + love of language/stories etc* in the centre of this circle and drew an oval shape around these words. She then wrote, in turn, *ethics, music, history, philosophy, film, politics, religion, art* and *criticism* within the circumference of the circle, and drew lines between each of these words to separate them. The result to some extent resembles a pie chart.

I asked Liz why she had put *Literacy* into the map first and she replied that she could remember some of the first map she had drawn – and our conversation about it – and that literacy 'was at the forefront of [her] mind [...] the actual basic skills you need to do English' (*ibid.*). I asked her why *research skills* and she said that this was also 'absolutely at the front of my mind at the moment' as, for the purposes of the PGCE, she needed to do more to encourage sixth-form students to do independent study. And for *love of language/stories etc* 'because if you've got the first [*literacy*] but you haven't got the third, what's the point? And, in essence, everybody has the third (*ibid.*).

Of the words around the circumference of the circle, Liz first wrote *ethics* and

I asked her why this might have been. She told me that English was 'so much to do with communicating ideas' that ethics was an unavoidable part of it:

> … thinking about what's acceptable, what, if anything, is going to cause offence to other people, what do we need to have an understanding of when we are reading something, umm, or we're talking about something. (*ibid.*)

Here, Liz seemes to be operating a definition of ethics as a moral imperative to be sensitive to and to respect other people's positions and opinions as this relates to her work as a teacher of English.

I asked Liz whether she had studied the subjects (*ethics, music, history*, etc.) she had written onto the map of the subject knowledge of English:

> I did philosophy at A-level so I have some sort of grounding in that although I'm sure a lot of it is sort of vague and blurred now and I don't really remember it, but I remember the basics of studying it. History, as an actual subject I haven't studied since Year 9, but going to Parkton and the English Literature degree being structured the way it is you cannot help but study history within it. Umm, ethics, I've never studied as an actual thing although, obviously, it comes within philosophy, but I think, as I say, that was something I address every day in almost every lesson so it's always in the forefront of my mind and deciding myself how to deal with situations. (*ibid.*)

And when I asked her whether these various subjects around the circle were emerging from the centre or feeding into it, she said that she intended both but she also wanted to 'make it all part of a whole, so there was no separation, the whole being, English literature' (*ibid.*). I checked that she had intended to say English literature:

> Umm … it's the difficulty of the terminology isn't it? I mean, I would say that generally you think of English as English Literature, and, obviously, language is involved but in a way, language is part of the literacy skills you acquire … but you often use literature as the stimulus. So, I guess, yeah, I would say English Literature. (*ibid.*)

It is likely that this is why literature as a separate item is absent from Liz's second map. This exchange provides an important example of the importance of working with the maps in the context of the interview transcripts.

When we came to look at the first and second maps together, Liz noticed 'definite circular theme' (*ibid.*). She remembered putting in the literacy skills heart in the first (see Fig. 7.2) as an effort 'to redeem herself' – 'I think you said, "oh, there are no literacy skills"' – but wrongly speculated that it was the first thing that she had drawn (*ibid.*). I asked Liz to try to account for the changes in the maps. The first reason she gave was 'more time in the classroom' during which she had come to realize that 'the absolute basics of skill are the most important thing' (*ibid.*). But she also linked this to a reordering of the way she was thinking:

I suppose maybe it's to do with the order of things now, and initially, I would have gone, right, English Literature, OK, English Literature just is but other things feed into it so then come in the satellite subjects, which, in this diagram seem to be very much discrete

	Liz Map 1	Liz Map2	Liz Map 3
NCats	0	0	0
ASK	3	5	2
Nodes	9	10	(9)
Links	26	0	0
Linear Connectivity	2.88	0	0

in themselves but in some ways feeding information in. But in this one, they're kind of interrelated and informing each other. So I suppose now, I think of the skills first but when I think of the whole subject, I'm thinking it's a whole product, it's like the cake that's produced by all of these other ingredients. Whereas before, maybe this was kind of like, this was the meal and these are just condiments ((laughs)). (*ibid.*)

In the third interview, Liz said that she was going to find the anticipated map drawing task 'really difficult' because 'I can pretty much remember what I did last time so now my brain is going "shall I do the same or should I deliberately do it differently?"' (Liz 3).

I suggested that she draw the map to represent what she thought 'today[.] the 12th of June' (*ibid.*). Then, as Liz was drawing the map (see Fig. 7.3), she asked me to clarify whether she was drawing a map of the *subject knowledge* of English or of the *teaching* of English. In turn, I asked her to make this distinction explicit. She responded:

… I think that the teaching of English would involve your relationship between you as a teacher and the students as well as all the elements of English whereas English as a subject as, it's that, a subject that you could do by yourself, hence it wouldn't involve a relationship between you and anyone else. (*ibid.*)

Figure 7.3: Liz's Map 3

At this point, she had completed what turned out to be about half the map and had begun with *Literature + Language* at the centre around which she had drawn a heart and started to enter words around this (beginning with *Ethics*). I asked her to complete the drawing 'as it is in relation to the subject itself' (*ibid.*) to which she replied: 'OK, but I'm still going to include personal history' (*ibid.*). When she had completed the drawing, I asked her what she would have done differently if it had been a map of the teaching of English:

> I probably shouldn't have put what I wanted to put but I would have wanted to almost put your relationship with your students almost as the central piece of it. Because I think without any kind of relationship, without any kind of respect or trust or understanding going on, none of it is going to go into the person's head. So although you're repeatedly told during your PGCE you shouldn't want to be your students' friend and that shouldn't be important, I think it is, because if I don't like the person who's telling me something, I probably won't listen, so I think that is important. (*ibid.*)

I asked her whether the map would have looked different on the page and she said that she would have made it 'more of a hierarchy', the student–teacher relationship at the top:

> ... and then had a kind of pyramid effect with literature and language on the next layer and then probably all of these things I've put around literature and language as maybe kind of foundation stones. (*ibid.*)

Theology, she told me, was important in relation to her recent experience of teaching Marlowe's *The Jew of Malta* at A-level, because 'the religion of the person writing and the religion of the time is massively important in the text' (*ibid.*). She also mentioned Walker's *The Colour Purple* in the same connection. I wondered whether, given what she had told me about her recollection of the previous maps, Liz had consciously reproduced a similar set of terms (*ethics, theology, philosophy*, etc.) in this map, but when we came to compare all three, Liz's strongest reaction came when comparing the first map and the third: 'OK, wow, hey look, there's a heart in that one too ((laugh))' (*ibid.*). The apparently genuine surprise was interesting. I asked her why she had used a heart in the map she'd just drawn:

> Liz: I suppose it is to do with bad pun really, this is the heart of what I'm talking about.
> VE: Which is literature and language?
> Liz: But also in that sad, I'm an English teacher kind of way ((laughs)).
> VE: Why do you say it's a sad thing to draw?
> Liz: Well, I think your students start seeing you as sad as you talk about books all the time and say 'here's ma'am going off on one'. (*ibid.*)

I asked Liz how much she could remember of the previous maps and she felt she could recall 'quite a lot', 'pretty much visually' (*ibid.*). She noticed that literacy wasn't on the map she had just drawn, even though it had figured on previous maps (*ibid.*). She said that she could remember that the previous one looked 'more like a slice of pie' (*ibid.*) but that she couldn't remember the words she had written in the 'bubbles' (as she described them) in the first one. Liz described the differences between the three maps she had drawn over the period of the research:

> … that one's saying these things are part of it but they are on the periphery and they can be part of it if they want to but you can take them or leave them. That pie is saying to me, but that's all one thing and it's all integral and this [the third map] is sort of very floaty floaty. I don't know what's happened here, that's quite bad. (*ibid.*)

Liz said that she 'prefer[red] that one' (*ibid.*), the second map she had drawn near the end of her PGCE year. This was because it was 'a lot more integrated, it's totally together and part of itself and love of language and stories, that's more me' (*ibid.*). Liz speculated that the changes in her maps might have been related to her development as a teacher:

> … like I've been saying, the creativity in my lessons has been diminishing … maybe this says that I'm feeling less that everything is integral and together because I've got to focus on this whole literature and language part and these bits sort of fall away. (*ibid.*)

Liz appeared to be unhappy about the changes she perceived in her maps and her tone of voice expressed regret that her third (and what she knew would be the final map in the research) was not like the second, about which she said towards the end of the interview: 'I feel like it ought to be more me, the togetherness, the structured' (*ibid.*).

Describing the maps

There are significant differences in the maps produced by Liz over the period. These are mainly organizational. There are also significant similarities between the maps in terms of their content.

Qualitative

In terms of organizational type, there are some significant changes in the maps over the period. The first is bounded and, although there is a large block at the centre, cannot be categorized as 'one-centred' as the links do not radiate outwards but inwards. This suggests a centripetal relationship between the elements, one of bringing something to bear on the main block rather than being influenced by it. The second map is also bounded with a clear centre. Here, there are no arrows to indicate the terms of the relationship; rather, the elements around the centre are arranged like the segments of a pie chart, implying that they are a part of the whole. To this extent, it could be categorized as one-centred. The third map is unbounded and with a clearly discernible single centre, even though there are no links with the other elements to suggest that they are emanating from the centre. Instead, they are arranged around the centre. These changes represent significantly different ways of structuring and organizing the images over time.

Liz's first map is notable for the constellation of words orbiting and influencing the central block. *Politics, philosophy, music, art, theology* and *history* are each located within an oval shape with a one-way arrow to the centre and are linked parts of the encircling ring. *Literacy skills* is closer to the central block, out of the encircling ring, is not located within an oval shape and the first 'l' of *literacy* is not capitalized. Even though it also has an arrow to the centre, it is recognizably of a different order to the other six elements and was added after I had posed a question once the drawing was finished. The central block is also interesting in that the words *English Lit* and *Language* are within both an oval and a rectangular shape and there is a zigzag line separating *Lit* from *Language*, left from right. In the centre of the block – and along the zigzag line – is a heart image.

In Liz's second map, *Literacy + research skills + love of language/stories etc* are within an oval shape at the centre. 'English' is not written anywhere on this map. Instead of a constellation of words, on this map, words are written in the segments of what could be described as a pie chart. To the six words used in the first map, three others are now added: *film, criticism* and *ethics*. This method of organizing the image conveys the sense of there being parts of a whole arranged around a core, the core being *Literacy + research skills + love of language/stories etc.*

In the third map, Liz uses no lines to indicate relationships. Again, 'English' does not appear on this map. At the centre is a heart image, recalling Liz's first map. The difference here is that the heart image is used in outline to surround *Literature + Language* at the centre of the map. The use of a plus sign to join *Literature* and *Language* within the heart shape is reminiscent of the use of plus signs and heart images in graffiti. Eight terms are now arranged around the heart image: *history, philosophy, theology* and *politics* – these have been present in all three maps; *other 'arts'* – previously maps have included references to music, art and film; *ethics* – retained from the second map; and two distinctively different items, *personal history* and *cultural context*.

There are various levels of conceptualization – in terms of the depiction of detail – discernible in all three maps, although perhaps less so in the third. In the first map, more detail is present around the central block. Not only are the words *English Lit* and *Language* located within two differently shaped blocks, but the block (and the words) are cut in two by a zigzag line on which there is a heart image and the block is shown as being *subject to* links with six other elements. Additionally, the words *literacy skills* are linked to the heart image. This accumulation of detail around the central block – and the implication that the central block is subject to elements from an outer ring – is notable. In Liz's second map, again it is the accumulation of detail at the centre that is notable – the conjoining of *Literacy + research skills + love of language/stories etc* with plus signs. And in the third, rather more sparse map, a limited level of detail is identifiable in the central image of the heart in outline with the words *Literature + Language* joined by a plus sign. In Liz's maps, however, I think it is more difficult to identify particular areas or sections where there is more detailed depiction as the maps seem to have meaning as a whole rather than as an assembly of elements; that is, they seem to be structured by one visual metaphor. In the first map, this might be that of a constellation; in the second, a pie chart; and in the third, the iconography of the ('cupid's') heart.

Numerical

It was relatively straightforward to use the procedures outlined in Chapter 4 to make a numerical description of Liz's three maps.

Table 7.1: Numerical description of Liz's maps

In Liz's maps, we see that the National Curriculum attainment targets are not mentioned at all (see Table 7.1). It is also apparent that the number of different areas of subject knowledge mentioned increases in the second map before decreasing again in the third to a figure below that of the first. The measure of linear connectivity decreases after the first map and is zero in the second and third. Indeed, the nature of the relationships between the various nodes in the second and third maps is not represented in a linear fashion at all.

The purposes of English teaching

In the first interview, Liz said that there were two purposes to her English teaching: the first she gave as wanting her students to understand texts 'in the right context' and have 'an overview of where things fit' (*ibid.*). The second was that they should have confidence to 'approach any book or poem' and not think 'I can't read that because it is too difficult or too complex for me' (*ibid.*). Liz said that she wanted her students to 'pick it up, have a go, and if you don't like it it's fine to not like things' (*ibid.*).

Liz saw 'basic skills' as an important part of English – students would be 'unable to comprehend any of the rest of it to any depth' (*ibid.*) – but resisted any confusion between English and literacy, something she saw as a contemporary concern. The government, in her view, were trying to 'subtly change' English lessons in the primary and secondary schools into literacy lessons (*ibid.*). For Liz, this was 'not what English[.] is'; English was more than this (*ibid.*).

Nevertheless, 'basic skills' were an important aspect of her motivations for wanting to become an English teacher in the first place. Although the first motivation she gave was communicating her 'passion' for English 'onto other people', she also mentioned teaching 'those skills that will enable people to continue in life' (*ibid.*). It is also interesting to note that Liz stressed that the 'joy' of English teaching was that she wasn't 'just giving them your subject that's very closed off, you're giving them skills to deal with every other area of life' (*ibid.*).

During the second interview, Liz stressed that although she wanted to 'giv[e] the students something they will find exciting', she also sensed that 'you do have to give them things, even though you think they will be bored with it, you think will benefit them' (Liz 2). It was not clear what Liz expected her students to be bored by but she again came back to the idea that it was important to develop 'basic skills' and, perhaps, that this should come first, before you can 'do English':

> … the actual basic skills that you need to be able to do English. So you need to be able to read and write and do both of those things on a coherent manner, you need to be able to create, umm, communicate verbally. (*ibid.*)

But Liz was also certain that *love of language/stories etc* was a vital prerequisite, perhaps in a motivational sense, saying: 'if you've got the first [literacy] but you haven't got the third [*love of language/stories etc*], what's the point?' (*ibid.*). It was during this interview that Liz raised the question as to whether she was drawing English or English Literature, coming to the position that 'generally you think of English as English Literature' (*ibid.*).

Towards the end of her NQT year at Kiplings, Liz said that the 'creativity' of her English teaching was 'constantly being compromised' by the assessment and examination systems (*ibid.*). She gave the example of being asked to teach Golding's *Lord of the Flies* for GCSE in six weeks, simply not enough time to do what she would have liked to have done:

> I mean really simple things like when you're starting to read the novel try and create a map of what the island looks like and where are things on the island … maybe reading extracts from other books, maybe reading extracts from *Coral Island* or other kind of dystopias. But we had no time. I would have liked to have done so much more contextual work and much more reading around the novel, but you never really have time, do you? (*ibid.*)

Nevertheless, Liz still professed a playful and pleasurable intent to her English teaching and said that, with a hypothetical class of 11-year olds, her main aim:

… would be for them to enjoy it and for them to enjoy playing around with the words that they knew and finding new ones … Because if they enjoy it, they'll work harder and they'll go for it in a bigger way later on. (*ibid.*)

Towards the end of this final interview, Liz also returned to the question of the constitution of English in relation to its purposes. She recognized that some English teachers make claims about the uniqueness of their subject whilst appearing to dismiss others – 'English is everything, Science is rubbish', as she put it (*ibid.*). English, for Liz,

… is not one of those subjects that can exist on its own, you can't in a vacuum simply write something having no experience of anything else. So I think English lends itself to being something cross-curricular, because you can start with a theme which lots of other people can get involved with. And in a way, in English, you can kind of do anything you like with that theme, whilst assisting the other subjects to do the bits they can do. (*ibid.*)

Epistemological stance

Liz had told me early on that she disliked both the decontextualized fragmentation of texts (Liz 1) and what she called a 'prescriptive approach to literature' (*ibid.*). She recalled the lesson from her own experience as a student in school where she had been asked to underline examples of alliteration in Coleridge's *Rime of the Ancient Mariner.* It was the 'breaking [.] into its component parts' that concerned her; the poem 'ended up not meaning anything' (*ibid.*). Another example – also from her own school experience – was where teachers said things like 'this is what this poem means' and if the students thought any different: 'you're wrong' (*ibid.*).

Expertise in English was a difficult concept to define for Liz. She described it as being 'as difficult a question as what constitutes gifted and talented' (*ibid.*). This was because English relates 'to so many other subjects' that to be an expert in English was to be 'an expert also in English history, colonial history, philosophy, history of art, music' (*ibid.*). She came to the opinion that, to be an expert, it was necessary to be 'an expert in a particular author, or sort of period' (*ibid.*).

In the second interview, we talked about the narratives Liz had written in the preceding months and had sent to me. In the first narrative, she had described a lesson in which she had asked the students to underline any words in a photocopied horoscope with which they were unfamiliar. She wrote, 'I allocated about ten minutes maximum to this activity on my planning, thinking that it would be boring for the students' (Liz's first narrative).

She had expected that 'nobody was going to admit any word that they didn't know' (Liz 2). In fact, she had only planned the activity in the first place as it was on the Peak Down English department's 'centralized' schemes of work and, as we spoke about the narrative, she characterized her reasoning at this stage as being that of a 'green teacher ... I was thinking, oh, it's on the scheme so I have to do it' (*ibid.*). As the students became very engaged in this activity – 'it was almost a matter of pride to say, I don't know this' (*ibid.*) – Liz recalled in interview that her first reaction was: 'this just isn't going to work' (*ibid.*). In the narrative, though, she wrote that she had realised this was an 'incredibly valuable' activity (Liz's first narrative) and:

> ... what an unusual experience this was in the classroom and let the activity go on for 25 minutes, with the children helping each other to work out the definitions of different words for each other. (*ibid.*)

In the discussion that followed, Liz commented on the assumptions that she felt teachers sometimes made about what students know. Very often these assumptions were unfounded, she felt, because (referring to this horoscope lesson):

> ... knowledge comes through years of picking up the paper and looking through it, or reading a teenage magazine or whatever. And children who are only 11 or 12 don't have that amount of time to gain that knowledge. (*ibid.*)

In another narrative, Liz had written:

> I think that one of the things that scared me most before I began training in earnest was the idea of not knowing something. In both senses of being asked to teach something I knew nothing about and in the more frightening case of being confronted with an inquiry in the classroom. (Liz's second narrative)

I asked her why she had used the word 'scared' and she explained that this reflected her concerns about the expectations at Parkton as an undergraduate, 'from being in that system and being expected to be very clever' (Liz 2). This also applied outside of Parkton, she said, as people had high expectations of Parkton graduates. This was compounded by:

> ... the idea that teachers are supposed to be know everything and if you don't know something you look stupid and the kids pick up on it, and they are going to treat you differently. (*ibid.*)

Importantly, however, Liz said: 'that's not the case, actually. That I've found' (*ibid.*). In the narrative we were discussing, Liz had written about being asked 'Why is Caliban called Caliban?', to which she had replied: 'I don't know, that's a very good question, I will try to find out the answer for the next lesson'

(Liz's third narrative). Liz wrote that she always tried to 'keep her word' in these situations. In the interview, she said that the 'I don't know' answer was:

> … the main bit that shows I've grown in confidence because before I would never have said I don't know. No way, I probably would have bluffed. (Liz 2)

At Kiplings, Liz told me about the silence in her lessons and how she 'interrupt[ed]' students 'just to be sure that they know what they are doing' (Liz 3). She had contrasted this with the noise and energy of Peak Down. In her view, the girls at Kiplings often found it 'awkward' to ask questions. She thought it was important to build relationships with students 'because if I don't like the person who's telling me something, I probably won't listen' (*ibid.*).

She told me about a lesson in which a student had asked her about why, in the (passive voice) sentence 'the dog was kicked by me', the 'I' of the active version ('I kicked the dog') had become 'me'. She didn't have an immediate answer but recalled her brain 'working overtime' and

> I thought, well, it's something to do with cases and in the end I said to her, for the moment, all that matters is that you know that's what you do […] but I will find out for you. (*ibid.*)

Liz said that not knowing an answer to this sort of question did 'bother her' and whilst she was 'perfectly willing to say I don't know' (*ibid.*), it was nonetheless an 'irritation' that she put down to not being 'taught any language since I was about their age' (*ibid.*).

Liz's reflections on her development

At the time of the second interview, Liz was able to see that being able to answer a student's question with 'I don't know' confounded certain cultural expectations of teachers but was nevertheless legitimate. She saw this as an aspect of her growing confidence. In the same interview, she was aware of being 'influenced by the people I've taught with' and of 'teach[ing] in a similar way to the way they teach' (Liz 2). In the third interview, Liz also seemed to be aware of opting into a particular English teacher identity, referring to her use of a heart on the map she drew as being used 'in that sad, I'm an English teacher sort of way' (Liz 3). She was also interested and somewhat disconcerted by her comparison of the maps she had drawn over the period.

8

Personal trajectories of participation: interpreting beginning teachers' development

Chapters 5, 6 and 7 consisted of in-depth case studies of the development of three beginning teachers' thinking about the subject knowledge of English. They offered a detailed, substantive answer to the question of *what* these beginning teachers thought and how this thinking about English subject knowledge developed over a two-year period. The purpose of this chapter is to present an interpretation, at a more conceptual level, across the cases in pursuit of theoretical generalisations about the processes of development and to establish how these cases might be understood as prototypes (Langemeyer and Nissen 2005).

The chapter is in three parts: the first briefly brings all three cases into view again and focuses on the key dynamics in the development of the individual beginning teachers' thinking. I am using the term 'key dynamic' to describe a significant intellectual tension – perhaps in the form of a contradiction – that is a force in both stimulating and structuring change. The second draws out common dimensions to this development. 'Common dimensions' is used to indicate similarities in developmental processes in conceptual terms across the three cases. The third part discusses three important, systemic concepts derived from my analysis of the cases that informs a reconfiguration of the theoretical framework outlined in Chapter 4 to focus more explicitly on the question of individual-within-system development. Through this, I show how the development of the beginning teachers' thinking about the subject knowledge of English might be described as a personal trajectory of participation in the practices of multiple settings informed and oriented by the affective concepts of stances or dispositions and bounded by the cultural identity of the English teacher and the cultural myths of teaching and teacher education.

Key dynamics in individual development

The three case studies were organized under headings developed from the theoretical framework in Chapter 4, itself generated from my earlier sociocultural argument about knowledge and cognition. In particular, and drawing from Davis and Sumara's nested model of 'individual knowing, collective knowledge and cultural identity' (Davis and Sumara 2000: 834), I proposed a systemic approach to analysing thinking about subject knowledge focused on the reflexive interactions between permeable layers of *culture*, *activity* and *agent*. Therefore, in trying to answer the question what and how the beginning teachers thought about the subject knowledge of school English and whether that thinking changed or developed, I was concerned to take account of the role of the educational settings in which they were learning to teach, their prior experience of English as a subject, their beliefs about the purposes for teaching and learning English, and their epistemological stance. In writing the case studies, I sought to preserve the complexities and contradictions in the beginning teachers' attempts to articulate their experience to me as researcher and render it as coherent. I deliberately resisted any urge to seek 'narrative unity' and sought instead to see how the dynamics of change for each beginning teacher arose partly out of conflicts and tensions that were *felt*.

Ann: 'you can do something'

For Ann, the 'why' question was important throughout and a key dynamic in the development of her thinking – from her initial motivation to enter teaching after working with adults with literacy difficulties through to the critical literacy focus of St Helen's, to her engagement with the theme of the IFTE conference and her questioning of 'what are we actually teaching?' in the third interview (Ann 3). This 'why teach English' question emerged in her reflections on her participation in the various settings and highlights the permeability of this organizing heading ('setting for learning to teach') with the 'purposes of English teaching' heading. Her experience as student teacher at St Helen's, for example, allowed her to remake her experience of her own schooling and her experience at her first PGCE school, Peak Down, and the focus of this remaking is the sense of purpose to the practice of English teaching in these settings: her perceptions of the critical literacy rationale at St Helen's is compared to the sometimes formulaic and 'getting on with it' approach at her own school and at Peak Down. And later, in her Induction year, the IFTE conference stimulated a remaking of her perceptions of Abbotts, again related to the purposes of English teaching:

> … should we be teaching things like ethics and values and social morality, or should we be teaching so that this student can answer, can get a grade B at GCSE? (Ann 3)

Ann's experience at St Helen's was influential in remaking her perceptions of her own school experience of English as 'just reading and reading and reading' (Ann 3). In comparison to the variation in learning activities at St Helen's (Ann 2), Ann felt her own experience of English in school to be dull and formulaic. Ann also saw aspects of her own schooling in the 'strong emphasis on the classroom reader' at Abbotts (Ann 3). Nevertheless, although Ann's perceptions of the emphasis on whole-class reading of novels in her own schooling and at Peak Down and Abbotts were quite negative by the time of the third interview, there was never-theless a contradiction present in the first interview when she referred to the 'guilty' pleasure of 'taking the kids through the text' (Ann 1). The tension here was between something she enjoyed personally as a student/reader and the different practices of English teaching in which she has participated, especially at St Helen's.

From the time of the first interview, Ann talked about the 'vastness' of English (Ann 1) and the difficulty of specifying the knowledge that 'makes it up'. Also, from this time onwards, Ann was aware of the political dimension to questions of subject constitution; for example, in her early references to the importance of personal, social and historical 'context' (Ann 1, Ann 2). This became much more explicitly related to questions of the purposes of English teaching during her experience at St Helen's, where she drew on the language of critical literacy and feminism: she sought the 'empowerment' of students (Ann 2) and to pay attention to issues of gender stereotyping (*ibid.*).

The question of subject constitution and the purposes of teaching English became most explicitly interrelated and most obviously political in the third interview after Ann's participation in the IFTE conference. In her third map of subject knowledge, 'English' became dispersed to the fragile boundary of the image to indicate that 'definitions are slightly breaking down' (Ann 3) and the items contained within the map were substantively different.

Grace: 'not as easy as it sounds'
Grace associated the PGCE course with subject knowledge auditing and the optional sessions arranged by the course tutor. She recalled the course tutor's presentation of the audit as 'here is your subject audit, these are things you need to know' (Grace 1). The 'compartmentalization' of knowledge was also a recurrent theme in the interviews. Grace thought that her head of department's influence on schemes of work at Park Girls School made them 'quite hard work' because of this compartmentalization: 'this is why you're doing it, this is what you are going to achieve' (Grace 1). Nevertheless, by the time of the third interview in her Induction Year at Green Road Community School, Grace had remade her experience of Park Girls as somewhere where the English teaching *lacked* explicitness and, in contrast to her current experience at Green Road, where tasks didn't need to be broken down for learners. This remaking of her experience at Park Girls through her participation in the practices of Green Road English teaching was quite profound– remaking something that she had found quite constricting at the time as now somehow *too* open and lacking in structure. Unlike Ann – where the focus for this remaking seemed to be the purposes of English teaching – the focus for Grace's own remaking of her own experience seems to be epistemological.

The three key settings in which Grace learned to teach were each perceived as holding a particular stance or orientation to knowledge related to objectivism (the

PGCE) and degrees of compartmentalization and fragmentation (Park Girls and Green Road). Although Green Road seems to have exerted a powerful influence on the way Grace remade her previous experience, it is also apparent that Grace was not fully in sympathy with the practices of Green Road English teaching. She described it as 'very prescribed now' and somewhat lacking in 'creativity' (Grace 3). She said that sometimes she had 'gone home and cried my eyes out' (*ibid.*) and contrasted what and how she had been expected to teach here with some new planning she had undertaken that she described as 'back to my own knowledge' (*ibid.*). In this way, Grace's previous experience continued to have some influence on her current perceptions, and the practices of Green Road were held in tension with her own set of beliefs about English *and* about knowledge.

By the time of her third interview towards the end of her Induction year, for example, Grace was associating her improved 'ability to relay [English subject knowledge] to the kids' (Grace 3) with aspects of linguistic terminology whilst simultaneously complaining that the students quickly forget this (*ibid.*). This apparent contradiction – it's now easier to 'relay' knowledge (thanks to terminology) but the students don't seem to remember it – seem to arise out of Grace's participation in the practices of English teaching at Green Road. This contradiction suggests that her earlier understanding of the distinction between a decontextualized, auditable subject knowledge and a more contextualized and situated (arguably, pedagogic) understanding of teachers' professional knowledge was now in tension with the prevailing epistemological stance in the English department at Green Road.

Epistemological stance is a key dynamic in Grace's development. Her sense of the contextual relevance and social dimensions to knowledge were first tested by the subject knowledge audit procedure in the PGCE course and later directly challenged by the objectivism of the practices of English teaching at Green Road. On reflection, Grace is aware of how her thinking has been shaped by the Green Road setting and her participation in its English teaching practices. She said that 'what they say often makes sense but I am not sure how deeply embedded that is' (Grace 3).

Liz: 'communicate passion onto other people'

For Liz, the Parkton PGCE course was associated in part with some active sessions on teaching poetry, Shakespeare and drama in which she and her fellow beginning teachers participated 'almost … in the role of students' (Liz 1) but more generally with a fairly rigid approach to planning lessons: 'let's have your standard plan, you must put how much time you're going to allocate and try to stick to that … so you can get through everything' (*ibid.*). Nevertheless, even by the time of the third interview, Liz still strongly recalled the poetry sessions taught by a tutor whose ideas she described as 'inspiring' (Liz 3). A key dynamic in the development of her thinking about the subject knowledge of English is the tension between her individual agency and creativity as a reader and teacher and the curricularization of knowledge.

This tension between 'inspiration' and relative prescription continues in Liz's perceptions of practice at Peak Down County High School and Kiplings, her Induction year school. At Peak Down, she had noted the requirement to 'stick to the schemes of work' (*ibid.*) and to use 'centralized banks of information' (*ibid.*). At Kiplings, she notes that her teaching 'in terms of solid methods has improved, but my teaching in terms of creativity has taken a step back' (*ibid.*) and she associates this with time and syllabus constraints. Indeed, towards the end of her Induction year, she is considering leaving secondary school teaching to find something 'more free and creative' (*ibid.*).

Flexible and creative approaches to English were valued by Liz in her own experiences and contrasted with what she referred to as a 'prescriptive approach' (Liz 2). In the second interview she recalled being inspired by a teacher who 'wouldn't just stick to the exam syllabus … She would treat you as an individual' (*ibid.*). She strongly associated this inspiration with the study of literature (English, it seemed, *was* English Literature, for Liz), particularly poetry, and saw herself as someone who was 'very playful with text and language' (Liz 1).

Liz's definition of a creative approach to English is often implicit and understood in relation to what it is not, however. 'Sticking' to the exam syllabus (meaning, perhaps, interpreting the syllabus minimally and mechanistically) wasn't creative, neither was 'breaking literature into its component parts', an activity she recalled in relation to Coleridge's *Rime of the Ancient Mariner* (*ibid.*). Additionally, an 'issues-based' approach to studying literature that she had experienced in school (associated with *Roll of Thunder, Hear My Cry*) wasn't creative and was criticized for being 'transparent' (*ibid.*). She was aware of how these recollections of her schooling were informing her development as an English teacher (*ibid.*) in a context of high pressure to achieve good examination results.

The parts of her English degree that she enjoyed the most were the Anglo-Saxon and Middle English element. In a written narrative, she described how – having studied it for three years and having 'developed a real passion for it' – she was 'determined to include it in classroom teaching' (Liz's second narrative). Although she had waited a year and resat her A-levels in order to get to Parkton, she didn't like the rapid pace of reading and response in the English degree there. She had 'struggled' with practical criticism and with expectations of a weekly turnaround in her reading and said that she 'loathed' having to skim something once in order to be able to form an opinion (Liz 3). Nevertheless, in the third interview, she also talked about 'emulat[ing] the Parkton structure of teaching' in her own planning at Kiplings with the students expected to 'do' a different form of poetry every week (*ibid.*). There is perhaps the sense that this tightly-packed, linear structure is acceptable if it provides opportunities to 'communicate [her] passion' (Liz 1).

In the third interview, Liz also shows she is aware of herself in relation to a particular form of cultural identity, the 'sad English teacher' who 'talks about books all the time' (Liz 3) and does so in a knowingly humorous way. However, there is more regret in her reaction to a comparison of the three maps of English subject knowledge that she had drawn, especially as she knows this is the end of the period of the research. She says she feels the second map 'ought to be more like me, the togetherness, the structured' (*ibid.*); there is a sense that, for her, the third map – with all its 'floaty floaty' qualities – is an inappropriate, end-point representation of the development of her thinking.

The problem of the individual in sociocultural analyses
Although identifying individual key dynamics might appear to be accepting individ-

	Ann 1	Ann 2	Ann 3	Grace 1	Grace 2	Grace 3
NCats	2	3	3	3	3	1
ASK	6	10	4	16	9	9
Nodes	9	8	(11)	22	14	(5)
Links	9	31	0	50	23	(6)
Linear Connectivity	1	3.87	0	2.27	1.64	(1)
Organizational type	One-centred Unbounded	Bounded One-centred	Bounded Unconnected	Unbounded Linear	Unbounded One-centred	Bounded One-centred (unconnected)
Distinctive features	Repetition and emphasis: grammar, language, context Detailed depiction: *literature* and *language*	Repetition represented in a more complex interrelated way. Interrelationships annotated in some detail Detailed depiction: *writing* and *literature*	Appearance of three distinctively different items: values/ethics, linguistics, cultural studies Detailed depiction: the boundary (*English*)	Division of 'literature' into historical fields Shakespeare mentioned specifically Detailed depiction: *NCats*	ICT, Independent study and KS3EF included in elements of subject knowledge Shakespeare continues to be mentioned Detailed depiction: *literature*	Appearance of six distinctively different items concerned with examinations and testing Shakespeare not mentioned Less detailed depiction: overlapping section ('common English')

Table 8.1: Summary of numerical description of participants' maps of English subject knowledge plus their organizational types and qualitatively distinctive features

ualist, inside-the-head understandings of knowledge and thinking, my purpose in doing so is to emphasize once again the particularity and the relational aspects of each beginning teacher's development, even when they have been part of the same teacher education programme and have taught in the same schools. I am also foregrounding the individual perspective at this point to acknowledge that for each of the beginning teachers, their development is experienced as personal and located rather than necessarily systemic. I have also endeavoured to tease out the reflexive and reciprocal nature of the relationships between the individual subject and the object-oriented systems in which they have been participating.

So, for Ann, the key dynamic was a tension between socially critical and instrumental purposes of teaching English and a remaking of her thinking about what a socially critical purpose entails. A key dynamic in the development of

Liz 1	Liz 2	Liz 3
0	0	0
3	5	2
9	10	(9)
26	0	0
2.88	0	0
Bounded (radiating in)	Bounded One-centred	Unbounded Unconnected
Other/subjects disciplines seen to inform (one-way relationship in)	Greater number of other subjects/ disciplines inter-related	Image of heart at the centre refers back to Liz's first image
Literacy skills at the 'heart'	Detailed depiction: central core (*literacy, research skills, love of language/stories etc*)	Appearance of two distinctively different items: *personal history, cultural context*
Detailed depiction: central block (*English Lit* and *Language*)		Detailed depiction: central heart image (*Literature + Language*)

Grace's thinking was a tension between (in Hillocks's terms) objectivist and constructivist epistemological stances in relation to improved educational and social outcomes for her students. And for Liz, it is possible to trace the dynamic tension between her personal agency and creativity as a reader and teacher and the effects of curricularisation in schools. These key dynamics in the development of all three beginning teachers' thinking are in a relation both to their participation in the activity systems of the settings in which they are learning to teach *and* to their own biographies. Although these case studies demonstrate the distinctiveness of the development in each case, it is also possible to draw out some common dimensions to the process of development at a conceptual level that are useful in interpretative and theoretical terms.

Common dimensions to development

Six common dimensions to the development of the beginning teachers' thinking about subject knowledge can be identified through a lateral analysis of the case studies.

1. Complex chronologies

Over the period of the research, each beginning teacher was actively constructing and working on a representation of their thinking to me during the interviews, the drawing of the maps and the writing of narratives. The development of their thinking about English subject knowledge was seen – including by the beginning teachers themselves – as being in a relation to their participation in the practices available to them in various settings and in relation to the cultural arena, specifically the cultural identity of English teaching in England. Thus Ann's thinking about the socially critical purpose of teaching English was extended by her participation in the IFTE conference. But current participation also enabled the beginning teachers to remake their prior participation as an aspect of their biography and refashion the thinking developed in previous settings. Grace, as we have seen, at first almost parodies the relatively explicit, objectives-led teaching at Park Girls School only to remake this as too implicit and therefore unsatisfactory following her participation in the practices of English teaching at Green Road. Liz talks about the pressure she felt to come up with immediate responses to texts on a weekly basis at Parkton but then incorporates this type of planning into her teaching at Kiplings. And Ann remakes her experience at Peak Down County High School (and aspects of her own schooling) through the lens of her participation in the practices at St Helen's with its media specialism. In terms of development, the process for these beginning teachers is hardly linear in the sense of going from A to B to C, accumulating bits of information as they move towards an idealized and complete whole. Instead, their development is characterized by a complex chronology where the past is not left behind but is, in a sense, continuous; the past is remade and reinterpreted through the present with a view towards a future identity (becoming an English teacher). T.S. Eliot explored this understanding of time in *Four Quartets*: 'It seems, as one becomes older, / That the past has another pattern, and ceases to be a mere sequence' (Eliot 1974: 208–9).

In her study of beginning teachers' 'struggle for voice', Britzman also noticed that 'a different sense of time fashioned how they talked about their educational biographies in relation to learning to teach' (Britzman 2003: 249) and noted that chronology was a problematic concept:

> A linear and literal sense of time could not account for the ways in which student teachers produce their identities. And they do produce them, not as if they moved through an orderly experiential continuum, but as if identities already constituted a cacophony of beckonings and involuntary returns. (*ibid.*: 249–50)

For the three beginning teachers in my study, the development of their thinking was structured in part by complex chronologies that also had a 'cross-contextual' (Dreier 1999: 22) dimension. The chronology of their development, in other words, is related to their participation *across* contexts. I will return to this point in the next section of the chapter.

2. Making little ticks: the audit paradox

The 4/98 QTS Standards required 'providers' of initial teacher education to check and then fill 'gaps' in trainees' subject knowledge, as laid down in the Initial Teacher Training National Curricula. Although reactions to the practice of subject knowledge auditing varied across the three beginning teachers, their later comments all suggested that the audit had had some unintentional effects. Both Ann and Liz – on the Parkton PGCE course – came to understand that they 'didn't need to know everything' (Ann 2) and that they 'knew a lot more than we thought we did' (Liz 1). Grace – at Newchester – questioned the notion of 'transfer' from one context to another and distinguished between what she might learn in her tutor's 'subject knowledge enhancement workshops' and being able to teach related concepts in the classroom (Grace 2). Paradoxically, being subject to the audit process stimulated these beginning teachers to think more seriously about knowledge and teaching whilst critically rejecting the audit's objectivist intent, even if their initial reaction had been panic and 'oh my God grammar' (Ann 2).

3. Biography as participation

An important aspect of each case study was the beginning teachers' background in English, something I referred to in the case study headings as their 'English biography'. Although this heading might appear to be rather individualistic and to be suggesting that this section of the data was concerned with what had previously gone on inside that beginning teachers' head, the case studies show how each beginning teachers' 'English biography' is composed of their participation in the practices of multiple educational settings. So their experience of being taught English in schools and at university – that is, their participation as a learner in the activity systems of these different settings – was also subject to being remade by their participation in the practices of current settings. In this way, 'English biography' is not a stable, linear concept concerned with 'explaining' why a beginning teacher thinks the way she does but is rather a highly dynamic concept that is also being *worked on* by the beginning teacher in current practices.

4. Subject constitution as purpose

In each case study, the selection of conceptual tools that together constitute the subject English were seen to be in a direct relation to the beginning teachers' conceptions of the purposes of teaching English. So, for example, as Ann's conception of the purpose of teaching English becomes more explicitly socially critical (although still in tension with a more instrumental aim), the areas of subject knowledge that make up her maps change and she has a different rationale for their selection. Similarly, as Grace puts herself under pressure at Green Road to achieve the very best examination results for her students, her sense of subject constitution almost disappears and is replaced by the appropriation of concepts from the arenas of policy and the National Curriculum assessment regime. She herself described it as 'less subject-based' (Grace 3). And Liz, who started by conceiving of the subject as English Literature, and seeing it as constituted by imports from other domains of knowledge, comes to a (in her own terms) less secure understanding of the relationships between different domains of knowledge and places literature and language at the heart of her map, conveying her own purpose of English teaching – 'communicating passion'.

The constitution of English in terms of its subject knowledge varies across the three beginning teachers and within each case. This constitution is informed partly by the individual beginning teacher's conceptions of purpose for teaching English (conceived of as being formed through their participation in previous settings) and partly by the prevailing subject paradigms and pedagogies in the settings in which they are currently learning.

5. Objectivist and constructivist stances in tension

In Chapter 3, I had suggested that Hillocks' (1999) primary categories of *either* 'objectivist' *or* 'constructivist' epistemological stances were not adequate as a view of pedagogy in practice and might not prove fully adequate analytically. In fact, there was no simple progression in any of the three cases from one epistemological stance to another. Instead, in each case, objectivist and constructivist epistemological stances are in tension throughout the process of development, having different emphases according to the goals of a particular practice. Ann, for example, finds the objectification of conceptual differences useful in her attention to linguistic and media studies terminology and thinks this empowers students. Yet she also learns to exploit her lack of knowledge about horror films when teaching a Year 9 class at St Helen's and sees that this creates a different kind of pedagogic relationship. Grace partly accepts the need for an objectivist epistemology at Green Road but simultaneously recognizes that her students don't seem to retain what they have learned. And Liz rejects the fragmentation of texts and 'transparent' didacticism but plans a poetry scheme of work that takes on some aspects of her Parkton experience that made her uncomfortable as a learner.

To an important extent, then, the case studies do show that Hillocks's binary categorization isn't that useful when trying to describe the complex and perhaps rather messy business of learning something like teaching, especially the teaching of English. Objectivist and constructivist epistemological stances are perhaps better thought of as concepts that figure in these beginning teachers' development rather than as factors that determine it.

6. Maps of English subject knowledge: changes in representational strategies

The maps drawn by the beginning teachers in the course of the three interview proved to be useful in terms of mediation and in stimulating reflection on development. There were substantive changes in the content of their maps over time associated, as I mentioned above, with the interrelationship between subject constitution and the purposes of teaching it. There were also major changes in the organization of these maps as visual images over the period of the research.

Table 8.1 below assembles in summary display form the numerical analyses of the beginning teachers' maps of English subject knowledge previously presented separately in the case studies along with their organizational types and qualitatively distinctive features.

In each case, over the course of the three maps, the following changes can be seen to have taken place:

- in terms of linear connectivity (a measure of the relationships between elements of the map represented by straight lines), there is a decrease from the first to the third map;
- in terms of organizational type, a move from either an image with a clear boundary to an unbounded image, or *vice versa*;
- in terms of areas of subject knowledge, a decrease in the number mentioned from the first to the third image;
- in the third map, distinctively different terms appear for the first time in all three cases.

It is interesting to note that the decrease in linear connectivity and the decrease in the number of areas of subject knowledge in the final maps drawn and discussed towards the end of the second year does not suggest that these images themselves are any less complex nor that we should infer that the beginning teachers' thinking is less complex. Rather, in the final interview we see the beginning teachers attempting to use different representational strategies to convey their thinking, sometimes (as in the case of Ann) consciously so. In all three cases, it is perhaps the move to unconnectedness that is most striking with Liz describing her third map as 'floaty floaty' and expressing some regret that this wasn't the map she would have liked as an end point in the research, Ann focusing on the fragile boundary that gives English its identity, and Grace trying to group relatively more items than the other two within policy-defined intersecting circles. The complexity of the three beginning teachers' thinking, therefore, and their efforts to represent it, is suggested not by lines in a hierarchical diagram but through attention to the space between the elements of the image and the use of meaningful organizational devices such as zigzag lines (Ann), the conventions of the Venn diagram (Grace) and the graffiti-like heart image (Liz).

In this chapter, I have so far suggested specific key dynamics in the development of the individual beginning teachers' thinking about the subject knowledge of English. I have also identified six common conceptual dimensions to the processes of development across the cases. In the final section, I briefly review the theoretical framework outlined in Chapter 4 in the light of the three case studies and identify some systemic concepts that might be used to reconfigure that framework with a specific focus on the nature of individual development.

Some key concepts in the development of the beginning teachers' thinking

The socioculturally informed, theoretical framework outlined in Chapter 4 placed the creation of knowledge within a dynamic system consisting of three interacting and reflexive layers: *culture, activity* and *agent*. In the case studies, the development of the beginning teachers' thinking is presented as an aspect of their *individual knowing* that is formed in practice – or through their participation in the activity systems of multiple settings – and in relation to the cultural arena, particularly the cultural identity of the secondary English teacher in England. In this way, the beginning teachers' thinking can be considered as a means of intellectually working on and towards that identity, as part of becoming an English teacher. However, rather than seeing *individual knowing* as an attribute residing solely inside the individual's head, the case studies have explicitly shown what was implicit in the model which is that *individual knowing* is developed through participation in practice in settings and in relation to a cultural identity. Thus, the distinction between *individual knowing* and *collective knowledge* can be explained as a difference in analytic focus on the same phenomenon: analysing *individual knowing* requires a focus on the individual's agentic participation in practices whereas analysing *collective knowledge* requires a focus on the division of labour within a community of practice and how its 'rule-governed behaviour' operates (Edwards *et al.* 2002: 39).

   The focus in my research was on *individual knowing* and has attempted to show its development as arising out of participation in practices – at the level of collective, conceptual work – and as culturally and historically nested. It might be useful, therefore, to extend the theoretical framework from Chapter 4 by reconfiguring it more directly on the analysis of *individual knowing*, that is, the development of the beginning teachers' thinking about subject knowledge. In doing so, I believe it is important to take account of the following concepts that I am suggesting are useful in interpreting the development of *individual knowing* in the case studies.

Dispositions and stances: formative records of experience

In the three case studies, how the beginning teacher *feels* about a conceptual tool (e.g. an area of English subject knowledge) influences their appropriation of that tool. That is to say, there is a strongly affective dimension to the beginning teachers' *individual knowing*, not in the sense of them expressing certain aesthetic or emotional qualities, but rather that the development of their thinking – as it arises out of their participation in practices – is informed by how they feel about prior (or, indeed, simultaneous) participation in practices in other settings. This development arises out of contradictions and conflicts at the conceptual level that are often felt as troubling and sometimes as painful. Damasio (2000), writing from the perspective of neurophysiology, uses the term *dispositions* to describe how our emotional and bodily reactions to our environment structure our thinking and consciousness. Dispositions, according to Damasio, are emotional and sensory 'records which are dormant and implicit' (Damasio 2000: 160) that have been developed through our interactions in the social world. They are implicit

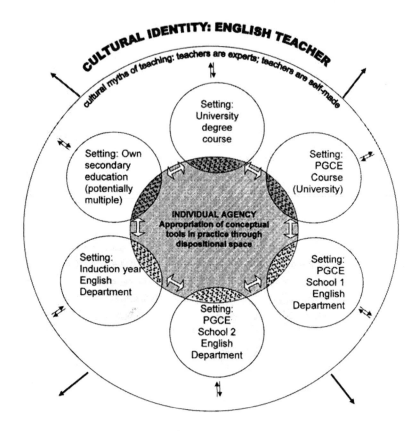

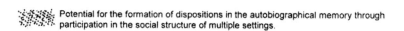

Potential for the formation of dispositions in the autobiographical memory through participation in the social structure of multiple settings.

Potential for the reconfiguration of dispositions across participation in multiple settings.

Figure 8.1: The development of the beginning teachers' thinking about the subject knowledge of English as a personal trajectory of participation in the practices of multiple settings

records of how we have felt about our participation in multiple settings that inform how we make sense of both current and past experience. Dispositions are an aspect of the autobiographical memory and, as such, subject to change and modification as we become older and as we learn.

The concept of disposition can assist our understanding of the way in which the beginning teachers remake their *individual knowing* through participation in practice. The beginning teachers' dispositions towards English and English teaching are both working on their current participation in practice and *being* worked on through this practice. It is through these beginning teachers' dispositional space in the autobiographical memory that their current and previous participation is interpreted and reinterpreted and that time comes to develop 'another pattern, and ceases to be a mere sequence' (Eliot 1974: 208–9).

Dreier (1999, 2000), writing as a sociocultural psychologist, uses the term 'stances' to represent a similar concept. Stances, according to Dreier, 'are elaborated by contrasting and comparing understandings and orientations from diverse local participations and concerns' (Dreier 1999: 14). They too are formative in that they help to structure individuals' 'orientations' in their ongoing social practice:

> … stances guide persons in their transitions between diverse contexts so that they may reorient themselves and redirect their activities according to their concerns in the present context, but also so as to keep on pursuing particular concerns and stances across contexts. (*ibid.*: 15)

Dreier's concept of stances is in some respects more useful than Hillocks's notion of epistemological stance in the analysis of the development of the beginning teachers' thinking as Dreier is not advancing stance as a single, defining characteristic but as multiple orientations that work on and are worked on through social practice. Dreier's concept of stances, like Damasio's dispositions, also suggests how the development of *individual knowing* has a cross-contextual dimension and how the individual exercises their agency in the configuration of their participation in the practices of multiple settings. The concepts of stances and dispositions are useful in this analysis as they bring in the affective and the embodied dimensions of thinking and knowledge. They also refer back to the notions of 'conceptions of purpose' and 'values' in research about teachers' subject knowledge but necessarily reinterpret these as being partly composed through participation in practice.

Personal trajectories of participation

Two of the three beginning teachers with whom I worked were students on the same PGCE course and were also placed (at different times and for different durations) at the same school. Yet Ann and Liz perceived aspects of their PGCE course and of Peak Down County High School very differently and, as settings, the Parkton PGCE and Peak Down both afforded very different opportunities for development. The case studies of the development of Ann's and Liz's thinking demonstrate, then, that it is not a question of what is *a priori* 'in' the environment or setting for learning but how the beginning teachers perceived that environment, how they 'picked up' information within it (Greeno *et al.* 1996). For Ann and Liz, the affordances (Greeno 1994) of these environments were different.

In developing the concept of stances, Dreier suggested that: 'The particular way subjects configure their participation in the present context does not depend on that context alone' (Dreier 1999: 11). Like Damasio (and his concept of dispositions), Dreier argues that the individual's participation in the practices of settings is informed by that individual's stances (or dispositions). That is, participation in practice is dispositionally informed or given an orientation by a person's stance (or stances). This allows for the possibility of individuals proceeding through the same setting resulting in different forms of participation. For Dreier, this leads to an argument for developing 'theories about complex personal trajectories of participation in structures of social practice' (*ibid*.: 29).

The theoretical framework outlined in Chapter 4 might be usefully reconfigured and extended by conceptualizing the development of *individual knowing* as a personal trajectory of participation in the practices of multiple settings. Viewing the development of the beginning teachers' thinking about the subject knowledge of English as a personal trajectory of participation in settings allows us to see the dynamic and reflexive nature of this work and to acknowledge that rather than seeming simply to pass through or 'float above' contexts and settings (as might be inferred from the tripartite division in Chapter 4's framework – *culture, activity, agent),* individuals actively participate in contexts and settings and potentially help to shape them, a possibility Lave and Wenger referred to as 'the continuity-displacement contradiction' (Lave and Wenger 1991). Dreier describes the individual work involved in developing such a trajectory thus: 'In the course of our trajectory of participation we re-flect, i.e. re-consider, re-evaluate, and re-configure our participations and concerns in the composition of our personal social practice in and across varying constellations of social contexts' (Dreier 1999: 13).

In doing so, Dreier draws attention to the complex, *cross-contextual* sense of direction to an individual's trajectory (*ibid*.: 22) that shows how chronology in terms of development can be problematic. For Dreier, traditional narratives of development conceptualize time in the abstract and 'lose the relation of time-space' (*ibid*.: 24). The three case studies presented here try to show how the chronology of the development of the beginning teachers' thinking is not straightforwardly linear and is in a relation to their participation in settings such that past and present participation are continually working on and being worked on in practice. Chapter 4's theoretical framework might be reconfigured from the perspective of *individual knowing* to foreground the concept of development as a personal, cross-contextual trajectory of participation.

Struggling with the cultural myths of teaching and teacher education
The beginning teachers' intellectual work on subject knowledge takes place in and

across multiple settings that in turn are in a relationship with aspects of the cultural arena (including political economy). Their work has as its object the cultural identity of the secondary English teacher in England and the case studies show how this work is partly constrained by certain powerful, idealised conceptions that work to shape how that cultural identity is understood in practice. Britzman (1986) interpreted these idealized conceptions as mythic and identified three cultural myths of teaching and teacher education. She defined cultural myth (after Barthes 1985) as follows: 'Cultural myths provide a set of ideal images, definitions, justifications and measures for thought and activity, and sustain a naturalised view of the reality it seeks to encode' (Britzman 1986: 448).

Britzman argued that such cultural myths 'valorise the individual and make inconsequential the institutional constraints which frame the teacher's work' (*ibid.*). In this way, she is also arguing against the *a priori* individual that passes through or 'floats above' contexts and is drawing attention – most obviously at the cultural level – to the sometimes repressive constraints on both *collective knowledge* and *individual knowing*. In developing a cultural identity as a secondary English teacher, the beginning teachers with whom I worked were also learning to negotiate – through the practices of their settings – their relationship with these cultural myths. Britzman elaborated the three cultural myths as *Everything depends on the teacher*, *The teacher as expert* and *Teachers are self-made*. With reference to the three case studies presented here, the two most relevant are *The teacher as expert* and *Teachers are self-made*.

Britzman asserted that 'the fear most commonly articulated by prospective teachers is that they will never know enough to teach' (*ibid.*: 450). This fear is apparent in all three case studies and was often a theme in their written narratives. The beginning teachers feared not knowing and *being seen* not to know in front of a class, whether this was in relation to grammar, poetic metre or literary history. They had also all been presented with an objective list of things that English teachers should know as part of the subject audit process and had been startled or panicked initially. In this way, the audit process reinforced the myth of *Teacher as expert* and did so quite explicitly from early in the career. It is to the credit of the beginning teachers that they each negotiated this myth in the course of their development and came to the understanding, first, that they didn't need to know everything (and that was alright) and, second, explicitly so in Grace's case, that what we learn in one setting is not simply 'transferred' to another.

Nevertheless, the cultural myth of *Teacher as expert* was a powerful factor in the development of their thinking about the subject knowledge of English. In addition to reinforcing a view of knowledge as a commodity that can be audited it also, as Britzman points out, 'reinforces the image of teacher as autonomous individual' (*ibid.*: 450).

Portraying the teacher as a 'rugged individual' is also an effect of the third, and for Britzman, most repressive cultural myth, *Teachers are self-made*. Britzman associates this myth with 'anti-intellectualism' and a rush to accumulate classroom experience: 'the myth that teachers are self-made serves to cloak the social relationships and the context of school structure by exaggerating personal autonomy … if one cannot make the grade, one is not meant to be a teacher (*ibid*.: 452).

The three case studies presented here show how the 'making' of the beginning teacher (specifically in relation to their thinking about the subject knowledge of English) is a complex process arising out of their participation in settings and that their perceptions of these settings shape their development. This is not a deterministic proposition but one that acknowledges that the schools and subject departments in which the beginning teachers were learning to teach extended certain forms of participation to them and denied them others. All three beginning teachers were aware of how this process worked to a greater or lesser extent; Grace, for example, however upset at times that she wasn't 'making' it, also realized how her development at Green Road was being informed by the social relationships she had established there but was also informed by ideas developed in previous settings (Grace 3).

Reconfiguring the theoretical framework to focus more explicitly on the development of *individual knowing*

The framework elaborated in Chapter 4 provided a useful perspective from which to analyse the development of the beginning teachers' thinking about subject knowledge. It was intended to be a dynamic model at the systemic level in which there were three dimensions of knowing: 'individual knowing', 'collective knowledge' and 'cultural identity' (Davis and Sumara 2000: 834). In proposing a model that focused on interactive and reflexive relationships between permeable layers of *culture, activity* and *agent* it enabled me to show in the case studies how what the individual beginning teacher was thinking was established in relation to their agentic participation in the systemic, object and goal-oriented practices of multiple settings (from their own schooling to the PGCE placement and Induction year's schools) and in relation to the cultural arena, specifically the cultural identity of the secondary English teacher in England. However, the framework might be reconfigured to focus more directly on the individual-within-system's development rather than the operation of the knowledge-creating system *per se*. Figure 8.1 offers such a reconfiguration of the framework in terms of the development of the beginning teachers' thinking about the subject knowledge of school English (an aspect of their individual knowing) as a personal trajectory of participation in the practices of multiple settings.

The model presented here – whilst still social and systemic – differs from Chapter 4's framework in that the individual agent is at the centre, situated both within and between their settings, partly composed by their participation within them, rather than as an apparently separate item in a system. This can be interpreted as a reconfiguration of the earlier framework in three ways: first, in the focus on individual development rather than the operation of the system; second, for the way in which settings for activity can be multiple, better reflecting an ecological understanding of development; and third, the model itself now describes the nature of the interactions between what I earlier referred to as 'layers' through the concepts of stances/dispositions, personal trajectories and cultural myths.

The reconfigured model is bounded by the particular cultural identity under study – the secondary English teacher – and framed by certain cultural myths of teaching and teacher education. The arrows leading out from the outer circle in different directions (this circle representing the cultural arena) are meant to indicate that this is subject to change and variation historically and the smaller pairs of arrows just inside the outer circle are meant to show how that change in the cultural arena is partly stimulated by practice in the various settings. These pairs of arrows also indicate the influence of the cultural arena and the cultural myths on practice in settings.

The model focuses at its centre on *individual knowing* but situates the individual and sees their agency as partly composed of participation in multiple settings within a particular cultural arena: the individual is conceptualized as a person-in-contexts. The shaded areas in the overlap between the individual and their multiple settings show the potential for stances or dispositions to be formed through participation in these settings. The double-headed white arrows within the centre circle of *individual knowing* suggest the multiple possibilities for stances and dispositions developed in one setting to orient or inform participation in other settings and for there to be a complex chronological relationship between current and past participation.

In taking account of the concepts of stances and dispositions, personal trajectories of participation, and certain cultural myths of teaching and teacher education, such a reconfigured model allows for individual agency in the sense of active participation whilst also acknowledging that this participation is oriented by stances or informed by dispositions that have also been developed through participation in practice. Rather than seeing the individual beginning teacher as someone who has passed through or 'floated above' their setting, the reconfigured model explicitly allows us to see that the individual actively participates in those settings and, indeed, that who they are and what they think (in these cases, about the subject knowledge of English) is partly composed of their current and previous participation.

This chapter has shown how the development of the beginning teachers' thinking about the subject knowledge of English might be described as a personal trajectory of participation in the practices of multiple settings informed and oriented by the affective concepts of stances or dispositions and bounded by the cultural identity of the English teacher and the cultural myths of teaching and teacher education. As such, it challenges Piagetian-like views of 'genetic' stage-schemes of development, objectivist understandings of knowledge and individualistic conceptualisations of teachers' thinking and knowledge.

9

From 'making little ticks' to building professional communities: some implications for teacher education

This book has presented a small-scale, in-depth study of beginning teachers' thinking about the subject knowledge of English over a two-year period as they learned to teach. It has also interpreted the development of their thinking in terms of the underlying processes and has offered a re-conceptualization of development itself. Overall, the research has established both substantive findings about the development of the beginning teachers' thinking about English subject knowledge and offered a formal, conceptual elaboration of a way of interpreting teachers' thinking, knowledge and development that claims prototypical significance (Langemeyer and Nissen 2005). For example, I have shown that reflection on the purposes of English teaching was an important thread in the beginning teachers' development rather than a simple concern *per se* about, for example, grammar. But I have also re-interpreted the concept of 'purpose' – important in previous research such as that of Grossman (1990), Gudmunsdottir (1991) and Medwell *et al.* (1998) – as being formed at least in part through participation in multiple settings. Further, I have also shown how 'purpose', as a concept, needs to be considered with a range of other concepts in an analysis of teachers' knowledge and thinking.

The case studies in Chapters 5, 6 and 7 demonstrate the vivid particularity and rich complexity of the beginning teachers' thinking and the tensions and contradictions in their development. These case studies confirm the importance of subject knowledge in a wider examination of the development of teachers' thinking but in contrast to the narrow and fragmented approach to auditable 'content' dominant in the arena of teacher education policy in England at the time of the research. As such, they might stand as critical cases that interrogate objectivist models of teachers' knowledge.

The research also demonstrates the relevance of a sociocultural perspective on studying teachers' thinking. In doing so, it suggests ways in which a focus on systemic categories of *culture*, *activity* and *agent* might be reconciled with a complementary focus on personal trajectories of participation in multiple settings. Through emphasizing and studying in-depth the beginning teachers' accounts and perceptions of their participation in multiple educational settings whilst learning to teach, my research confirms the need to revise individualist and purely cognitive theories of teachers' thinking – theories that, for example, have focused on the staged construction of schema. I have suggested that this revision might be accomplished by foregrounding participation in collective practice in settings and I have demonstrated the relevance of the concepts of stances and dispositions, personal trajectories and the cultural myths of teaching and teacher education. In particular, the research reinterprets the concept of development away from merely cumulative, linear or 'vertical' (Engeström 1996:1) versions to embrace complex chronologies and the concept of 'horizontal' trajectories across social worlds (*ibid.*). In so doing, it indicates the continued relevance of the concept of development but within an adequate understanding of how this process might be constituted by a 'cacophony of beckonings' (Britzman 2003: 250).

There is a sense in which experienced teacher educators might instinctively understand some of these insights into teacher development. Teacher educators notice developmental trajectories of beginning teachers that they sometimes describe as 'idiosyncratic'; they might wonder how this student became that sort of teacher, what one school or department usually 'does' to its student teachers, and why this or that student didn't make it. In the previous chapter, I offered a conceptualization of development that might help to explain such apparent idiosyncrasies, understood rather as dispositionally informed, personal trajectories of participation in social systems. In this chapter, I conclude the book by briefly suggesting some interrelated pedagogic implications of this conceptualization – that is to say, of not understanding teachers' subject knowledge as an *object*.

Concluding: pedagogical implications

Minds, 'gaps' and audits: taking knowledge seriously

The statutory requirement to audit subject knowledge in initial teacher education in England was dropped in 2002 following the introduction of new QTS Standards. Nevertheless, my impression from talking to colleagues in the teacher education community over the last few years has been that the 'audit' is still alive and remains a core part of what goes on in some pre-service courses, especially the PGCE. So early in 2006, a colleague and I asked 20 secondary English teacher educators whether they operated audit procedures and, if so, why. Nineteen out of twenty said that they did.

Amongst the 19, the most common reason given was – to quote one colleague directly – 'Ofsted like it!' Quite often, the approval of Ofsted coincided with a rationale focused on 'benchmarking' where beginning teachers were 'at' and 'meeting their individual needs'. The 'gap' metaphor was also common in the answers to our questions with a strong interest in identifying deficits in individual student teachers' educational achievements ('coverage' and 'quality'), sometimes (although not always) along the lines of a generational complaint about what graduates or school-leavers don't know 'these days'. It came as something of a relief to find one colleague saying that the use of an audit also 'hopefully made [student teachers] realize that no-one can know everything'.

My point here is not to criticize my colleagues for their attention to subject knowledge but to emphasize the power of the knowledge-as-object metaphor for liberal governments looking for managerialist solutions to the problem of improving education 'brick-by-brick'. Moreover, the real power of the instruments of audit, as Marilyn Strathern has observed, is that they endure (Strathern 2000), to be cynical, even after the funding has run out. States specify operations and commodities to be counted (audited) under the guise of making institutions and professions democratically accountable and enforce these procedures temporarily. But in introducing audit, the state's concern 'may be less to improve day-to-day direction than to ensure that internal controls, in the form of monitoring techniques, are in place' (*ibid.*: 4). From this perspective, the success of the subject knowledge audit in teacher education in England is startling: more than four years after the statutory requirement to audit came to an end (and the funding for the elaborate system of extended Ofsted inspections ran out), many student teachers are still being asked to 'make little ticks' (as Ann put it) and their ticks are being taken seriously in matters of assessment.

My impression, based upon the case studies of Ann, Grace and Liz, and upon my own experiences as a teacher educator, is that the audit has a powerfully negative symbolic effect that beginning teachers do well to counter. It creates anxiety and fear about knowledge and teaching at the start of pre-service courses when beginning teachers are usually pretty good at creating these strong emotions for themselves. The apparent message from the teacher education programme to the student teacher is that there is indeed a universal codification of knowledge that teachers must accumulate and that must be ticked off. More than that, the message is that knowledge is fixed and given and utterly disembedded from any social context whatsoever. In the circumstances, it is remarkable that beginning teachers move from 'Oh my God, grammar' to realizing that they 'don't need to be the language guru'; it is also reassuring that most beginning teachers don't seem to 'transfer' the lessons that the audit teaches and don't audit their own students in schools. And although teacher educators in England (and of course I include myself in this discussion) might say that the audit stimulates student teachers to think about what they *do* know or to 'realise that no one can know everything', is a checklist designed to encourage feelings of inadequacy against an objectivist codification the best way of achieving these ends? Although the paradoxical effect of the subject knowledge audit in building confidence later on was observed in the three beginning teachers with whom I worked, it seems to me that teacher educators' opportunities for 'duplicitous discourse' have become institutionalized. A relatively small – and statutorily possible – shift in practice would allow teacher educators to take subject knowledge much more seriously and this might have beneficial consequences for teachers, for students in schools and for teacher education itself.

Transforming the object of activity: subject knowledge in practice

If subject knowledge is understood as being as much amongst participants in a field as it is within them, then subject knowledge becomes something that can be worked on by those participants as much as it works on them. Subject knowledge needs to be understood not in the sense of a teacher's individual transformation (usually seen as 'downwards') from the relevant, superior (usually, university) discipline but as a form of expertise that exists amongst people who engage in the same kind of practice. In the case studies presented in this book, the form of expertise is secondary school English teaching and it can only follow on from what I have been arguing that the experts in this area are those experienced English teachers (wherever they are located) who are evaluated as such by their professional communities. In this way, we might re-conceptualize teachers' subject knowledge as knowledge created in the *transformation of the object* where the object (the problem on which the professional community is working) is the expert teaching of (in this analysis) English in schools. This seems a better way of understanding the kind of knowledge that must be developed in and for the specific activity systems of teaching than metaphors such as subject knowledge or pedagogical content knowledge. The effect of such metaphors (intended or otherwise) is to distinguish between certain high-status kinds of knowledge that are fixed and universal (subjects or disciplines) and lower status forms of (albeit valued and valuable) 'professional' knowledge that depends on 'use-value' and context. This distinction ignores the dynamic social tensions and cultural variations that have driven the historical development of high-status subjects and disciplines (Toulmin 1972); this distinction, in other words, is sociological rather than epistemological.

There are at least two important implications of this assertion for teacher education. The first is that serious attention needs to be paid to knowledge *in practice* and that this involves working in and with the settings in which student teachers learn in order to open up new horizons for practice. The key settings in secondary PGCE courses in England are school subject departments where student teachers spend two-thirds of their time. This would involve collective relationships between university-based teacher educators, school-based mentors, other teachers in the school department, and beginning teachers, where the focus is on the development of knowledge within that setting *and* within the teacher education partnership with the goal of positively transforming the system. This would be a significant shift in the roles and ways of working that teacher educators have operated recently in England and would itself provide a ground for much needed research into teacher education and teacher development.

For example, working within a paradigm of participatory and interventionist methodologies, teacher education researchers might collaborate with school subject departments in the tradition of developmental work research (Engeström 1991). The purpose of this kind of research is to support change in organizations and systems by providing participants with the analytic tools of activity theory (Engeström 1999) as they engage in a cycle of what Engeström called 'expansive learning'. One of the potentially productive foci to explore in the development of the teacher education work of schools would be – in activity theory terms – the possibilities of a shared object: that is to say, to build understanding of how the problem on which the department is working (e.g. effective English teaching) – the object of the activity system – is contested. By exposing and exploring such contradictions and tensions (contradictions and tensions suggested by this research) with participants, the aim would be to support positive change in practice and the creation of new knowledge.

A second implication of the assertion that subject knowledge is more accurately knowledge created in transforming the object is the need to rebuild and re-energize professional communities and networks outside the school setting. Recently, in England, the opportunities for teachers to work professionally outside their own schools have diminished as a result of the changing roles of the LEA and the subject teaching associations. Whereas LEAs were once sources of professional development, support and highly distributed, bottom-up initiatives such as the National Oracy Project, more often than not they are now franchisees of central government in the implementation and monitoring of highly centralized, top-down initiatives such as the National Literacy Strategy. My impression is that subject teaching associations' roles have also changed and, in some cases, while sales of their classroom resources have gone up, their memberships have declined. The annual conference of NATE, for example, now struggles to attract more than 200 teachers each year compared to the much larger events that were held even as recently as the early 1990s (see Goodwyn 2001). This isn't a criticism of NATE but an example of how the roles of subject teaching associations have become diminished and the limited extent to which teachers now participate in networks of practice beyond their own school. It seems to me that teacher educators have a potentially important role to play in both collective work with schools and departments and in extended professional networks by supporting teachers in partnerships that take knowledge seriously. As many have pointed out (e.g. Brown *et al.* 1989, Putnam and Borko 2000, Edwards *et al.* 2002), it seems reasonable to assume that knowledge-creating young people require knowledge-creating teachers.

Supporting personal trajectories across teacher education settings

The school-based nature of graduate-level teacher education in England means that student teachers work in a minimum of two schools through their PGCE year. As I have shown in this book, the movement between these schools, and, indeed, between these settings and the other educational settings in which they are currently and have previously participated in conceptual work, is characterized by complex chronologies and a process of personal remaking that is highly affective, embodied and recursive. Understanding teachers' development in this way means paying attention to the capacity of beginning teachers to learn in these different social settings. Development is not understood so much as a 'vertical', individual accumulation of particular bits of knowledge and skills but as the capacity for joint, knowledge-creating work towards shared goals, to transform and expand the object of the activity – a capacity for what Edwards (2006, 2002) has called 'relational agency'. Developing relational agency becomes a responsibility of teacher education in its collective work with schools and departments as does supporting beginning teachers in developing their responsiveness to learners within their own classrooms.

Again, there is a sense in which teacher educators already understand the need to organize learning environments for their student teachers and to focus some of this work on the school setting. But my impression is that very often this work takes the form of the 'quality assurance' of the individual student teachers' entitlement to practise in terms defined by the school setting. Sometimes, unfortunately, it turns into arbitration. In other words, it is an individualistic kind of teacher education in which many things have to be left unsaid and the trick becomes getting the student in and out of the teaching context without causing harm to either. Edwards suggests that this is a consequence of setting up school-based teacher education as 'a site for participatory learning [but] without the interactional support that one might expect to accompany it' (Edwards 2002: 11). However, focusing the work of school-based teacher education at the more collective level, as I suggested earlier, might lead to the development of just the kind of reciprocal and responsive capacity for learning – for 'recognising and accessing' (*ibid.*: 9) resources held within the community – that one would also hope to see developed in relation to young people in schools.

Finally, one aspect of helping student teachers to develop agency becomes helping them to uncover and to explore their own subjectivities and the way that their personal trajectories of participation have been composed. An important part of this will be through examining how and where stances and dispositions about knowledge and about teaching have been formed and how these may orient their ongoing participation in the multiple settings of a teacher education programme. In this way, joint work on the object of activity can also be seen as working back on subjects' developing subjectivities which in turn transforms how those subjects work on the object. Exposing this reciprocal and 'trans-actional' (Stetsenko 2005) relationship between subjects and the object of activity can be achieved through reflexive biographical work of a kind that doesn't seek to render the individual as a sort of sponge on a linear develop-mental trajectory but as a complex work-in-progress that is working on the system as well as being worked on by it in the course of participation. English teachers of my generation and older would certainly understand this as taking the same approach to beginning teachers' learning as we have to school students' learning, which is to say, understanding learning as Mina Shaughnessy understood it, 'as a constant and often troubling reformulation of the world' rather than 'a steady flow of truth into a void' (Shaughnessy 1987: 70).

The pedagogical implications that I have briefly touched on here are, of course, interrelated. Fundamentally, these interrelationships arise out of the conceptualizations of knowledge and development with which I have been working. Understanding teachers' knowledge and development in these ways means making teacher education a humane and relational activity as well as a professional and practical one. This doesn't require us to sentimentalize the process nor to romanticize teachers. But it does ask us to conceptualize teacher development as something complex, personal and conceptual involving the sometimes painful remaking of worlds and crossing of borders rather than the simple ascent of a ladder having successfully avoided 'gaps'.

Notes

1. Introduction

1   Readers outside the UK can find a glossary of England-specific terminology and jargon at the end of this book.
2   'Tools', in a sociocultural analysis, is used to describe the artefacts or concepts used in human action towards development (see Wertsch 1991; Kozulin 1998).
3   'Object', in a sociocultural analysis, is used (after Leont'ev) to describe the material goal or problem to be worked *on* or towards: 'the object of an activity is its true motive' (Leont'ev 1978: 62). Object is therefore understood as something that is capable of being transformed rather than in the sense of a simple objective.

2. Working on and being worked on: developing knowledge in practice

1   In much of the research referred to in this chapter, cognition is the starting point for a discussion that focuses on knowledge and thinking from diverse (e.g. neurological, sociological, anthropological or ecological) perspectives. As Davis and Sumara point out, 'a main contribution of these varied discourses to understandings of cognition has been the realisation that such phenomena as thought and learning are not strictly brain-based events' (2000: 829).
2   'Activity' within this perspective has a specific meaning: '[a]ctivities are defined as enduring, intellectually planned sequences of behaviour, directed toward particular objects and goals' (Yinger and Hendricks-Lee 1993: 103).

3. Know, understand and be able to do: professionalizing knowledge

1   An alternative, more critical view is that the ITTNCs in Primary and Secondary English were intended to be a preparation to teach the National

Literacy Strategy and the Key Stage 3 English Framework rather than an increasingly marginalised National Curriculum.

2 For an account of the development of the QTS Standards framework that underpinned the ITTNCs see Reynolds 1999 and Hextall and Mahony 2000.

3 The seven ITTNCs included in Circular 4/98 were Primary English, Mathematics and Science, Secondary English, Mathematics and Science, and the ITTNC 'for the use of ICT in subject teaching'.

4 Poulson refers to a study by Bennett and Carre (1993), for example, which 'found trainee teachers' subject knowledge, across a range of subjects, to be limited when they were tested at the beginning and the end of their training' (Poulson 2001: 44). Other studies referred to include Wragg, Bennett and Carre (1989) and Aubrey (1997).

5 This is certainly apparent in some of Shulman's and his students' early work: Wilson and Wineburg (1988), for example, refer to the 'lectures' and 'mini-lectures' of the history teachers they were studying.

6 Daw's article is also interesting for its acknowledgement that, despite being one criterion in assessing the quality of teaching in schools, subject knowledge is rarely mentioned in Ofsted inspection reports when 'providing explanations for both the excellence of the best teaching or the deficiencies of the worst' (Daw 2000: 6).

7 Bernstein's distinction between 'collection' and 'integrative' codes refers to the way in which curricula may be organized. Those organized by collection codes emphasize the discrete nature of subjects and present them as an increasingly specialized and hierarchical collection of knowledge separate from other subjects and from lived experience. The integrative code, on the other hand, organizes subjects in an interrelated way so that connections with the learner's experience are emphasized.

8 The variation is also noted in a survey conducted in 1997 by the Council for College and University English (CCUE) for the higher education Quality Assurance Agency (CCUE 1997).

4. Culture, activity, agent: designing the research

1 'Layers' is used to indicate that the interactions are complex within the system and the space therein, i.e. they are not two-dimensional or simply linear and can and do overlap.

2 Values and beliefs is used here in preference to ideology. The dimension of values (a set of personal judgements about a way of life that might be shared) and beliefs (propositional statements arising out of those values) is a set of personal commitments that usually operate self-consciously whereas ideology is usually understood as operating on a

subconscious level and as leading to the interpellation of a particular form of subjectivity.

3 The names of the universities have been changed for reasons explained later in this chapter.

5. Anne: thinking about the subject knowledge of English

1 The name and number in brackets at the end of a quotation indicates the interview from which the quotation was taken. Comments on transcripts and extracts from narratives are identified separately.

2 Ann's own account of her teaching about the genre of email doesn't necessarily appear to coincide with this view, however, and will be discussed later.

References

Adamcyzk, P. and Willson, M. (1996) 'Using concept maps with trainee teachers', *Physics Education*, 31 (6): 374–81.

Ball, S. J. (1981) *Beachside Comprehensive: A Case-Study of Secondary Schooling*, Cambridge: Cambridge University Press.

Ball, S. J. and Lacey, C. (1980) 'Subject disciplines as the opportunity for group action: a measured critique of subject sub-cultures', in Woods, P. (ed.) *Teacher Strategies: Explorations in the Sociology of the School*, London: Croom Helm.

Banks, F., Leach, J. and Moon, B. (1999) 'New understandings of teachers' pedagogic knowledge', in Leach, J. and Moon, B. (eds) (2000) *Learners and Pedagogy*, London: Paul Chapman.

Barnes, D. (1976) *From Communication to Curriculum*, London: Penguin.

Barnes, D., Barnes, D. with Clarke, S. (1984) *Versions of English*, London: Heinemann.

Barthes, R. (1985) *Mythologies*, New York, NY: Hill and Wang.

Bassey, M. (1999) *Case Study Research in Educational Settings*, Buckingham: Open University Press.

Baxter Magolda, M. B. (1987) 'The affective dimension of learning: faculty-student relationships that enhance intellectual development', *College Student Journal*, 21: 46–58.

Belenky, M. F., Clinchy, B. M., Goldberger, N. R. and Tarule, J. M. (1986) *Women's Ways of Knowing: The Development of Self, Voice and Mind*, New York, NY: Basic Books.

Bell, A. H. R. (ed.) (1984) *Social Researching: Politics, Problems, Practice*, London: Routledge and Kegan Paul.

Bernstein, B. (1972) *Class, Codes and control, Vol. 1: Theoretical Studies towards a Sociology of Language*, London: Routledge and Kegan Paul.

———, (1996) *Pedagogy, Symbolic Control and Identity: Theory, Research, Critique*, London: Taylor and Francis.

Betts, P. and Frost, L. (2000) 'Subject knowledge AND teacher preparation', *Education Canada*, 40 (1): 38–9.

Blackledge, A. (1998) 'The institutionalisation of inequality: the Initial Teacher Training National Curriculum for Primary English as cultural hegemony', *Educational Review*, 50 (1): 55–64.

Borko, H., Livingston, C., McCaleb, J. and Mauro, L. (1988) 'Students teachers' planning and post-lesson reflections: patterns and implications for teacher preparation', in Calderhead, J. (ed.), *Teachers' Professional Learning*, London: the Falmer Press.

Britzman, D. P. (1986) 'Cultural myths in the making of a teacher: biography and social structure in teacher education', *Harvard Educational Review*, 56 (4): 442–56.

——, (1991) *Practice Makes Practice: A Critical Study of Learning to Teach*, Albany, NY: State University of New York Press.

——, (2004) *Practice Makes Practice: A Critical Study of Learning to Teach*, revised edition, Albany, NY: State University of New York Press.

Bronfenbrenner, U. (1979) *The Ecology of Human Development. Experiments by Nature and Design*, Cambridge, MA: Harvard University Press.

Brown, A. and Dowling, P. (1998) *Doing Research/Reading Research. A Mode of Interrogation for Education*, London: The Falmer Press.

Brown, J. S., Collins, C. and Duguid, P. (1989) 'Situated cognition and the culture of learning', *Educational Researcher*, 18 (1): 32–42.

Bruner, J. (1986) *Actual Minds, Possible Worlds*, Cambridge, MA: Harvard University Press.

Bullough, R. V. (2001) 'Pedagogical content knowledge circa 1907 and 1987: a study in the history of an idea', *Teaching and Teacher Education*, 17: 656–66.

Burgess, T., Turvey, A. and Quarshie, R. (2000) 'Teaching grammar: working with student teachers', *Changing English*, 7 (1): 7–21.

Calderhead, J. (ed.) (1987) *Exploring Teachers' Thinking*, London: Cassell.

——, (ed.) (1988) *Teachers' Professional Learning*, London: The Falmer Press.

Calderhead, J. and Shorrock, S. B. (1997) *Understanding Teacher Education. Case Studies in the Development of Beginning Teachers*, London: The Falmer Press.

Carlgren, I., Handal, G. and Vaage, S. (eds) (1994) *Teachers' Minds and Actions: Research on Teachers' Thinking and Practice*, London: The Falmer Press.

Carnegie Task Force on Teaching as a Profession (1986) *A Nation Prepared: Teachers for the 21st Century*, Washington, DC: Carnegie Forum on Education and the Economy.

Carter, K. (1993) 'The place of story in the study of teaching and teacher education', *Educational Researcher*, 22 (1): 5–12.

——, (1994) 'Preservice teachers' well-remembered events and the acquisition of event-structured knowledge', *Journal of Curriculum Studies*, 26 (3): 235–52.

Chevellard, Y. (1991) *La Transposition didachtique du savoir savant au savoir en-seigné*, Paris: La Pensée Sauvage.

Clandinin, J. D. and Connelly, F. M. (2000) *Narrative Inquiry: Experience and Story in Qualitative Research*, San Francisco, CA: Jossey-Bass Publishers.

Clark, C. M. (1989) 'Asking the right questions about teacher preparation: contributions of research on teacher thinking', in Lowyck, J. and Clark, C. M. (eds) *Teacher Thinking and Professional Action*, Leuven, NL: Leuven University Press.

Clark, C. M. and Peterson, P. L. (1986) 'Teachers' thought processes', in Wittrock, M.C. (ed.) *Handbook of Research on Teaching*, New York, NY: Macmillan.

Cochran, K., DeRuiter, J. A. and King, R. A. (1993) 'Pedagogical content knowing: an integrative model for teacher preparation', *Journal of Teacher Education*, 44 (4): 263–73.

Cole, M. (1996) *Cultural Psychology*, Cambridge, MA: Harvard University Press.

Connelly, F. M. and Clandinin, J. D. (1986) 'On narrative method, personal philosophy, and narrative unities in the story of teaching', *Journal of Research in Science Teaching*, 23 (4): 293–310.

Conle, C. (2000) 'Narrative inquiry: research tool and medium for professional development', *European Journal of Teacher Education*, 23 (1): 49–63.

Council for College and University English (CCUE) (1997) *The English Curriculum: Diversity and Standards. A Report Delivered to the Quality Assurance Agency*, Luton: CCUE.

Craig, C. J. (1997) 'Telling stories: accessing beginning teacher knowledge', *Teaching Education*, 9 (1): 61–8.

Crystal, D. (2004) *The Stories of English*, London: Allen Lane.

Damasio, A. (2000) *The Feeling of What Happens: Body, Emotion and the Making of Consciousness*, London: Vintage.

Darling-Hammond, L. and Youngs, P. (2002) 'Defining "highly qualified teachers": what does "scientifically-based research" actually tell us?', *Educational Researcher* (December): 13–25.

Davies, C. (1996) *What is English Teaching?*, Buckingham: Open University Press.

Davis, B. and Sumara, D. J. (1997) 'Cognition, complexity, and teacher education', *Harvard Educational Review*, 67 (1): 105–25.

———, (2000) 'Curriculum forms: on the assumed shapes of knowing and knowledge', *Journal of Curriculum Studies*, 32 (6): 821–45.

Daw, P. (2000) '"The gaps I mean" – subject knowledge and the training of English teachers', *English in Education*, 34 (2): 3–15.

Denzin, N. and Lincoln, Y. (eds) (1994) *Handbook of Qualitive Research*, London: Sage.

DES (Department of Education and Science) (1975) *A Language for Life* (The Bullock Report), London: HMSO.

——, (1983) *Teaching Quality*, London: HMSO.

——, (1989) *The National Curriculum: English*, London: HMSO.

DfE (Department for Education) (1993) *The Initial Training of Primary Teachers* (Circular 14/93), London: DfE.

DfES (Department for Education and Employment) (1997) *Requirements for Courses of Initial Teacher Training – The Primary Initial Teacher Training National Curricula* (Circular 10/97), London: DfES.

——, (1998a) *Teaching: High Status, High Standards. Requirements for Courses of Initial Teacher Training* (Circular 4/98), London: DfEE.

——, (1998b) *The National Literacy Strategy: Framework for Teaching*, London: DfEE.

——, (2001) *Framework for Teaching English in Years 7, 8 and 9 (Key Stage 3 National Strategy)*, London: DfEE.

Dewey, J. (1902) 'The Child and the Curriculum' in Boydston, J. A. (ed.), *John Dewey: The Middle Works, 1899–1924, Volume 2: 1902–1903*, Carbondale, IL: Southern Illinois University Press.

Dixon, J. (1975) *Growth through English: Set in the Perspective of the Seventies*, Oxford: Oxford University Press.

Doecke, B., Brown, J. and Loughran, J. (2000) 'Teacher talk: the role of story and anecdote in constructing professional knowledge for beginning teachers', *Teaching and Teacher Education*, 16 (3): 335–48.

Dreier, O. (1999) 'Personal trajectories of participation across contexts of social practice', *Outlines: Critical Social Studies* 1 (1): 5–32.

——, (2000) 'Psychotherapy in clients' trajectories across contexts', in Mattingly, C. and Garro, L. (eds) *Narratives and the Cultural Construction of Illness and Healing*, Berkeley, CA: University of California Press.

Eagleton, T. (1983) *Literary Theory: An Introduction*, Oxford: Basil Blackwell.

Edwards, A. (2002) 'Developing understandings of agency and disposition in sociocultural accounts of learning to teach', paper presented at the annual meeting of the American Educational Research Association, New Orleans.

——, (2006) 'Relational agency: learning to be a resourceful practitioner', *International Journal of Educational Research*, 32 (1): 168–82.

Edwards, A. and Wiseman, P. (2005) 'Creating new forms of interprofessional practice in distributed networks', paper presented at ISCAR Conference, Seville.

Edwards, A., Gilroy, P. and Hartley, D. (2002) *Rethinking Teacher Education: Collaborative Responses to Uncertainty*, London: RoutledgeFalmer.

Eisner, E. and Peshkin, A. (eds) (1990) *Qualitative Inquiry in Education: The Continuing Debate*, New York, NY: Teachers College Press.

Elbaz, F. (1983) *Teacher Thinking: A Study of Practical Knowledge*, London: Croom Helm.

———, (1991) 'Research on teacher's knowledge: the evolution of a discourse', *Journal of Curriculum Studies*, 23 (1): 1–19.

Eliot, T. S. (1974) 'The dry salvages', in Eliot, T. S. *Collected Poems 1909–1972*, London: Faber.

Engeström, Y. (1991) 'Developmental work research: Reconstructing expertise through expansive learning', in Nurminen, M. I., and Weir, G. R. S. (eds) *Human Jobs and Computer Interfaces*, Amsterdam, NL: Elsevier.

———, (1996) 'Development as breaking away and opening up: a challenge to Vygotsky and Piaget', paper presented to the 2nd Conference for Socio-Cultural Research: Vygotsky – Piaget, Geneva, 15 September available at http://lchc.ucsd.edu/MCA/Paper/Engestrom/Engestrom.html, accessed 15 December 2006.

———, (1999) 'Innovative learning in work teams: analysing cycles of knowledge creation in practice', in Engeström, Y., Miettinen, R. and Punamäki, R. (eds) *Perspectives on Activity Theory*, Cambridge, MA: Cambridge University Press.

Eraut, M. (1994) *Developing Professional Knowledge and Competence*, London: The Falmer Press.

Esland, G. M. (1971) 'Teaching and learning as the organisation of knowledge', in Young, M. F. D. (ed.) *Knowledge and Control*, London: Collier-Macmillan.

Esland, G. M. and Dale, R. (eds) (1973) *School and Society*, Milton Keynes: Open University.

Feiman-Nemser, S. and Parker, M. B. (1990) 'Making subject matter part of the conversation in learning to teach', *Journal of Teacher Education*, 41 (3): 32–43.

Ferry, B. (1996) 'Probing personal knowledge: the use of a computer-based tool to help preservice teachers map subject matter knowledge', *Research in Science Education*, 26 (1): 233–45.

Finch, J. (1984) '"It's great to have someone to talk to": the ethics and politics of interviewing women', in Bell, A. H. R. (ed.) *Social Researching: Politics, Problems, Practice*, London: Routledge and Kegan Paul.

Ford, G. W. and Pugno, L. (eds) (1964) *The Structure of Knowledge and the Curriculum*, Chicago, IL: Rand McNally and Co.

Fuller, F. F. and Bown, O. H. (1975) 'Becoming a teacher', in Ryan, K. (ed.) *Teacher Education: The Seventy-Fourth Yearbook of the National Society for the Study of Education*, Chicago, IL: University of Chicago Press.

Furlong, J., Barton, L., Miles, S. Whiting, C. and Whitty, G. (2000) *Teacher Education in Transition: Re-forming Professionalism?*, Buckingham: Open University Press.

Gallagher, C. and Greenblatt, S. (2001) *Practising New Historicism*, Chicago, IL: University of Chicago Press.

Gibson, J. J. (1966) *The Senses Considered as Perceptual Systems*, Boston, MA: Houghton Mifflin.

———, (1979) *The Ecological Approach to Visual Perception*, Boston, MA: Houghton Mifflin.

Gilroy, D. P. (1993) 'Reflections on Schön: an epistemological critique and a practical alternative', in Gilroy, D. P. and Smith, M. (eds) *International Analyses of Teacher Education*, Oxford: Carfax.

Goffman, E. (1959) *The Presentation of Self in Everyday Life*, Garden City, NY: Doubleday.

Goodson, I. F. with Anstead, C. J. and Marshall Mangan, J. (1998) *Subject Knowledge: Readings for the Study of School Subjects*, London: The Falmer Press.

Goodwyn, A. (2001) 'Second tier professionals: English teachers in England', *L1 – Educational Studies in Language and Literature*, 1 (2): 149–61.

Gosden, P. H. J. (ed.) (1969) *How They Were Taught*, Oxford: Basil Blackwell.

Goswami, D. and Stillman, P. R. (eds) (1987) *Reclaiming the Classroom: Teacher Research as an Agency for Change*, Porstmouth, NH: Boynton/Cook Publishers.

Graham, J. (1997) 'The Initial Teacher Training National Curriculum for Primary English 1997. A most unnecessary document', *Changing English*, 4 (2): 241–9.

Greeno, J. (1994) 'Gibson's affordances', *Psychological Review*, 101 (2): 336–42.

Greeno, J. G., Collins, A. M. and Resnick, L. (1996) 'Cognition and learning', in Berliner, D. and Calfee, R. (eds) *Handbook of Educational Psychology*, New York, NY: Macmillan.

Grossman, P. (1989) 'A study in contrast: sources of pedagogical content knowledge for secondary English', *Journal of Teacher Education* (September–October): 24–31.

———, (1990) *The Making of a Teacher: Teacher Knowledge and Teacher Education*, New York, NY: Teachers College Press.

Grossman, P. L. and Stodolsky, S. (1995) 'Content as context: The role of school subjects in secondary school teaching', *Educational Researcher*, 24 (1): 5–11.

Guba, E. G. and Lincoln, Y. S. (1994) 'Competing Paradigms in qualitative research', in Denzin, N. and Lincoln, Y. (eds) *Handbook of Qualitative Research*, London: Sage.

Gudmunsdottir, S. (1991) 'Values in pedagogical content knowledge', *Journal of Teacher Education*, 41 (3): 44–52.

Gudmunsdottir, S. and Shulman, L. S. (1987) 'Pedagogical content knowledge in social studies', *Scandinavian Journal of Educational Research*, 31 (2): 59–70.

Halim, L. and Meerah, S. M. (2002) 'Science trainee teachers' pedagogical content knowledge and its influence on physics teaching', *Research in Science and Technological Education*, 20 (2): 215–25.

Hardman, F. and Williamson, J. (1993) 'Student teachers and models of English', *Journal of Education for Teaching*, 19 (3): 279–92.

Hextall, I. and Mahony, P. (2000) 'Consultation and the management of consent: Standards for Qualified Teacher Status', *British Educational Research Journal*, 26 (3): 324–42.

Hillocks, G., Jr. (1999) *Ways of Thinking, Ways of Teaching*, New York, NY: Teachers College Press.

Hoffman, N. (1981) *Women's 'True' Profession*, Old Westbury, NY: Feminist Press.

Holmes Group (The) (1986) *Tomorrow's Teachers: A Report of the Holmes Group*, East Lansing, MI: Author.

Hood, P. (2002) 'Perspectives on knowledge utilization in education', available at www.nekia.org/files/Hood_paper_Knowledge_Utilization.doc; accessed 31 March 2006.

Hoyle, E. and John, P. D. (1995) *Professional Knowledge and Professional Practice*, London: Cassell.

Huberman, M. (1983) 'Recipes for busy kitchens: a situational analysis of routine knowledge use in schools', *Knowledge: Creation, Diffusion, Utilization*, 4 (4): 478–510.

Hunter, I. (1988) *Culture and Government: The Emergence of Literary Education*, London: Macmillan.

Jones, K. (2003) *Education in Britain: 1944 to the Present*, Cambridge: Polity Press.

Kagan, D. M. (1992) 'Professional growth among preservice and beginning teachers', *Review of Educational Research*, 62: 129–69.

Keiny, S. (1994) 'Teachers' professional development as a process of conceptual change', in Carlgren, I., Handal, G. and Vaage, S. (eds) *Teachers' Minds and Actions: Research on Teachers' Thinking and Practice*, London: The Falmer Press.

Kelly, G. A. (1955) *The Psychology of Personal Constructs* (vols 1–2), New York, NY: W. W. Norton and Company.

——, (1963) *Theory of Personality: The Psychology of Personal Constructs*, New York, NY: W. W. Norton and Company.

Kozulin, A. (1998) *Psychological Tools: A Sociocultural Approach to Education*, Cambridge, MA: Harvard University Press.

Labaree, D. F. (1992) 'Power, knowledge, and the rationalization of teaching: a genealogy of the movement to professionalize teaching', *Harvard Educational Review*, 62 (2): 123–53.

Lacey, C. (1977) *The Socialisation of Teachers*, London: Methuen.

Langemeyer, I. and Nissen, M. (2005) 'Activity theory', in Somekh, B. and Lewin, C. (eds) *Research Methods in the Social Sciences*, London: Sage.

Lave, J. (1988) *Cognition in Practice, Mind, Mathematics and Culture in Everyday Life*, Cambridge: Cambridge University Press.

Lave, J. and Wenger, E. (1991) *Situated Learning: Legitimate Peripheral Participation*, Cambridge: Cambridge University Press.

Leach, J. and Moon, B. (2000) 'Pedagogy, information and communications technology and teachers' professional knowledge', *The Curriculum Journal*, 11 (3): 385–404.

Leach, J. and Moon, B. (eds) (1999) *Learners and Pedagogy*, London: Paul Chapman.

Leinhardt, G. (1988) 'Situated knowledge and expertise in teaching', in Calderhead, J. (ed.) *Teachers' Professional Learning*, London: The Falmer Press.

Leinhardt, G. and Smith, D. (1985) 'Expertise in mathematics instruction: subject matter knowledge', *Journal of Educational Psychology*, 77: 247–71.

Lenton, G. and Turner, G. (1999) 'Student-teachers' grasp of science concepts', *School Science Review*, 81 (295): 67–72.

Leont'ev, A. N. (1978) *Activity, Consciousness and Personality*, Englewood Cliffs, NJ: Prentice Hall.

Lortie, D. C. (1975) *Schoolteacher: A Sociological Study*, Chicago, IL: University of Chiacgo Press.

Lowyck, J. and Clark, C. M. (eds) (1989) *Teacher Thinking and Professional Action*, Leuven, NL: Leuven University Press.

Luke, A. (2003) Opening address, 7th Conference of the International Federation for the Teaching of English (IFTE), University of Melbourne, 5–8 July.

Lyotard, J.-F. (1984) *The Postmodern Condition: A Report on Knowledge*, Manchester: University of Manchester Press.

McCormick, R. and Paechter, C. (eds) (1999) *Learning and Knowledge*, London: Paul Chapman/The Open University.

McEwan, H. and Bull, B. (1991) 'The pedagogic nature of subject matter knowledge', *American Educational Research Journal*, 28 (2): 316–34.

McIntyre, D. (ed.) (1997) *Teacher Education Research in a New Context: The Oxford Internship Scheme*, London: Paul Chapman.

McIntyre, D. and Morrison, A. (1977) 'Priorities in research into classroom life and teacher education', *Scottish Educational Studies*, 9 (1): 4–12.

McNamara, D. (1991) 'Subject knowledge and its application: problems and possibilities for teacher educators', *Journal of Education for Teaching*, 17 (2): 113–28.

McNamara, D. and Desforges, C. (1978) 'The social sciences, teacher education and the objectification of craft knowledge', *British Journal of Teacher Education*, 4 (1): 17–36.

Marshall, B. (1998) 'What they should be learning and how they should be taught', *English in Education*, 32 (1): 4–9.

Marshall, B., Turvey, A. and Brindley, S. (2001) 'English teachers – born or made: a longitudinal study on the socialisation of English teachers', *Changing English*, 8 (2): 189–201.

Mason, J. (1996) *Qualitative Researching*, London: Sage.

Mathieson, M. (1975) *The Preachers of Culture*, London: Allen and Unwin.

Mavers, D., Somekh, B. and Restorick, J. (2002) 'Interpreting the externalised images of pupils' conceptions of ICT: methods for the analysis of concept maps', *Computers and Education*, 38: 187–207.

Medway, P. (1980) *Finding a Language*, London: Chameleon Books; cited in Rosen, H. (1981) *Neither Bleak House Nor Liberty Hall: English in the Curriculum*, London: University of London Institute of Education.

Medwell, J., Wray, D., Poulson, L. and Fox, R. (1998) *Effective Teachers of Literacy: A Report of a Research Project Commissioned by the Teacher Training Agency*, Exeter: University of Exeter.

Merriam, S. B. (1988) *Case Study Research in Education*, San Francisco, CA: Jossey Bass.

Miles, M. B. and Huberman, A. M. (1994) *Qualitative Data Analysis: An Expanded Sourcebook. 2nd Edition*, Thousand Oaks, CA: Sage.

Mishler, E. G. (1986) *Research Interviewing: Context and Narrative*, Cambridge, MA: Harvard University Press.

Murray, F. (ed.) (1996) *The Teacher Educator's Handbook: Building a Knowledge Base for the Preparation of Teachers*, San Francisco, CA: Jossey Bass.

Muspratt, S. and Luke, A. (eds) (1997) *Constructing Critical Literacies: Teaching and Learning Textual Practice*, Cresskill, NJ: Hampton Press.

National Statistics and Department for Education and Skills (DfES) (2005) *Education Statistics: School Workforce in England. 2004 edition*, London: The Stationery Office.

Nurminen, M. I., and Weir, G. R. S. (eds) *Human Jobs and Computer Interfaces*, Amsterdam, NL: Elsevier.

Oakshott, M. (1962) *Rationalism in Politics: And Other Essays,* London: Methuen.

Payne, G. and Payne, J. (2004) *Key Concepts in Social Research,* London: Sage.

Pearson, M. and Somekh, B. (2003) 'Concept-mapping as a research tool: a study of primary children's representations of information and communication technologies (ICT)', *Education and Information Technologies,* 8 (1): 5–22.

Perry, W. G. (1970) *Forms of Intellectual and Ethical Development in the College Years: A Scheme,* New York, NY: Holt, Rinehart and Wilson.

Piaget, J. (1950) *Introduction à l'épistemologie génétique,* Paris: Presses Univ. de France.

———, (1971) *Biology and Knowledge,* Chicago, IL: University of Chicago Press.

Polkinghorne, D. (1995) 'Narrative configuration in qualitative analysis', in Hatch, J. A. and Wisniewski, R. (eds) *Life History and Narrative,* London: The Falmer Press.

Poulson, L. (2001) 'Paradigm lost? Subject knowledge, primary teachers and education policy', *British Journal of Educational Studies,* 49 (1): 40–55.

Pring, R. (2000) *Philosophy of Educational Research,* London: Continuum.

Putnam, R. T. and Borko, H. (2000) 'What do new views of knowledge and thinking have to say about research on teacher learning?', *Educational Researcher,* 29 (1): 4–15.

Reynolds, M. (1999) 'Standards and professional practice: the TTA and initial teacher training', *British Journal of Educational Studies,* 47 (3): 247–60.

Rosen, H. (1981) *Neither Bleak House nor Liberty Hall: English in the Curriculum,* London: University of London Institute of Education.

Rosenblatt, L. (1978) *The Reader, the Text, the Poem,* Carbondale, IL: Southern Illinois University Press.

Roth, W.-M. (1999) 'Authentic school science: intellectual traditions', in McCormick, R. and Paechter, C. (eds) *Learning and Knowledge,* London: Paul Chapman/The Open University.

Ryan, K. (ed.) (1975) *Teacher Education: The Seventy-Fourth Yearbook of the National Society for the Study of Education,* Chicago, IL: University of Chicago Press.

Sachs, J. (2003) *The Activist Teaching Profession,* Buckingham: Open University Press.

Sacks, H., Schegloff, E. A. and Jefferson, G. (1978) 'A simple systematics for the organization of turn-taking for conversation', in J. Schenkein (ed.) *Studies in the Organization of Conversational Interaction,* New York, NY: Academic Press.

Sampson, G. (1921) *English for the English: A Chapter on National Education*, Cambridge: Cambridge University Press.

Sanders, S. E. and Morris, H. (2000) 'Exposing student teachers' content knowledge: empowerment or debilitation?' *Educational Studies*, 26 (4): 397–408.

Scheffler, I. (1965) *Conditions of Knowledge: An Introduction to Epistemology and Education*, Chicago, IL: University of Chicago Press.

Schön, D. (1983) *The Reflective Practitioner: How Professionals Think in Action*, New York, NY: Basic Books.

Schön, D. and Rein, M. (1994) *Frame Reflection: Towards the Resolution of Intractable Policy Controversies*, New York: Basic Books.

Schwab, J. J. (1964) 'The structure of disciplines: meanings and significance', in Ford, G. W. and Pugno, L. (eds) *The Structure of Knowledge and the Curriculum*, Chicago, IL: Rand McNally.

Shaughnessy, M. (1987) 'Diving in: an introduction to basic writing', in Goswami, D. and Stillman, P. R. (eds) *Reclaiming the Classroom: Teacher Research as an Agency for Change*, Portsmouth, NH: Boynton/Cook Publishers.

Shulman, L. S. (1984) 'The missing paradigm in research on teaching', lecture presented to the Research and Development Center for Teacher Education, Austin, Texas.

——, (1986) 'Paradigms and research programs in the study of teaching: a contemporary perspective', in Wittrock, M. C. (ed.) *Handbook of Research on Teaching*, New York, NY: Macmillan.

——, (1987) 'Knowledge and teaching: foundations of the new reform', *Harvard Educational Review*, 57 (1): 1–22.

——, (1999) 'Introduction' to Hillocks, G., Jr., *Ways of Thinking, Ways of Teaching*, New York, NY: Teachers College Press.

Shulman, L. S. and Shulman, J. H. (2004) 'How and what teachers learn: a shifting perspective', *Journal of Curriculum Studies*, 36 (2): 257–71.

Siskin, L. S. (1994) *Realms of Knowledge: Academic Departments in Secondary Schools*, London: The Falmer Press.

Smagorinsky, P., Cook, L. S. and Johnson, T. S. (2003) 'The twisting path of concept development in learning to teach', *Teachers College Record*, 105: 1399–936.

Sockett, H. T. (1987) 'Has Shulman got the strategy right?', *Harvard Educational Review*, 57 (2): 208–19.

Somekh, B. and Lewin, C. (eds) (2005) *Research Methods in the Social Sciences*, London: Sage.

Stark, S. and Torrance, H. (2005) 'Case study', in Somekh, B. and Lewin, C. (eds) *Research Methods in the Social Sciences*, London: Sage.

Stetsenko, A. (2005) 'Activity as object-related: resolving the dichotomy of individual and collective planes of activity', *Mind, Culture and Activity*, 12 (1): 70–88.

Strathern, M. (2000) 'New accountabilities: anthropological studies in audit, ethics and the academy', in Strathern, M. (ed.) *Audit Cultures: Anthropological Studies in Accountability, Ethics and the Academy,* London: Routledge.

Thornton, S. (2003) 'What counts as subject matter knowledge for teaching?', paper presented at the Annual Meeting of the American Educational Research Association, Chicago, 21–5 April 2003; ERIC document ED 477 504.

Tom, A. (1984) *Teaching as a Moral Craft,* New York, NY: Longman.

Toulmin, S. (1972) *Human Understanding* Volume 1. General Introduction, Oxford: Clarendon Press.

——, (1999) 'Knowledge as shared procedures', in Engeström, Y., Miettinen, R. and Punamäki, R. (eds) *Perspectives on Activity Theory,* Cambridge: Cambridge University Press.

Turner-Bissett, R. (1999) 'The knowledge bases of the expert teacher', *British Educational Research Journal,* 25 (1): 39–55.

Usher, R. and Edwards, R. (1994) *Postmodernism and Education: Different Voices, Different Worlds,* London: Routledge.

Verret, M. (1975) *Le temps des crudes,* Paris: Librarie Honorés Champion.

Viswanathan, G. (1989) *Masks of Conquest: Literary Study and British Rule in India,* New York, NY: Columbia University Press.

Vygotsky, L. S. (1974) *Mind in Society,* Cambridge, MA: Harvard University Press.

——, (1986) *Thought and Language,* Cambridge, MA: MIT Press.

——, (1987) *The Collected Works of L. S. Vygotsky: Vol. 1 Problems of General Psychology. Including the Volume Thinking and Speech,* New York: Plenum (trans Minick, N.).

Wertsch, J. V. (1991) *Voices of the Mind: A Sociocultural Approach to Mediated Action,* Cambridge, MA: Harvard University Press.

Wilson, G. C. (1964) 'The structure of English', in Ford, G. W. and Pugno, L. (eds) *The Structure of Knowledge and the Curriculum,* Chicago, IL: Rand McNally and Co.

Wilson, S. M., Floden, R. E. and Ferrini-Mundy (2002) 'Teacher preparation research: an insider's view from the outside', *Journal of Teacher Education,* 53 (3): 190–204.

Wilson, S. M. and Wineburg, S. (1988) 'Peering at history through different lenses: the role of disciplinary perspectives in teaching history', *Teachers College Record,* 89 (4): 525–39.

Wineburg, S. (1997) 'Beyond "breadth and depth": subject matter knowledge and assessment', *Theory into Practice*, 36 (4): 255–302.

Wittgenstein, L. (1972) *Preliminary Studies for the 'Philosophical Investigations'*, Oxford: Blackwell.

Wittrock, M. C. (ed.) (1986) *Handbook of Research on Teaching*, New York: Macmillan.

Woods, P. (ed.) (1980) *Teacher Strategies: Explorations in the Sociology of the School*, London: Croom Helm.

Wyse, D. and Jones, R. (2002) 'Circular arguments: teachers and texts', *Changing English*, 9 (1): 77–84.

Yaakobi, D. and Sharan, S. (1985) 'Teacher beliefs and practices: the discipline carries the message', *Journal of Education for Teaching*, 11 (2): 187–99.

Yinger, R. and Hendricks-Lee, M. (1993) 'Working knowledge in teaching', in Day, C., Calderhead, J. and Denicolo, P. (eds) *Research on Teacher Thinking: Understanding Professional Development*, London: The Falmer Press.

Young, M. F. D. (ed.) (1971) *Knowledge and Control: New Directions for the Sociology of Education*, London: Collier-Macmillan.

	INTERVIEW 1	INTERVIEW 2	INTERVIEW 3
1	Educational background in English as a school and university subject	Educational background in English as a school and university subject	Educational background in English as a school and university subject
2	Concept of expertise in English	Current perspective on PGCE course and subject knowledge auditing	Comparing own education in English to PGCE and Induction year's schools
3	Mapping English subject knowledge (task)	Hypothetical: free choice of teaching	Reflection on induction year
4	Motivations for becoming a teacher	Reading and analysing written narratives together	Reflections on current teaching
5	Purposes for teaching and learning English	Mapping English subject knowledge, including comparison with previous map (task)	Reflections on development as a teacher
6	School students' difficulties with English	Purposes for teaching and learning English	Mapping English subject knowledge, including comparison with previous maps (task)
7	Reflections on current teaching	Reflections on current teaching	Hypothetical: free choice of teaching
8	Perceptions of PGCE course and subject knowledge auditing	Reflection on PGCE year as a whole	Purposes for teaching and learning English

Glossary

AS/A2/A-level These are relatively new examinations usually taken by students between the ages of 16 and 18. They are modular exams with the AS taken after the first year and A2 at the end of a two-year course in particular subject areas. They are sometimes still referred to as A-levels.

Beacon school An early form of 'specialist' status available to schools that made successful bids to central government. Part of a larger effort to mark out certain schools as highly performing.

Benefits Agency A non-executive government agency that manages the welfare system for individuals and families on low incomes or with health problems and disabilities.

CATE Council for the Accreditation of Teacher Education. An organization set up in 1992 to accredit teacher eduction programmes in England and Wales. One of the criteria for accreditation was that teacher educators had 'recent and relevant' experience in schools. CATE was superceded by the Teacher Training Agency (TTA).

CCUE Council for College and University English. An organization representing university teachers of English in the UK.

Comprehensive school The type of state, secondary (high) school that enrols all students between the ages of 11 and 16 or 18 regardless of their 'ability'. They are usually contrasted with selective grammar schools (which can also be state-funded) and private schools.

DfES/DfE/ DfEE/DES Department for Education and Skills. The current designation of the ministry within the government in England responsible for education and schooling. Previously known as the Department for Education (DfE), Department for Education and Employment (DfEE) and the Department for Education and Science (DES).

EAL English as an Additional Language. The acronym used to refer to school students for whom English is not their first language (English language learners).

Further education college The type of college initially intended to provide day-release provision for apprentices and some adult education. Their scope has expanded over time to encompass academic, community and basic skills learning.

GCSE	The General Certificate of Secondary Education. This is the major school examination usually taken by students aged 16. In England, league tables (rank orders) are published to show the relative performance of schools on the basis of the percentage of their pupils gaining 5 A* to C grades in GCSE examinations.
GCSE Anthology	Since the early 1990s, the GCSE English examination has required English teachers to teach partly from a prescribed anthology of literary texts, mostly poetry.
GNVQ	General National Vocational Qualification. A qualification in a vocational school subject such as Leisure and Tourism.
HMI	Her Majesty's Inspector(s) of Schools. With a long history of independent work in improving the quality of education and schooling (Matthew Arnold was one nineteenth-century example), HMI underwent radical change in the early 1990s. Their work was brought under the control of Ofsted and the number of HMIs was cut significantly. However, the enlarged school inspection system managed by Ofsted was then franchised out to teams of freelance inspectors who bid for contracts. Senior figures at Ofsted, however, remain HMIs.
IFTE	International Federation for the Teaching of English. Founded as an umbrella association of the English teaching association in the UK, US, Canada, Australia and New Zealand. The US affiliate – NCTE (National Council of Teachers of English) – withdrew from IFTE in 2004.
Induction standards	Performance statements that new teachers must demonstrate at the end of their first (employed) year of teaching.
Induction year	The first, employed year of teaching following the pre-service programme. The beginning teacher has to demonstrate achievement of Induction Standards in order for QTS to be confirmed.
ITE	Initial Teacher Education (in preference to Initial Teaching Training) – also known as pre-service teacher education.
ITTNC	The Initial Teacher Training National Curricula brought in for primary and secondary core subjects following government Circular 4/98. The ITTNC specified what student teachers should be taught by the teacher education programmes.
Key Stage 3 English Framework	A centralized framework for teaching English imposed by the New Labour Government on secondary schools in 1999/2000 on the heels of the National Literacy Strategy in the primary (elementary) phase. It applies to the teaching of students aged between 11 and 14 (Years 7 to 9).
LEA	Local Education Authority. Organisations set up by local government in England at the city and county level to coordinate and monitor the provision of education services (including schools). Although technically responsible to locally elected politicians (councillors), recent

	Conservative and New Labour national governments have pulled much of the power of the LEA back to the centre. Similar to the US system of school districts.
Mentor	The usual designation of the experienced teacher responsible for a student teacher's development in schools.
NATE	National Association for the Teaching of English. An organization established in 1964 to represent the views of English teachers in British schools.
National Literacy Strategy	The centralized framework for teaching literacy in the primary phase (Years 1 to 6) imposed by the New Labour Government in 1997/8. The first few years of the Strategy's implementation was evaluated by a team from the Ontario Institute for Studies in Education under Michael Fullan.
Non-executive government agency	An organization set up by central government to implement (but not direct) its policies. An advantage for government is that this is done 'at arm's length'.
NQT	Newly Qualified Teacher.
Ofsted	The Office for Standards in Education. The non-executive government agency responsible for inspecting schools and colleges, teacher education and childcare organizations. On the basis of Ofsted inspection results, the TTA allocates funding to what it refers to as teacher education 'providers'.
Pre-/post-1992 universities	The distinction between universities that existed before 1992 (the 'old' universities) and those colleges of higher education and polytechnics that have been redesignated as universities since 1992 (the 'new' universities).
Private finance initiative	An initiative of the New Labour Government that has sought private/public capital partnerships in the construction of new schools and hospitals.
PGCE	Postgraduate Certificate of Education. The one year, graduate-level course that is the main route into high school teaching in England. The government requires that two-thirds of this course is spent in schools.
QTS	Qualified Teacher Status. The government accreditation that is bestowed upon those who pass teacher education courses such as the PGCE. In order to be recommended for QTS, student teachers need to demonstrate achievement of certain performance Standards.
SATS	End of Key Stage 3 tests taken by all Year 9 students in state schools in England. 'SATS' is frequently used to describe these tests but has never been used officially and the tests bear no similarity to SATS in the US.
Setting/sets	Selecting and organizing groups and classes of students on the basis of their perceived 'ability'. Known in the US as 'tracking'.

Index

duced.

Year 9/   Year groups of students
                    in schools in England
                    are designated from
Year 10, etc.   Reception
                    (Kindergarten) through
                    to Year 6 (the primary
                    phase) and Year 7 to
                    Year 11 (the secondary
                    phase, to age 16).
                    Students in Year 9
                    would be 13/14 years
                    of age.

Appendix A

The progression of questioning foci across the three interview schedules

Appendix B

A note on transcription

All interviews were recorded (with the permission of the participants) and fully transcribed with the help of a transcription machine. Although I did not intend to use the transcripts for the purposes of conversational or discourse analysis, I adapted my transcription conventions from those developed by Sacks *et al.* (1978). The relatively limited number of conventions I operated are shown below:

Interviewer:

Speak ers' roles/n ames are separa ted from their utter- ances by colons .

...   Three dots indicat

	e an untimed pause.
//	Double obliques indicate the point at which overlap by the next speaker begins.
(don't)	Words between parentheses represent the best guess of talk that was difficult to hear.
(? ?)	Blank spaces inside parentheses with occasional question marks indicate uncertain or inaudible talk.
(( ))	Material between double quotes provides paralinguistic information, e.g. laughter.

Lightning Source UK Ltd.
Milton Keynes UK
27 May 2010
154785UK00001B/27/P